CHILD POVERTY, EVIDENCE AND POLICY

Mainstreaming children in international development

Nicola Jones and Andy Sumner

First published in Great Britain in 2011 by

The Policy Press
University of Bristol
Fourth Floor
Beacon House
Queen's Road
Bristol BS8 1QU
UK

Tel +44 (0)117 331 4054
Fax +44 (0)117 331 4093
e-mail tpp-info@bristol.ac.uk
www.policypress.co.uk

North American office:
The Policy Press
c/o International Specialized Books Services (ISBS)
920 NE 58th Avenue, Suite 300
Portland, OR 97213-3786, USA
Tel +1 503 287 3093
Fax +1 503 280 8832
e-mail info@isbs.com

British Library Cataloguing in Publication Data
A catalogue record for this book is available from the British Library.

Library of Congress Cataloging-in-Publication Data
A catalog record for this book has been requested.

ISBN 978 1 84742 445 7 paperback
ISBN 978 1 84742 446 4 hardcover

The right of Nicola Jones and Andy Sumner to be identified as authors of this work has been
asserted by them in accordance with the 1988 Copyright, Designs and Patents Act.

Cover design by Robin Hawes
Front cover: image kindly supplied by Anthony Robbins
Printed and bound in Great Britain by TJ International, Padstow
The Policy Press uses environmentally responsible print partners

Contents

List of figures, tables and boxes

Figures

Tables

Boxes

Acknowledgements

I would like to thank Elizabeth Presler-Marshall for research support and Yuri Van der Leest and Roo Griffiths for editorial support; dear friends and colleagues in Ethiopia, India and Peru for inspiring conversations over the years; and Paul for his patience and support.

Nicola Jones
Fellow, Overseas Development Institute, London, UK

I would like to thank the following for research support: Chetna Desai, Ben Mann, Richard Mallet, Ricardo Santos and Graca Sousa. I would also like to thank family, friends and colleagues past and present for their support.

Andy Sumner
Fellow, Institute of Development Studies,
University of Sussex, UK

List of acronyms

3D	three-dimensional
AACT	Asia Against Child Trafficking
ACP	African, Caribbean and Pacific
ACPF	African Child Policy Forum
ADC	Austrian Development Cooperation
AIDS	Acquired Immune Deficiency Syndrome
ANDI	News Agency for Children's Rights (Brazil)
ANPPCAN	African Network for the Prevention and Protection against Child Abuse and Neglect
BMZ	Federal Ministry for Economic Cooperation and Development (Germany)
BTC	Belgian Technical Cooperation
CACL	Campaign Against Child Labour (India)
CASACIDN	Argentinean Committee for the Follow-up of the UNCRC
CASSA	Campaign Against Sex Selective Abortion (India)
CCDC	Caribbean Child Development Centre
CEANIM	Centre for the Study and Care of Children and Women (Chile)
CEDAW	Convention on the Elimination of all forms of Discrimination Against Women
CENDIF	Centre for Childhood and Family Research (Venezuela)
CHIN	Children in Need Network (Zambia)
CHIP	Childhood Poverty Research and Policy Centre (UK)
CIDA	Canadian International Development Agency
CIES	Consortium for Social and Economic Research (Peru)
CIESPI	International Centre for Research and Policy on Childhood (Brazil)
CINDE	International Centre for Education and Human Development (Colombia)
CLOSE	Committee for Liaison between Social Organisations for the Defence of Child Rights (Benin)
CODESRIA	Council for the Development of Social Science Research in Africa

PPA	participatory poverty assessment
PRA	participatory rural appraisal
PRSP	Poverty Reduction Strategy Paper
PST CRRC	Psychosocial Support and Children's Rights Resource Centre (Philippines)
RAPID	Research and Policy in Development (ODI)
RECOUP	Research Consortium on Educational Outcomes and Poverty (UK)
REPOA	Research on Poverty Alleviation (Tanzania)
RISALC	Latin American and Caribbean Network of Social Institutions (Chile)
SEASUCS	Southeast Asia Coalition to Stop the Use of Child Soldiers
Sida	Swedish International Development Cooperation Agency
SIGI	Social Institutions Gender Index (OECD)
SIMPOC	Statistical Information and Monitoring Programme on Child Labour (ILO)
SOAWR	Solidarity for African Women's Rights
TISS	Tata Institute for Social Sciences (India)
UCRNN	Uganda Child Rights NGO Network
UDHR	Universal Declaration on Human Rights
UK	United Kingdom
UN	United Nations
UNCRC	United Nations Convention on the Rights of the Child
UNDESA	United Nations Department for Economic and Social Affairs
UNDP	United Nations Development Programme
UNICEF	United Nations Children's Fund
UNPD	United Nations Population Division
US	United States
WB	well-being lens
WeD	Well-being in Developing Countries (ESRC)
WHO	World Health Organization

Introduction

I.1 What is this book about?

This book is about child poverty, evidence and policy. It is about how children's *visibility, voice and vision* in *ideas, networks and institutions* can be mainstreamed in development research and policy (see Figure I.1).

Children (younger than 18 years old) account for, on average, over a third of the population in developing countries and almost half in the least-developed countries. Not only are a large proportion of these children poor, but the impacts of poverty suffered during childhood are often enduring and irreversible. We use the lens of '3D well-being' to convey a holistic understanding of child poverty and well-being, meaning that research and policy are approached from multiple angles and with multiple understandings of power and policy change.

There is, of course, a wealth of literature on child poverty. An important development has been a child-centred approach based on children as active agents in terms of voice (in decision-making in communities and societies), vision (of deprivation and well-being) and visibility (in terms of the local meaning ascribed to or social construction of childhood). Our book asks: how can we understand child poverty and well-being? What types of knowledge are being generated about the nature, extent and trends in child poverty and well-being in developing-country contexts? How can this evidence catalyse change to support children's visibility, voice and vision? Finally, how do these questions play out in different contexts?

I.2 Who is this book for?

This book is primarily for a 'policy audience', meaning those working within or seeking to influence policy by drawing on and/or generating evidence that seeks to promote children's visibility, voice and vision. This includes those working within and outside governments as children's champions, whether it be for international or local non-governmental organisations (NGOs) and civil society organisations (CSOs), the United Nations Children's Fund (UNICEF) or as civil servants located in social and economic ministries and children's and women's agencies around the world.

The book may also be of interest to those working in international development and poverty reduction more generally, those studying

Figure i.1: Approach taken in this book

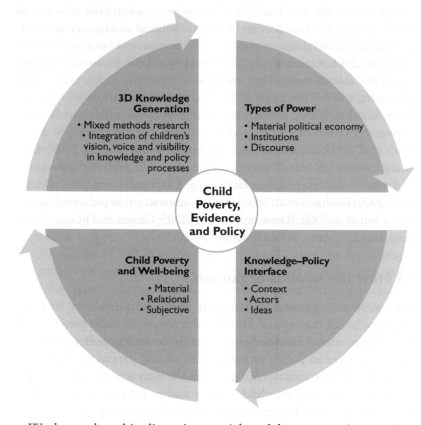

We hope that this discussion enriches debate on mainstreaming children in development research and policy globally, and welcome feedback and discussion.

Note

[1] These case studies draw on empirical research conducted by the authors as an adjunct to phase 1 of the Department for International Development (DFID)-funded child research project, Young Lives, now based at the University of Oxford. During 2003–06, Jones was policy coordinator at *Save the Children UK* (at the time a core partner of the Young Lives project). For 2006–07, Sumner was a Higher Education Funding Council for England-funded Visiting Research Fellow at the London School of Hygiene and Tropical Medicine (the lead academic institution in phase I of the Young Lives project).

Part One

Child poverty, evidence and policy: perspectives and approaches

ONE

Child poverty and well-being

1.1 Introduction

Children (if one takes the *United Nations Convention of the Rights of the Child* [UNCRC] definition of less than 18 years old) account for an average of 37% of the population in developing countries and 49% in the least-developed countries (UNICEF, 2005:12). Demographics are not the only reason, however, to advocate for a greater focus on child poverty and well-being in development research and policy: children are more likely to be poor, making up a disproportionate number of the total poor (Gordon et al, 2004; Barrientos and DeJong, 2009). The different ways in which adults and children experience poverty is key to advocating for a greater focus on and understanding of child poverty and well-being.

Such difference manifests itself in various ways. Child poverty is distinct from adult poverty and well-being because children's needs and capabilities differ both from those of adults, and from those of other children depending on their life-stage, amongst other factors (Moore and Lippman, 2005; Subrahamanian, 2005a, 2005b). The long-term impacts of poverty experienced during childhood are also well documented in terms of wasting, stunting, delayed school enrolment and reduced grade completion, and exposure to physical and emotional abuse and neglect (Gerhardt, 2004; Corak, 2006; Smith and Moore, 2006; Bird, 2007).

There is, of course, a wealth of literature on child poverty. An important development has been a child-centred approach based on children as active agents in terms of voice (in decision-making in communities and societies), vision (of deprivation and well-being) and visibility (in terms of the local meaning ascribed to or social construction of childhood). A substantial body of literature around children's voice in terms of child participation and agency in knowledge generation, policy processes and decision-making at various levels is emerging (e.g. Boyden and Ennew, 1997; White and Choudhury, 2007; Redmond, 2008, 2009). There is also a rich literature on children's perspectives on poverty and/or well-being and how children understand and perceive their well-being (e.g. Woodhead, 2001; Ben-Arieh, 2005; Fattore et al,

2007; Johnston, 2008; Redmond, 2008; 2009; Crivello et al, 2009). In addition, there is extensive research on children's visibility in terms of the social construction of childhood and how the nature, norms and conventions around childhood and what childhood is or should be are context-determined/specific (e.g. in Peru, Ames and Rojas, 2009; in Ethiopia, Camfield and Tafere, 2009).

In this chapter we discuss how child poverty differs from adult poverty, and present a 'human well-being' or 'three-dimensional (3D) human well-being' approach.[1] Although such an approach builds on much previous thinking regarding poverty and well-being, it is a relatively recent development, especially with regard to thinking about children, childhoods and related policy interventions (see Camfield et al, 2009a, 2009b). The chapter is structured as follows: Section 1.2 discusses the nature of child poverty and child well-being. Section 1.3 introduces the 'human well-being' approach. Section 1.4 asks what this approach means for children before Section 1.5 concludes.

1.2 Perspectives on child poverty

Childhood poverty can be defined and conceptualised in various ways that emphasise the differences between child and adult poverty to varying extents. In its 2007 Resolution on the rights of the child, the United Nations (UN) General Assembly adopted a definition of child poverty that acknowledges, albeit in a somewhat limited way, the *differential experience* of poverty in childhood. The definition highlighted that its impacts are both more severe and also potentially longer lasting than those of poverty experienced in adulthood:

> Children living in poverty are deprived of nutrition, water and sanitation facilities, access to basic health-care services, shelter, education, participation and protection, and that while a severe lack of goods and services hurts every human being, it is most threatening and harmful to children, leaving them unable to enjoy their rights, to reach their full potential and to participate as full members of the society.[2]

Although there is relatively little consensus on what conceptual frameworks are most appropriate for understanding childhood poverty (Harper et al, 2003), rights-based approaches have become dominant in international policy discourses and have emerged as the primary instrument for thinking about childhood poverty at UNICEF and amongst international NGOs.[3] Rights-based approaches to child poverty draw upon the set of basic needs codified in the legal instrument of the UNCRC (adopted in 1989 and effective from 1990). Ratified by 189 countries, the UNCRC is one of the most universal of human rights conventions.[4] However, the UNCRC is more than just a legal codification. Its transformative power lies in its potential as a tool by which children and their advocates may demand the realisation of four broad clusters of rights – child survival (nutrition, health, water and sanitation), child development (education and psychological development), child protection (from violence, abuse, exploitation and neglect) and child participation (in community decisions that affect children's lives) – and hold 'duty-bearers' (i.e. governments) accountable for ensuring progress in advancing children's well-being.[5] To this end, the UN Committee on the Rights of the Child has actively encouraged countries to 'domesticate' the UNCRC by incorporating it into national action plans for children that have legal standing within countries.

A 'rights-based' approach to poverty is based on the notion that poverty is itself a violation of human rights. Definitions steer between the general and more specific. For example, Hausermann's (1999: 31) approach is more general, defining it as an 'approach to development that stresses liberty, equality and empowerment', whereas Maxwell (1999: 1) conceptualises it more specifically as an approach that, 'sets the achievement of human rights as an objective of development.... [invoking] the international apparatus [of] rights accountability in support of development action'. The significance of the latter is that, as noted earlier, it allows for a focus on the accountability that duty-bearers (e.g. parents, educators and local, regional and state governments) have in ensuring that children's rights are fulfilled. Importantly, the UNCRC recognises that different states, especially in the developing world, have different capacities to uphold these rights, and therefore invokes the principle of 'progressive realisation'. The convention specifies that states have a responsibility to demonstrate how their record of fulfilling children's rights is improving over time relative to their resource base and capacities. In order to support countries in this process, various targets on rights were set at UN conferences in the 1990s, including:

- to halve extreme poverty (Copenhagen, 1995);
- to attain universal primary education (Jomtien, 1990; Beijing, 1995; Copenhagen, 1995);
- to attain gender equality in education (Cairo, 1994; Beijing, 1995; Copenhagen, 1995);

9

- to reduce by two-thirds infant and under-five mortality (Cairo, 1994);
- to reduce by three-quarters maternal mortality (Cairo, 1994; Beijing, 1995); and
- to provide reproductive health care for all (Cairo, 1994).

The rights-based approach evident in the above declarations was interwoven with Amartya Sen's and the United Nations Development Programme's (UNDP's) *Human Development* approach to ultimately contribute to the emergence of the MDGs.[6] Sen and the UNDP argued that development is not based on fulfilling desire (utility or consumption measured by a proxy for income such as per capita gross domestic product [GDP]), as this does not take sufficient evaluative account of the physical condition of the individual or of a person's or child's *capabilities*. Sen (see, in particular, 1999), Nussbaum (see, in particular, 2000) and the UNDP (1990–present) have argued that attention should be paid to the capabilities – means, opportunities or substantive freedoms – which permit the achievement of a set of 'functionings' – things that human beings value in terms of 'being' and 'doing'.

Sen has argued that there is a broad set of conditions (including being fed, healthy, clothed and educated) that together constitute well-being. Individuals have a set of entitlements (command over commodities) that are created through a set of endowments (financial, human, natural, social and productive) and exchange (production and trade by the individual). These entitlements are traded for a set of opportunities (capabilities) in order to achieve a set of functionings (well-being outcomes). Although Sen resolutely refuses to name the capabilities, he does identify basic freedoms (1999: 38). Furthermore, in the case of poverty assessments and 'basic capabilities', Sen (1992: 44–5) notes that, '[i]n dealing with extreme poverty ... [capabilities might include] the ability to be well-nourished and well-sheltered ... escaping avoidable morbidity and premature mortality, and so forth'.

Development thus consists of removing various types of 'un-freedom' that leave people with little opportunity to exercise their reasoned agency:

> Development can be seen ... as a process of expanding the real freedoms that people enjoy ... the expansion of the 'capabilities' of persons to lead the kind of lives they value – and have reason to value. (Sen, 1999: xii, 1, 18)

The child poverty aspects of the MDGs that arose from the interweaving of rights and human development approaches are important for children because many are about child poverty directly and unambiguously (see Table 1.1), for example primary school enrolment and child malnutrition.

However, although there are a substantial number of child-focused indicators among the MDGs, they do not fully capture the distinctions between childhood and adult poverty. Further, it is well noted how MDG 1a (the dollar-a-day poverty measure – now $1.25/day) and 'traditional' proxy monetary measures of poverty and, more broadly, sources of data such as income and consumption, are deeply problematic when considering the well-being of children (see Box 1.1).

Box 1.1: Challenges in available indicators and child poverty

• Data are not collected from children themselves but from (usually male) heads of household or caregivers.
• Children's involvement in work may be in the informal or care economies, which are often not visible. Non-market channels are especially important in shaping gender dimensions of childhood poverty.
• Children's access to and control of income or expenditures may be extremely marginal, especially as resources and power are typically distributed unequally within households).

Moreover, the MDGs also overlook key dimensions of children's experiences of poverty, such as the absence of protection from violence, abuse and neglect, and opportunities, or lack of them, to participate in community decision-making.

Table 1.1: Mapping UN rights instruments and key MDGs

Rights instrument	MDG 1	MDG 2	MDG 3	MDGs 4–7
	Income and nutrition	Education	Gender equality in education	Health and environment
UDHR	23, 25, 26.1	26.1	–	25.1
CEDAW	14.2	10; 14.2d	Pre; 2a; 3; 4.1;	12.1, 14.2b, 14.2h
UNCRC	27.1	23.3; 28	–	23.3, 24.1, 24.2e, 24.3

Note: Numbers refer to Article numbers in the respective Convention/Declaration.

In addition to the MDG indicators there are now numerous sets of child indicators (see Table 1.2). Indeed 'child indicators' is a major area of research, and has its own association, the International Society for Child Indicators.[7] A recent innovation, published in 2007, was the UNICEF Innocenti Centre's first Report Card on children's well-being. It included six dimensions of well-being: material well-being; health and safety; educational well-being; family and peer relationships; behaviours and risks; and subjective well-being. However, to date this scorecard only covers Organisation for Economic Co-operation and Development (OECD) countries due to data constraints.[8]

Another recent innovation is the set of indices produced by the *African Child Policy Forum* (ACPF), which is based in Addis Ababa and focuses on the 'child-friendliness' of policy in Africa.[9] The ACPF's 2009 report contains data on the records of governments throughout the region with regard to child protection (by legal and policy frameworks); basic service provision for children (efforts to meet basic needs assessed by budgetary allocation, service provision and achievement of outcomes); and child participation in consultations held to draft poverty-reduction strategy papers (PRSPs) or other national plans.

Finally, in terms of indicators that seek to address issues related to children's relational well-being, an important new development can be found in the OECD's Social Institutions Gender Index (SIGI). Although not specifically focused on children, unlike the UNDP's Gender Empowerment Measure (GEM), which is solely adult-focused, many of the indicators are relevant to childhood. The SIGI looks at five clusters of indicators, three of which relate to childhood: family code, physical integrity and son preference; only civil liberties and ownership rights are more pertinent to adulthood.[10] There are various other child indicator sets, indices and networks (see Table 1.2).

Whilst the above-mentioned analytical approaches have their uses, there is a need for an approach that can more comprehensively account for the differential experiences of children and identify how child poverty is distinct from adult poverty. An emergent approach that offers potential and is not mutually exclusive to many of the perspectives already discussed, but is holistic, is a 'human well-being' or '3D well-being' approach. It is important to note that although some of the other indices refer to 'well-being', the 3D well-being approach is conceptually specific.

Table 1.2: Selected sources of child poverty and well-being indicators

Organisation	Indicators and indices	Sources
ACPF	Child Friendliness of Policy Indices	www.africanchildinfo.net/africanreport08/
Bristol University; Gordon et al	Child deprivation indicators	www.bristol.ac.uk/poverty/child%20poverty.html#abpov
Child and Youth Network	Child and Youth Network Indicators	http://www.redbarnet.dk/Approaches/Logical_Framework/Indicators.aspx
Foundation for Child Well-being	Child Well-being Index	http://www.soc.duke.edu/~cwi/
OECD	Social Institutions and Gender Index	http://genderindex.org/
Save the Children	Child Development Index	www.savethechildren.org.uk/en/docs/child-development-index.pdf
UN	MDGs	www.un.org/millenniumgoals/
UNICEF	UNCRC Indicators	www.unicef.org/crc/
UNICEF Innocenti Research Centre	Child well-being index	www.unicef.org/media/files/ChildPovertyReport.pdf

1.3 What is a three-dimensional well-being approach?

'Human well-being' or 'three-dimensional (3D) human well-being' is emerging as a complement to more traditional and material ways of conceptualising and measuring poverty and deprivation. Although the concept of well-being has a long intellectual history, the quantity of published books and articles indicates that it has been particularly hotly debated over the last 10 years or so (see, for example, Lewis, 1996; Sen, 1999, 2009; Kahneman et al, 2004; Layard, 2006; McGillivray, 2006; McGillivray and Clarke, 2006; Gough and McGregor, 2007; McGregor, 2007; Samman, 2007; Alkire, 2008; Copestake, 2008; White, 2008; Deneulin and McGregor, 2009; Sumner et al, 2009). Evidence of this trend is most visible in the recent Sarkozy Commission, chaired by Amartya Sen, Joseph Stiglitz and Jean-Paul Fitoussi, which has provided one of the latest and strongest signposts of all with its conclusion that there is a need 'to shift emphasis from measuring economic production to measuring people's well-being' (Fitoussi et al, 2009: 10). There is further evidence in the OECD's *Measuring the Progress of Societies*, which suggests that current approaches to poverty, development and the goals of pro-poor policy are being rethought (Giovannini, 2009), and the UNDP Human Development Report Office's 20-year review of human development, released in 2010. One might also note the academic debate stimulated by the five-year, multi-country research undertaken by the Economic and Social Research Council's (ESRC's) Well-being in Developing Countries (known as WeD) network and the Oxford Poverty & Human Development Initiative (OPHI).

The approach to human well-being that is outlined here draws upon and synthesises various traditions (see discussion in McGregor, 2007). This well-being approach thus builds on human development and Sen's (1999) concepts of 'beings' and 'doings' (i.e. human development is about freedoms and what a person *can* do and be), focusing on the interactions between beings, doings and feelings. Robert Chambers' (2003) emphasis on the need for the development profession to listen to the voices of poor people and their perceptions and feelings about poverty has also been influential in shaping the notion of 3D human well-being.

'Three-dimensional human well-being' shifts our focus beyond incomes and narrow human development indicators such as the Human Development Index (HDI) to take account of what people can do and be, and how they feel about what they can do and be. Indeed, McGregor (2007: 317) defines well-being as the interplay of: 'the resources that a person is able to command; what they are able to achieve with those resources and what needs and goals they are able to meet; the meaning that they give to the goals they achieve and the processes in which they engage'.

Human well-being is thus 3D: it takes into account material well-being, subjective well-being and relational well-being, and their dynamic and evolving interactions. Policy that is intended to stimulate development processes cannot realistically focus on just one or two of these factors to the exclusion of the other(s). People's own perceptions and experience of life matter, as do their relationships and their material standards of living. The three dimensions of material, subjective and relational well-being are summarised in Table 1.3. The *material* dimension of well-being concerns 'practical welfare and standards of living', the *relational* concerns 'personal and social relations' and the *subjective* concerns 'values, perceptions, and experience' (White, 2008: 8). The well-being lens can take both the individual and the community as the unit of analysis.[11]

While many contemporary definitions of poverty go beyond measures of income to include more socio-cultural and subjective dimensions of deprivation (e.g. human development, rights-based approaches, social exclusion approaches and sustainable livelihoods), a well-being approach sharpens the focus of the 'traditional' poverty lens in at least two ways. First, its emphasis is on the *relational* and *the subjective*,

Table 1.3: 3D well-being – dimensions, areas of study, indicators and key determinants

Dimensions of well-being	Material	Relational	Subjective
What is to be studied	Objectively observable outcomes people are able to achieve	The extent to which people are able to engage with others in order to achieve particular needs and goals, and the nature of these engagements	The meanings that people give to the goals they achieve and the processes they engage in
Indicators	• Needs satisfaction indicators • Material asset indicators	• Multidimensional resource indicators • Human agency indicators	• Quality of life indicators
Key determinants	• Income, wealth, and assets • Employment and livelihood activities • Education and skills • Physical health and (dis)ability • Access to services and amenities • Environmental quality	• Relationships, love, and care • Networks of support and obligation • Relations with the state: law, politics, and welfare • Social, political, and cultural identities and inequalities • Violence, conflict, and (in)security • Scope for personal and collective action and influence	• Understanding of the sacred and moral order • Self-concept and personality • Hopes, fears, and aspirations • Sense of meaning/ meaninglessness • Levels of (dis)satisfaction • Trust and confidence

Sources: Gough and McGregor (2007); White (2008) and McGregor and Sumner (2010).

implying that what people feel they can do or be influences what they will actually be able to do and be. These feelings and perceptions are determined by people's experiences as well as by norms and values that are culturally and socially determined by their relationships. Examples include prevailing notions of 'normal' adult–child interactions or relationships at school, home and, in the case of child labour, at work.

Second, a well-being approach is about positives. It is arguably more respectful as it is based on what people and children *can* do/be/feel, rather than *deficits* in what they can do/be/feel. This resonates with Nancy Fraser's work (e.g. Fraser, 2000) on recognition, respect and issues of stigma, and in particular how labelling or 'othering' people as the 'poor' infers a status inferior to the 'non-poor'. It is also respectful in the sense that it is about self-determination and participation rather than exogenously defined well-being.

It is true, however, that the development community may be uncomfortable talking about 'positives', as it might seem to make light of deprivation as framed by Western-trained researchers, and as such risk making poverty analysis apolitical. But by focusing on the perceptual and relational, the concept of well-being is rendered inherently political in that it is about agency. This approach asks questions about who has what, who can do what, who feels good about what they can have and do, who commands resources, who is able to achieve their needs and goals with those resources, and who constructs meanings in terms of goals to be achieved and processes to achieve those goals. A well-being approach makes power more explicit – not only as material political economy (in Marx's terms), but also as discourse (i.e. Foucault), and as embedded in norms, values and conventions (i.e. North's institutions [1990] and Bourdieu's *habitus* [1990]) and the dynamic interaction of different types of power.

In short, if we take a '3D well-being' perspective, we can see that conventional approaches may capture the material dimensions of child well-being but less so other aspects, such as the relational and subjective dimensions of children's lives and the dynamic interaction of the material, relational and subjective in shaping outcomes for children.

1.4 3D well-being and child poverty

Standard material and human indicators of child development are important, but they do not provide sufficient information about whether particular children are flourishing in a specific society. Increasingly, however, as international agencies have engaged with children's own voices, a broader agenda has emerged. In Latin America and the Caribbean (LAC), for example, UNICEF (1999) has noted that perceptions of peace in society, family harmony, environmental health, food quality, access to schooling, ability to play in safety and the degree to which they are 'looked down on' by others are all important to children. There is now a voluminous literature on child participation. Redmond's reviews (2008, 2009) note that although adults (and *inter alia* policymakers) emphasise the material well-being of children, when asked, children themselves frequently drew attention to the relational aspects of well-being:

> What concerns children is not lack of resources per se, but exclusion from activities that other children appear to take for granted, and embarrassment and shame at not being able to participate on equal terms with other children. (Redmond, 2008: 12)

A 3D child well-being approach, to echo McGregor earlier, could thus be thought to be: what a child has, what a child can do with what s/he has, and how a child thinks about what s/he has and can do. It involves the interplay of the resources that children are able to command; what they are able to achieve with those resources and what needs and goals they are able to meet; the meaning that they give to the goals they achieve; and the processes in which they engage. This is, of course, not completely new, but rather constitutes a bringing together of dimensions. For example, in the UNCRC the material and relational aspects of child well-being are clear.[12] The former relate to child survival and child development in particular, and the latter to child participation and child protection. However, aspects of child development, participation and protection all relate to subjective aspects of well-being as well (see Table 1.4).

Three-dimensional well-being brings together well-being in a holistic way to ensure that important aspects of child poverty are not neglected, expanding the focus from the body/physiology to include the mind/psychology. Importantly for children and child poverty, it draws attention to their *current* well-being rather than only their future 'well becoming' as adults and citizens (Ben-Arieh, 2007). While a poverty lens orientates towards future well-being (i.e. schooling to facilitate labour-market participation, food to ensure health, etc), 3D well-being also emphasises 'newer' areas, notably the importance of the relational or relatedness (relationships), autonomy, enjoyment/ fun/play and social status.

Finally, a 3D child well-being approach can make an important contribution to understanding child well-being as it resonates strongly with children's own perceptions of exclusion and agency (see Camfield, 2009; Redmond, 2008; UNICEF, 2005). It is also non-imposing, in that it is about self-defined well-being and focuses on what children

Table 1.4: Mapping UNCRC Articles and 3D child well-being

	3D child well-being		
	Material well-being	**Relational well-being**	**Subjective well-being**
UNCRC Articles	• Child survival (nutrition, health, and water and sanitation) (6, 24, 27) • Child development (education and psychological development) (6, 28, 29)	• Child participation (in community decisions that affect children's lives) (12, 13, 31) • Child protection (from violence, abuse, exploitation and neglect) (19, 32, 33, 34, 35, 36, 37)	• Child psychological and emotional development (13, 14, 28, 29) • Child participation (12, 13, 31) and child protection (19, 32, 33, 34, 35, 36, 37)

Note: Numbers refer to Article numbers in UNCRC.

can do/be/feel, that is, their agency, rather than their deficits, avoiding the stigmatising and labelling of poor children.

Applying a well-being approach to understanding the processes of IGT offers a number of important insights. First, the non-material dimensions of well-being are essential components of transmission. We can disrupt IGT via: the disruption of the transmission of *material well-being*, that is, via interventions such as breastfeeding promotion to improve early childhood development; the disruption of the transmission of *subjective well-being,* that is, via changes in values/ thinking/consciousness and social conditioning; and the disruption of the transmission of *relational well-being,* that is, *changes in behaviour* and norms, conventions and institutions. An example would be public policy campaigns promoting the schooling of girls in Bangladesh relating to poor people's aspirations ('my girls will never go to school') or the multiple ways IGT is gendered by role models, values and ideas.

Second, the focus on agency makes sure we do not ignore opportunities to disrupt the transmission of ill-being/well-being via child agency. In this case, it is worth reflecting on the issues of child agency with regard to the 'voice' and 'visibility' of children. In terms of voice, children are legal minors with no right to vote or to make decisions without the approval of their legal guardian. Indeed, denial of voice in family, school and community decisions is still viewed as 'normal' and culturally acceptable in many parts of the developing and developed world. Despite the UNCRC principles having been agreed by almost all countries, children (especially younger children) typically have few opportunities or resources to advocate on their own behalf in decision-making processes. In terms of visibility or vision, children's limited voice is often compounded by a lack of legitimacy of children's perspectives in many societies and the invisibility of children in public policy debates (despite their numbers).

Child and adult agency is a crucial determinant of disrupted transmissions (Harper et al, 2003; Bird, 2007). Children, including poor children, have at least some degree of individual agency, but it is highly life-stage dependent, more relational in nature than that of adults because of children's dependence on adult protection and care, and both personal and context dependent (e.g. related to prevailing understandings of 'childhood'). An example of the latter point is the way Western understandings of childhood tend to conceptualise this as a life-stage free from work, but this is not the case in many countries (see, for example, research in India and Peru, notably Morrow and Vennam, 2009; Crivello, 2009).

There has been significant research on agency and poverty. Lister's (2004) taxonomy of the agency exercised by those in poverty recognises that adults' and children's agency can be good/progressive or bad/regressive. Lister's model has four quadrants (see Figure 1.1). The vertical axis is about the actions poor people (and children) take to improve their situation in the short term, and the horizontal axis is about long-term actions. This stretches from everyday matters of 'getting by' and 'getting back at' (meaning rebellious behaviour) to more strategic matters of 'getting out' and 'getting organised' (meaning collective action).

When Lister talks about getting by, she is referring to the little things people do in order to cope with everyday situations such as prioritising daily expenditures and juggling resources. Redmond (2008, 2009) applies this to children who take advantage of informal and ad hoc opportunities to earn income (agency in the material well-being domain), help parents with housework and childcare (agency in the relational well-being domain) and reappraise their daily situation in a positive light (agency in the subjective well-being domain). We can thus start to map child agency across 3D well-being domains (see Table 1.5).

Redmond argues that children's agency is generally exercised in the domains of the everyday and personal (getting by, getting back at). Children are less likely to exert agency that is strategic and political (getting out, getting organised), although children can do this, especially

Figure 1.1: Taxonomy of agency exercised by those in poverty

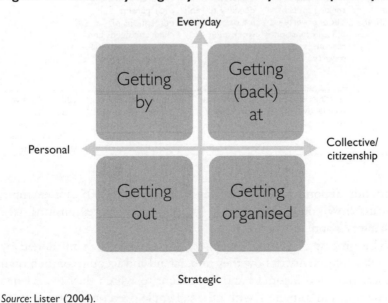

Source: Lister (2004).

Table 1.5: Redmond's taxonomies of child agency mapped across 3D well-being dimensions with examples

Type of child agency		Dimension of well-being with examples		
		Material	Relational	Subjective
Agency definition	Material political economy (i.e. Marx), and the available resources upon which children can call	Institutions (e.g. North), norms, and conventions, including the formal/informal 'rules of the game' or ways of doing things in terms of children–adult relationships	Power as discourse (i.e. Foucault) and embedded in values and ways of seeing the world, (e.g. the social construction of 'childhood')	
Everyday and personal	Getting by – coping strategies, personal and social resources, and augmenting resources through the informal economy	Taking advantage of informal and ad-hoc opportunities to earn income	Helping parents with housework and childcare	Reappraising daily situation in a positive light
	Getting back at – the channelling of anger and despair into activities and lifestyles that signal resistance to bureaucratic and social norms.	Petty crimes	Borderline non-compliance with rules and obligations of welfare receipts	Vandalism and drug/solvent use
Strategic and political	Getting out – seeking routes out of poverty via officially sanctioned responses to poverty	Children deciding to look for, or take on, work and/or education	Children influencing their parents' perceptions of children's needs and influencing parental decisions to look for work, seek education, etc.	
	Getting organised – collective responses	Child labour collectives/ unions	Collective self-help, political action and gendered action	Child collective action based on identity as children or child labourers, etc

with the support of adults, White and Choudhury (2007), for example, discuss how adults can provide 'supplements and extensions' (see Chapters 2 and 3).

The process of getting organised, for example, is constrained by people's subjectivity, or how they understand and account for their own experiences and identities and the extent to which they experience belonging and 'sameness' with others. People overcome constraints to getting organised via collective self-help and political action. Individual agency is, of course, a product of wider social forces. As Lister notes (2004: 128), it is not only about how those in poverty (including children) act, but also about how those in power act in relation to them – in this discussion, how poor as well as richer adults act in relation to poor children. Further, structures are perpetuated or modified by individual and collective action and non-action. What matters is not just the system of cultural norms, values, attitudes and behaviours that is transmitted across generations, but also the degree to which a person assumes or identifies herself with them (Shek et al, 2003; Shek, 2004).

In sum, child poverty and agency are distinct from adult poverty and agency because of the greater emphasis on children's relational well-being and the limited opportunities to voice their experiences of poverty and well-being (subjective well-being). What a 3D well-being lens brings to the discussion is the ability to think holistically across differing types of child and adult agency, and to explore the dynamic interaction across dimensions of well-being.

1.5 Conclusions

This chapter has introduced concepts of child poverty and well-being and asked how adult and child poverty differ. A holistic perspective on child poverty, that of '3D child well-being', has been proposed as a means of better understanding child poverty and well-being. What does such an approach offer? A 3D well-being approach can contribute to understanding child poverty in three ways. First, it puts children and their agency (what they *can* do and be) at the centre of analysis. It is thus a means in itself of achieving a child-centred analysis by bringing together understandings based on children as active agents in terms of voice (in decision-making in communities and societies), vision (of deprivation itself) and visibility (in terms of the subjectivities and the social construction of childhood conceptually). Second, it encourages a positive perspective on children in development by avoiding labelling certain children as 'poor' and thus applying the stigma that accompanies labels of inferiority.

Third, it explicitly integrates relational and subjective perspectives into the material dimension of well-being and recognises that the material, relational and subjective dimensions of children's lives are co-evolving, interdependent and dynamically interactive. In doing so, it leads development policy in new directions by focusing on all three dimensions and their interaction, rather than focusing primarily on material well-being. This is not to suggest that child nutrition, health or educational achievements are unimportant, but rather that the relational and subjective dimensions of well-being matter in attaining and shaping material well-being as well as in their own right.

Take, for example, the case of child nutrition. There are important aspects of material well-being such as actual allocation of food and water to children. However, there are also important aspects of relational well-being – personal and social relationships such as the agency of women and girls, individually or collectively, to negotiate gender equity in food and water for children – that play a role in shaping material well-being. Finally, there are important aspects of subjective well-being – values, perceptions and experiences – such as norms about who deserves the most and best food in the house and the practice of eating less during pregnancy to avoid too much weight gain, that also play a role in shaping material well-being.

Thus, 3D well-being offers a different way of understanding child poverty and child agency by recognising the distinctiveness of child poverty and well-being and placing children and their agency at the centre of an approach to understanding poverty and well-being and responding to it in a holistic way. In Chapter 2 we discuss knowledge generation and child poverty and well-being.

Notes

[1] This chapter draws on and develops ideas in Sumner (2010) 'Child Poverty, Well-being and Agency: What does a 3D Well-being Approach Contribute?', *Journal of International Development* 22: 1064–75; McGregor and Sumner (2010) 'Beyond Business as Usual. What Might 3-D Well-being Contribute to MDG Momentum?', *IDS Bulletin* 41(1): 104–12.

[2] http://www.unicef.org/media/media_38003.html

[3] We can draw a connection between child rights approaches, human development and the child-relevant Millennium Development Goals (MDGs, the UN's poverty targets for 2015).

[4] Only two countries have not signed and/or ratified it. One of the two countries is the USA, which, although it has signed the UNCRC, has failed to ratify it. The other country that is not a signatory is Somalia. By comparison, the Convention on the Elimination of all forms of Discrimination Against Women (CEDAW, adopted in 1979 and effective from 1981) has been signed and ratified by only 162 countries.

The UNCRC is part of a wider rights-based approach under which development is regarded as a combination of civil, social, economic and political rights. These rights are also enshrined in the Universal Declaration of Human Rights (UDHR, adopted in 1948), which has been signed by all countries.

[5] To simplify UNCRC implementation, monitoring and reporting, UNICEF has developed six thematic areas by grouping UNCRC articles under interconnected themes. These are: general measures of implementation; civil rights and freedom; family environment and alternative care; basic health and welfare; education, leisure and cultural activities; and special protection measures. There are also two optional UNCRC protocols on child labour and child trafficking.

[6] Although one might argue that the MDGs are needs-based rather than rights-based, both interpretations have their merits.

[7] www.childindicators.org

[8] In addition to the Innocenti Report Card, UNICEF uses a range of other indicators to capture a multidimensional understanding of child well-being, notably: the UNCRC monitoring and evaluation committee's thematic areas (37 indicators); the State of the World's Children (approximately 50 indicators); the UNICEF Medium Term Strategy Key Result Areas (15 indicators); UNCRC committee reporting – UNCRC Effort Index (100 questions); the UNICEF Medium Term Strategy questionnaire (baseline 2006) reporting questions (55 questions); and the 'World Fit for Children' report (21 indicators).

[9] See www.africanchildforum.org

[10] It is possible to calculate an aggregate score for each country on the basis of these three sub-indices (see the Appendix). Importantly, too, given the completeness of the data (compared to the limited number of countries covered by the UNICEF-supported and facilitated Multiple Indicator Cluster Survey [MICS], for instance – see discussion in Chapters 4–6), the SIGI is more amenable for identifying regional and subregional trends.

[11] The WeD group found that the relational and community aspects of well-being were particularly prominent in the developing countries they studied, but they were not able to compare this with findings from developed countries. 'Relatedness' in people's lives was central to well-being. Further, there was often a strong moral aspect of subjective well-being related to collective aspects of well-being and the community, rather than just related to individual preferences (see White, 2008).

[12] Subjective well-being was a component of the UNICEF Innocenti Research Centre OECD Report Card (UNICEF, 2005).

TWO

Knowledge generation and child poverty and well-being

2.1 Introduction

In this chapter, we extend our 3D thinking on child poverty and well-being to consider knowledge and evidence generation. Given this book's focus on the knowledge–policy interface around childhoods in the developing world, it is critical that we explore the knowledge base that underpins dominant understandings of childhood poverty and well-being. Questions that we need to consider include: how are multiple forms of 'expertise' accommodated? Whose 'evidence' prevails – that is, is perceived to be most credible – in policy debates and why? What accounts for the prevailing underinvestment in evidence about children, especially in developing countries? This chapter begins by briefly reviewing trends in thinking about the generation of evidence in development studies, and then discusses how these broader debates have played out in the case of childhood poverty and well-being. We focus particularly on emerging thinking about 3D approaches via combining research methods, and explore the particular challenges and opportunities of such approaches to child well-being.[1]

This chapter is structured as follows. Section 2.2 discusses the concepts of evidence-based policy. Section 2.3 is about knowledge generation and children. Section 2.4 discusses 3D approaches in general via mixing methods. Section 2.5 applies this debate to child poverty and well-being, and Section 2.6 concludes.

2.2 The evidence-based policy movement and its critics

To understand the interaction between knowledge and policy processes, it is important to look at the role of different types of knowledge in development policy. Early work on the link between knowledge and policy focused predominantly on the rational role of science and research (Laswell and Lerner, 1951), conceptualising the policy arena as one that ideally facilitates the production and application of technical expertise to solve policy problems. Models then began to incorporate an understanding of the pragmatic, political and often opportunistic ways in which policymakers draw on different sources. Here, the evidence-based policy movement sought to develop frameworks to understand the drivers of and barriers to research 'uptake' (Cracknell, 2001; Landry et al, 2003; Brehaut and Juzwishin, 2005; Young, 2005; Ammons and Rivenbark, 2008; Moynihan et al, 2008) with the normative goal of increasing the influence of research on policymaking. However, this school of thought has come under criticism for ignoring the political and epistemological dynamics of the production and use of particular sources of knowledge (Luke, 2003; Marston and Watts, 2003; Sanderson, 2004; Simons, 2004). By focusing on *evidence* (instead of the more complex meaning of *knowledge*), a value-free world versus the value-laden world of politics has been overemphasised:

> [W]e need to work within a broader conception of rationality to recognize the validity of the range of forms of intelligence that underpin 'practical wisdom', to acknowledge the essential role of fallible processes of crafting judgement in assembling what is to be accepted as 'evidence', and to incorporate deliberation, debate and argumentation in relation to the ends of policy and the ethical and moral implications of alternative courses of action. (Sanderson, 2004: 376)

As such, there has been a tendency for evidence-based policy studies, especially in the health sciences and economics, to prioritise some research techniques over others, setting experimental methods as the 'gold standard'[2] and paying lesser attention to more qualitative and participatory sources, such as public service users' views and local knowledge (Tilley and Laycock, 2000; Rycroft-Malone et al, 2004; see also Box 2.1). As we discuss later, there has been a move to address this bias, with *participatory development* explicitly seeking to counterbalance the top-down production of evidence by enabling bottom-up data generation. In this vein, rural development and poverty-reduction policies (such as PRSP processes) have seen systematic attempts to integrate local knowledge into the policymaking process (Jones and Villar, 2008; see also Chapter 4).

Box 2.1: What counts as rigorous evidence?

Academic rigour is often shaped by understandings of hierarchies of knowledge that privilege some methods and academic disciplines over others (e.g. quantitative methods, economics) and is a critical filter through which research evidence is consumed in policy processes. Typically, we think of reliability, replicability, generalisability and validity as criteria for evaluating social research. Drawing on Becker et al's (2006: 7–8) survey of social policy research quality, discussions of 'standards' provoke major debate, with many arguing that qualitative and quantitative approaches need to be judged by different – or 'alternative' – criteria because 'traditional' criteria assume that quantitative approaches are better.

It has also been suggested that the word 'rigour' is problematic because it is biased towards a perception of precision and assumes an association between objectivity and quantitative methods (David and Dodd, 2002: 281). As Boaz and Ashby (2003: 7) noted, while validity, reliability, replicability and generalisability are the prominent criteria used to judge quantitative research, they may not be appropriate criteria for qualitative research. For example, although some might advocate for replicability as a key quality determinant, others might argue that research is simply not replicable, not only because the context and people's lives will have changed from the exact point in time the research was conducted, but also because a different researcher would inevitably interact differently with participants. In short, as Becker et al (2006: 7–8) argue, because traditional criteria are biased towards quantitative approaches, alternative criteria should seek to be more inclusive. Thus, instead of thinking of 'truth' we could think of 'trustworthiness', validity could be replaced by credibility, generalisability by transferability of context, reliability by dependability, and objectivity by confirmability. Patton (2002) goes further by proposing lists of alternative quality criteria including 'traditional scientific', 'social constructivist', 'artistic and evocative', 'critical change' and 'evaluation standards and principles' (see Table 2.1). The 'critical change' criteria in particular may appeal to parts of the development studies research community as they include participatory learning approaches, noting their neo-Marxist and feminist roots, increasing consciousness of inequalities and injustice, and representations of the perspectives of the less powerful. Critical change criteria also have strong resonance with Lather's (1986) concept of catalytic validity, which entails an explicit concern for social transformation. It goes beyond the research principle of 'do no harm' and calls for research that:

> allow[s] marginalized voices to be heard, to challenge dominant discourses and to open up alternative perspectives and courses of action ... research process reorients, focuses, and energises participants towards knowing reality in order to transform it. (Lather, 1986: 69, 272)

Source: Sumner and Tribe (2008).

Table 2.1: Alternative quality criteria

Traditional scientific criteria (i.e. positivist)	Social constructivist criteria (i.e. relativist)	Artistic and evocative criteria	Critical change criteria (neo-Marxist, some feminist)	Evaluation standards and principles
• Objectivity (attempts to minimise bias)	• Subjectivity acknowledged and embraced	• Opens the world to us in some way	• Critical perspectives – increases consciousness of injustice	• Utility – no point doing it if it is not going to be useful to some audience
• Validity of data	• Trustworthiness and authenticity – fairness and coverage of others' perspectives	• Creativity	• Identifies nature and sources of inequalities and injustice	• Feasibility – no point if not practically or politically doable
• Systematic rigour of fieldwork practices		• Aesthetic quality	• Represents the perspective of the less powerful	• Propriety – fair and ethical
• Triangulation (for consistency of findings)	• Triangulation (to capture multiple perspectives)	• Interpretive vitality	• Makes visible the ways in which those with more power exercise and benefit from this power	• Accuracy
• Reliability of coding and pattern analysis (multiple coders)	• Reflexivity and praxis – understanding one's own background and how to act in the world	• Flows from self – embedded in lived experience	• Engages those with less power respectfully and collaboratively	• Systematic inquiry
• Correspondence of findings to reality	• Particularity – doing justice to unique cases	• Stimulating	• Builds capacity of those involved to take action	• Integrity/honesty and respect for people
• Strength of evidence supporting causal hypotheses	• Contributions to dialogue – encouraging multiple perspectives	• Provocative	• Identifies potential change-making strategies	• Responsibility to general public welfare
• Generalisability		• Connects with and moves the audience	• Consequential or catalytic validity	
• Contributions to theory		• Voice is distinct and expressive		
		• Feels 'true', 'authentic', and 'real'		
		• Case studies become literary works, blurring boundaries		

Source: Sumner and Tribe (2008), adapted from Patton (2002: 544).

A second important critique of the evidence-based policy approach concerns the understanding of *power*. By emphasising the instrumental role of research and its direct impact on policy decisions, there is a danger of obscuring the 'invisible' ways in which power is exercised. Gaventa (2006), based on the seminal work of Lukes (1974), focuses on the importance of the 'third dimension' of power – that is, the way in which power operates to shape people's preferences – and the role of policy discourses in influencing the parameters of policy decision-making. As such, both scholars and practitioners in this field increasingly appreciate that scientific knowledge is but one of several rival forces shaping the policy process, and subscribe to an *evidence-inspired* policy-making approach (Duncan, 2005), making research a key building block of policy formulation (Nutley et al, 2002).

Finally, there is a growing debate over the politicisation of science – as highlighted by recent heated debates on the nature and intensity of climate change. Monaghan (2008: 145) argues that evidence-based policy may at times be policy-based evidence, which he defines as 'the cherry-picking of favourable evidence to support an established policy position'.

2.3 Approaches to evidence generation on child poverty and well-being

Historically, evidence about childhood and childhood poverty in developing countries has been dominated by quantitative assessments of children's human capital development, such as nutritional status and school enrolment. Over the last decade and a half, in part inspired by the UNCRC, a much richer body of knowledge has emerged, including child-centred approaches that incorporate children's participation. As a result, the debates about evidence quality and what knowledge counts as 'legitimate' or 'most persuasive' discussed in the previous section have also surfaced in the field of childhood studies.

Quantitative researchers have focused on measuring the extent and causes of childhood poverty, especially infant mortality rates, child malnutrition (using anthropometric data), educational attainment and achievement,[3] and involvement in harmful forms of child labour (recent noteworthy examples include Cockburn, 2002; Gordon et al, 2004). These researchers have sought to address the disjuncture between childhood and adult/household-level poverty, especially as 'traditional' proxy monetary measures of poverty and sources of data such as income and consumption are problematic for children for the reasons noted in Chapter 1 (such as the possibility that non-market channels are more important in shaping childhood poverty; children's access to, and control of, income can be extremely marginal; and the likelihood that resources and power are distributed unequally within households and thus disaggregated data are essential – see Box 2.2).

Qualitative researchers have, by contrast, engaged less with discourses of poverty reduction, instead focusing more on aspects of well-being, including care, nurture, resilience, capabilities, rights, social capital, the creation of gendered identities and opportunities for participation and decision-making, among others (noteworthy examples include Graue and Walsh, 1998; Woodhead, 1999; Lloyd-Smith and Tarr, 2000; White, S., 2002). The 'thick description' and nuanced insights of qualitative analysis provide an understanding of the intra-household dynamics and/or social processes behind the numbers. In the case of participatory research, it also enables an understanding of children's experiences and perceptions of various forms of deprivation and vulnerability. This is critical as it shifts policy debates from preparing for children's future

---

Box 2.2: Age-disaggregated data collection

Age-disaggregated data, which enable policy advocates to make compelling arguments about the extent of childhood deprivation and the urgency to act (see Chapter 3), have only become available relatively recently. UNICEF's MICS (Multiple Indicator Cluster Swing), which was initiated in the mid-1990s, is one of the few internationally comparative data sources on childhood well-being. It was initially designed to focus on maternal/child health and nutrition, but subsequently expanded to include indicators on child education and protection, and is now in its fourth round, covering more than 100 countries. Important data constraints still exist, however, in relation to the impact of intra-household dynamics on child well-being, age-disaggregated budget outlays on child-related policies and longitudinal data that would allow analysts to trace the cumulative impacts of well-being or deprivation over the course of childhood and adulthood, and possibly intergenerationally. In 2000, the United Kingdom (UK) Department for International Development (DFID) established the Childhood Poverty Research and Policy Centre (CHIP), a multi-year childhood poverty research programme within its Chronic Poverty Research Centre, as well as Young Lives, a longitudinal study on childhood in four developing countries. In addition, the International Labour Organization (ILO) has established a Statistical Information and Monitoring Programme on Child Labour (SIMPOC) that coordinates national surveys in almost 60 countries. These types of programmes constitute important first steps in bridging the gap between data availability and knowledge and policy.

Source: See www.chronicpoverty.org and www.younglives.org.uk

'well becoming' to working towards their current 'well-being' (Ben-Arieh, 2006).[4]

Until relatively recently, quantitative and qualitative approaches to researching child poverty tended to be published in different types of journals – economics, epidemiology and development studies versus childhood studies, sociology, anthropology and gender studies, respectively – with relatively little crossover between the two. Gradually, however, links are being forged between the two disciplinary/methodological clusters, and mixed methods research on childhood well-being is emerging.

A central argument of this chapter is that the distinctiveness of children's well-being (noted in Chapter 1) means research on this topic in particular benefits from mixing methods and combining quantitative and qualitative analysis. In Chapter 1 we concluded that relational and subjective dimensions of children's well-being have been underemphasised, and that they matter when considering children's voice, vision and visibility and play a role in determining material dimensions of children's well-being. To recap, we concluded that childhood poverty and well-being are distinct from adult poverty and well-being on a number of levels. Better understanding of the dynamics and processes that might reinforce or reverse patterns of disadvantage or benefit is a matter of urgency in light of the growing body of scholarship on the life-course and the intergenerational impacts of childhood poverty.

Children have differing needs, wants and capacities depending on their stage of childhood (e.g. infancy, early childhood, middle childhood and adolescence). Over the course of the first decades of life, children undergo certain physical and neurological transformations that give rise to *evolving capacities* over time (e.g. Lansdown, 2005). These are, however, experienced in diverse ways as children are a *heterogeneous group* living in divergent socio-economic conditions with distinct needs and concerns. As Wood (1985: 2) argues, 'Children become "cases" which are "disorganised" from their own context and "re-organised" into the categories given by development intervention'. Whereas there is broad acceptance of 'gender' and 'sexuality' as social divisions that are not natural or 'god-given', but culturally constructed, recognition of childhood as a culturally constructed phenomenon, whereby children in different cultural contexts have divergent sets of rights and responsibilities, is more recent and little explored outside childhood studies circles (e.g. James and Prout, 1990; Platt, 2003). As such, processes of evidence generation need to take account of the complexities of childhood biological, neurological, social and moral development (e.g. Ridge, 2002; Yaqub, 2002).

We can posit that a further key differentiating experience is that childhood poverty and well-being are more intensely relational in nature: there is greater reliance on 'others', typically adults, for care and nurture; greater physiological and psychological vulnerability; and reduced autonomy/power – that is, children's conventional voicelessness has a particular quality and intensity. In recent years scholars have paid increasing attention to the relational nature of well-being and the importance of care, especially for young children and the elderly (e.g. Lewis, 2002; White, S., 2002; Folbre and Bittman, 2004). In order to understand child well-being, exploring intra-household dynamics and arrangements of care is critical given children's greater vulnerability and reliance on (usually) adult care (Marshall, 2003). However, as research on child-headed households and the gendered dimensions of child work has underscored, intra-household dynamics often entail children, especially girls, shouldering part of the care management burden, especially in large impoverished households (e.g. Kabeer, 2003). Although analyses of care dynamics usually lend themselves more readily to qualitative approaches, feminist economists are increasingly seeking to explore the impacts of intra-household allocations of resources and power quantitatively in order to draw greater policy attention to the political economy of care (e.g. Folbre, 2006).

Furthermore, a considerable body of research evidence has emphasised the ways children are situated and influenced not only by their household environment, but also by their neighbourhood, school and society (e.g. Becker et al, 1998; Ruel et al, 1999). Although the current emphasis on children as 'participant agents' in social relations (Mayall, 2002) who shape their circumstances and social structure is a necessary correction to conceptualisations of children as passive targets of social intervention, child well-being is ultimately more dependent on community and social influences than that of adults due to their unequal power and prevailing decision-making relations. As Sarah White (2002: 2) argues, '"child-centred" development practices must not be "child-only": social and economic justice for poor children must be tackled in the context of their families and communities'. In light of the above, this book argues that a 3D approach to knowledge generation about child poverty and well-being is essential to accurately capture and understand the complexities of child poverty and well-being.

2.4 Mixed-methods knowledge on childhood

To accept and promote cross-disciplinary approaches implies openness to the use of all available insights to gain a better understanding of phenomena.[5] Labels such as 'qual–quant', 'q-squared' or 'q-integrated' might suggest that mixed methods simply entails taking a quantitative method and adding a qualitative method, giving equal weight to each. However, there are numerous possible combinations, each imbued with assumptions regarding the respective roles, relative importance and desired sequencing of qualitative or quantitative methods.

At the outset, it is worth reminding ourselves what the terms 'qualitative' and 'quantitative' are used to refer to:

• types of methodology – the overall research strategy used to address the research questions or hypotheses;
• types of methods of data collection – that is, the specific methods;
• types of data collected – that is, the raw data;
• types of data analysis – that is, the techniques of analysis; and
• types of data output – that is, the data in the final report or study.

With regard to poverty research, Carvalho and White (1997: 1) characterise quantitative and qualitative approaches as follows:

> The quantitative approach ... typically uses random sample surveys and structured interviews to collect the data – mainly, quantifiable data – and analyzes it using statistical techniques. By contrast, the qualitative approach ... typically uses purposive sampling and semi-structured or interactive interviews to collect the data – mainly, data relating to people's judgment, preferences, priorities, and/ or perceptions about a subject – and analyzes it usually through sociological or anthropological research techniques.

Qualitative methods can also produce quantitative data, although the opposite is not true. Moser (2003), for instance, has championed the need for 'apt illustration' (as compared to anecdotal evidence) through quantifiable qualitative research:

> [There is a need to shift] goalposts as to the definition of robustness so that it becomes more 'inclusive' of quantifiable qualitative research. Only this can ensure that social issues do not remain confined to anecdotal boxes, but provide

information of equal comparability in poverty assessments.
(2003: 82)

Moser's work on violence in Colombia and Guatemala, which
quantifies and categorises insights from participatory research with
hundreds of urban poor people, was designed to break down the divide
between researchers and policymakers and make information about the
complexities of people's experiences 'accessible to more policymakers
not only within the research countries but also in a broader context'
(2004: 3).[6]

However, there is no guarantee that different approaches, methods
or data will be immediately synthesisable or even comparable. It
is interesting to question how one adjudicates situations when the
evidence is contradictory. Mixing might have different functions – to
enrich, explain or even contradict, rather than to confirm or refute. It
may even tell 'different stories' on the same subject, because quantitative
methods are good for specifying relationships (i.e. describing) and
qualitative methods for explaining and understanding relationships
(Thomas and Johnson, 2002: 1).

Brannen (2005: 12–14) lists four functions of combining methods:[7]

- elaboration or expansion ('the use of one type of data analysis adds
  to the understanding being gained by another');
- initiation ('the use of a first method sparks new hypotheses or
  research questions that can be pursued using a different method');
- complementary ('the data analyses from the two methods are
  juxtaposed and generate complementary insights that together create
  a bigger picture'); and
- contradictions ('simply juxtapose the contradictions for others to
  explore in further research').

One concrete example of mixing can be taken from poverty researchers
who have sought to combine quantitative approaches (to determine
the amount of poverty and where it is) and qualitative approaches
(to identify the causes and dynamics of poverty). They have done so
by combining household surveys and case studies from participatory
poverty assessments (PPAs). Table 2.2 sets out selected generic strengths
and weaknesses of surveys and PPAs.

Combination may take place during data collection by simultaneously
conducting a survey and a PPA in the same sample, or during the data-
analysis stage by merging results and/or synthesising findings into one
set of recommendations (see Table 2.3).

Table 2.2: Selected possible generic strengths and weaknesses of PPAs and surveys

	Strengths	Weaknesses
PPAs	• Richer definition of poverty • More insights into causal processes • Holistic – a set of relationships as a whole, not pre-selected attributes • Scope for attention to processes as well as snapshots of the situation • Feedback loop – new/more interviews for interrogating data • Focus on context and people's experiences	• Lack of generalisability (but the sample can be made more or less representative of the population) • Difficulty of verifying information • Limited systematic disaggregation • Possibility of unrepresentative participation • Potential for agenda framing by facilitators • Pitfalls in attitudinal data – arrival of a PPA team changes people's behaviour
Household surveys	• Aggregation and comparisons possible across time and with other data sets • Reliability of results measurable • Credibility of numbers with policymakers • Credibility of national statistics with policymakers • Allows simulation of different policy options • Correlations identify associations, raising questions of causality	• Misses what is not easily quantifiable • Sampling frame may miss significant members of the population • May fail to capture intra-household resource allocation • Assumes that numbers are objective and conclusive • Assumes that one question means the same thing in different cultural contexts

Sources: Appleton and Booth (2001), Carvalho and White (1997) and Chambers (2003)..

Table 2.3: Selected examples of combining qualitative and quantitative data collection and analysis

		Function	
		Combining	**Integrating**
Stage of research process	**Data collection**	• Conduct a simultaneous survey and PPA in the same sample (ideally nationally representative)	• Use surveys to identify subgroups for PPAs or use PPAs to identify survey questions
	Data analysis	• Synthesise findings into one set of results or merge outcomes from mixed teams of qualitative and quantitative researchers	• Use PPAs to confirm or refute the validity of surveys (or vice versa) • Use PPAs to enrich or explain information on processes in survey variables (or vice versa)

Sources: Constructed and expanded from text in Carvalho and White (1997), Shaffer (2003) and Thorbecke (2003).

At a more sophisticated level, integration might take place at the data-collection stage by using surveys to identify subgroups within PPAs or using PPAs to identify survey questions. At the data–analysis stage, integration could take place by PPAs and surveys confirming or refuting each other (e.g. using PPAs to confirm the validity of surveys, or vice versa), or by PPAs and surveys enriching/explaining each other's findings (e.g. using PPAs to obtain information on processes underpinning survey variables, or vice versa). In sum, the researcher needs to consider two questions, both of which are informed by the type of research problem and the question and/or hypothesis under investigation. First, is the 'dominant' method – that which will yield most of the data – qualitative or quantitative? Second, are the methods to be mixed sequentially or simultaneously?

So how do these methodological concerns play out in research on child well-being? We begin by discussing the relatively new field of participatory research with children, and then discuss examples of research where the mixing of methods was used to 'initiate' (generate new hypotheses), 'expand', 'combine' or 'contradict' the findings generated through a different methodological approach.

In order to capture the particular quality of children's 'voices', qualitative researchers interested in childhood have used participatory research methods such as play, song, drawing and photography to explore conventionally silenced perspectives (Alfini, 2006; see also Table 2.5 at the end of this chapter). As Selener (1997: 2) argues:

> The inclusion of direct testimony in the development debate can help to make it less of a monologue and more of a dialogue, as people's testimony begins to require answers and as their voices force the development establishment to be more accountable for their actions.

As discussed in Chapter 1, while adult researchers may emphasise children's health, nutritional and scholastic outcomes, participatory research with children suggests that relational and subjective deprivations are often equally important concerns, including insufficient time to play, lack of affection from family members, feelings of social exclusion by peers and shabby and/or dirty clothing.

The degree and duration of children's involvement in research varies considerably. Cahill (2007) argues that research *with* children is distinct from research *on* children, an argument resonating with the claim that children as project/research beneficiaries are quite different from children genuinely involved in decision-making and/or knowledge-generation processes. The extent of children's involvement in the research process depends largely on the perceptions of, and the methodology adopted by, the researcher(s). The majority of research is never truly participatory in the sense that children are not conferred equal 'co-researcher' status – partnerships are usually characterised by power imbalances (see Cahill, 2007). This is perhaps largely due to embedded discourses within the academy regarding children's capacities and reliability in a research context (Ben-Arieh, 2005), logistical obstacles to such long-term equitable engagement and, interestingly, the way in which participation is defined and interpreted by development agencies and professionals (White and Choudhury, 2007). In the latter case, it is suggested that as participation does not (as is sometimes claimed) unproblematically bypass issues of power, but rather introduces a *new* set of power relations, it can seldom be said that what is heard is an 'authentic' children's voice as discussed in Chapter 1.

Nonetheless, researchers undertaking studies *with* children have made significant efforts to even out the power differentials inherent in all research contexts. These include: involving children in the initial design of the research project, thereby transferring a sense of ownership over the process; employing not just one participatory technique, but a range of methods to ensure that children with differing skills, capacities and experiences can participate (particularly important for preventing the reproduction of patterns of social exclusion); tailoring the degree of adult facilitation in accordance with the nature of the research/techniques used; and taking creative and innovative approaches to overcome cultural and language barriers, such as the use of visual methods (Biggeri et al, 2006). A number of studies also speak of the importance of continued child involvement after the 'formal' research process has ended. Through a reciprocal approach (Pham and Jones, 2005), it is possible to involve child participants in processes of active research dissemination whereby findings are communicated directly to both local communities and key decision-makers (van Blerk and Ansell, 2007). If participation is genuinely about empowerment, and more importantly sustained, long-term empowerment, then researchers must ensure not only that children attain valuable skills and experiences through the process, but also that they – and their families and communities – gain a better understanding of the issues researched, and are given opportunities to use the findings to push for action and change.

Participatory approaches can be mixed with other approaches, resulting in – we would argue – a 3D approach to researching child well-being whereby research seeks to capture where, how and/or why children's well-being may be distinct from adult well-being in the material, relational and subjective dimensions (see Table 1.5). In this regard, a 3D understanding of child well-being clearly needs to pay particular attention to the temporal dimensions of child outcomes

a sensitive manner in order to balance cultural relativism and universal principles. Here a mixed methods approach might be able to provide the authority, moral weight and nuanced approach that James et al advocate. For instance, quantitative survey data on the incidence of child labour can be used to draw attention to the extent of involvement in harmful forms of child work, while qualitative research can capture the complex ways in which children, their families and communities ascribe meaning to work and the intra-household and socio-economic dynamics that need to be taken into account to eradicate exploitative forms of work in an effective and sustainable way. Woldehanna et al's (2005a) work on children's paid and unpaid work in Ethiopia is one example of such a mixed methods approach, which was used for policy engagement purposes during the country's second PRSP (Jones et al, 2009).

2.5 Conclusions

This chapter highlighted the importance of understanding debates about the process of generating evidence or knowledge that underpins key policy and practice decisions, and how these play out with regard to childhood poverty and well-being in developing country contexts. It emphasised that evidence is not a neutral concept, but is embedded within a set of power relations between knowledge producers and knowledge users. This is arguably particularly true in the case of evidence about childhood well-being, as children's perspectives are too often hidden or silenced in mainstream development debates. Indeed, the very process of being involved in a participatory research endeavour may open up new and potentially profound possibilities for children and change how they interact in their social worlds.

In order to capture the complexities of children's material, relational and subjective well-being, the second half of the chapter argued that a mixed methods approach combining quantitative and qualitative (both participatory and ethnographic) methodologies can best capture the multidimensionality and heterogeneity of childhoods and, indeed, lend new weight to the urgency of investing in genuinely cross-disciplinary approaches. In this vein, there is a particular need to develop more sophisticated methodologies for capturing intra-household dynamics, community–child relations and macro–micro policy linkages.

Table 2.5: Selected studies on children's participation in research and the ways in which power relations are understood

Reference (author(s)/date)	Definition/meaning of participation taken by author(s)	Type of study: conceptual or empirical (if empirical then nature of study methodology) and scope (i.e. country coverage)	Factors mediating children's participation		
			Power as narratives/ discourses	Power as actors/networks	Power as context/ institutions
Aitken and Herman (2009)	• Children should be involved in research design: the number of children living independently of adults is evidence of the potential competence of children and their agency in plans for improving livelihood • Participation can take many forms and operate at different levels in the research process	• Conceptual	• Perceptions of children's 'reduced capacity' to understand the consequence of actions, including participation in research activities • Conceptualisations of children as legal subjects • Potential disregard of children because their involvement does not fit the ideals of what is 'normal' and 'good' for a child • Operational ambiguity of 'participation' • Perceptions that provision and protection should be privileged over participation	• Aims and motivations of researchers • Consent of children/parents • Who is participation for? • Types of methods implemented by researchers: do children get a choice? • Relevancy of questions asked to children • Payment of participants • Skills of children as researchers	• Ethical considerations • Issues of confidentiality and privacy • Stage at which children are involved in the research process • Children's relations to wider population

(continued)

Table 2.5 (continued)

Reference (author(s)/ date)	Definition/meaning of participation taken by author(s)	Type of study: conceptual or empirical (if empirical then nature of study methodology) and scope (i.e. country coverage)	Factors mediating children's participation		
			Power as narratives/ discourses	Power as actors/networks	Power as context/ institutions
Ben-Arieh (2005)	• Children's active involvement in the study of their well-being – a natural consequence of the concept of child rights	• Conceptual	• Perceptions that: i) children should not take part in research due to age and low cognitive ability; and ii) children are unreliable and research with them produces low response rates	• Whether follow-up activities are conducted by researchers • Parental consent • Power disparities between children and researchers	• Stage at which children are involved in the research • Are children involved in the dissemination process? • Role of child participants (e.g. data collection, data analysis, etc.) • Anonymity of research
Biggeri et al (2006)	• Capability-based approach: children have and can define their capabilities • Taking children's views into account is important for overcoming assumptions inherent to adult-based understandings of children's capabilities	• Empirical: mixed methods approach looking at children's conceptualisations of their own capabilities • At 2004 'Children's World Congress on Child Labour', 104 child delegates first surveyed, then participatory focus group with South Asian child delegates, and case studies through in-depth interviews	• Prevailing attitudes towards children, based on the view that adults know best and act in children's best interests	• Age of child (different capabilities) • Motivations of adults: Using children to promote their own goals • Representativeness of child delegates/participants • Capacities of parents which influence those of their children • Decisions and actions of parents, guardians, and teachers • Expectations of researchers • Training/skills of interviewers • Children's education	• Ground rules of the research • Language barriers

(continued)

Reference (author(s)/date)	Definition/meaning of participation taken by author(s)	Type of study: conceptual or empirical (if empirical then nature of study methodology) and scope (i.e. country coverage)	Factors mediating children's participation		
			Power as narratives/discourses	Power as actors/networks	Power as context/institutions
Cahill (2007)	• Involvement of participants (co-researchers) throughout every stage of the research • Participants are active in all decision-making processes from deciding on the focus of the project to agenda setting and data analysis • Built on the idea that all people develop social theory through life experience	• Conceptual/empirical: small-scale participatory action research project in New York involving six collaborators/co-researchers at every stage of the research	• Dominant discourses embedded within academia about research with children	• Methods for expression employed by researcher • Power relations between researcher and participants • Role of the facilitator • Capacities of participants	• Tensions between producing academically robust and 'legitimate' results and effecting action
Camfield et al (2008)	• A child-focused perspective that emphasises participation provides a better understanding of children's experiences, and creates opportunities for them to contribute to discussions and interventions that affect their lives • Participation represents a valuable way of exploring children's understandings of well-being	• Conceptual	• Contrasting perspectives of children and adults • Stereotyping and idealising the vulnerable and invisible	• Power imbalances between child participants • Power of researcher • Types of methods utilised • Number of interviews conducted • Children's role in the research • Is research quantitative or qualitative?	• Power relations associated with setting the agenda and defining research questions

(continued)

Table 2.5 (continued)

Reference (author(s)/ date)	Definition/meaning of participation taken by author(s)	Type of study: conceptual or empirical (if empirical then nature of study methodology) and scope (i.e. country coverage)	Factors mediating children's participation		
			Power as narratives/ discourses	Power as actors/networks	Power as context/ institutions
Crivello et al (2009)	• Capturing children's 'standpoints' in contexts of poverty and considering their views and experiences informs more effective and integrated interventions. • Children are both competent social actors and 'experts in their own lives', and therefore constitute valuable sources of data	• Empirical: examination of three core qualitative methods for researching child well-being as adopted by Young Lives in Ethiopia, Peru, Vietnam, and India	• Discourses informing construction of methodologies (i.e. emphasis on survival and deprivation, or on resilience and agency)	• Age and varying capacities of child participants • Children's memories • Types of methods/techniques employed by researchers (including icebreakers, games, physical movement) • Degree of facilitation by adults • Extent of interaction among children in exercises	• Translation of concepts such as 'well-being' into different languages and cultures • Ethical issues associated with information-sharing in a group setting • If longitudinal study, importance of building rapports
Fattore et al (2007)	• Children should be involved in defining their understandings, perspectives, and standpoints of and on well-being • Giving these views serious consideration, and incorporating them into the identification of key domains that can be leveraged to monitor and measure important aspects of well-being at a population level	• Empirical: collaborative research project between New South Wales Commission for Children and Young People and University of Sydney (Australia) • Individual/group semi-structured interviews with 126 children; in-depth interviews with 95 (of the original 126) children; task-oriented project with 56 children	• Approaches to conceptualising/researching well-being • Policymakers' views towards significance of research carried out with children		• General reluctance to involve children at each stage of research and policy processes • Factors associated with local contexts

(continued)

Reference (author(s)/ date)	Definition/meaning of participation taken by author(s)	Type of study: conceptual or empirical (if empirical then nature of study methodology) and scope (i.e. country coverage)	Factors mediating children's participation		
			Power as narratives/ discourses	Power as actors/networks	Power as context/ institutions
Gallagher (2008)	• Foucauldian understanding of participation: power is relational and always involves a relationship between two entities • Participation does not entail the straightforward transfer of power from adult to child, but rather constitutes a messy, fraught and ambiguous process • Instances of participation are always different	• Conceptual/empirical: author's own experience in a Glaswegian school	• Concept of the 'powerless' child • Perceptions of a 'dominating adult–subordinate child' relationship • Children may perceive participatory initiatives as unwelcome interventions • Romanticisations of child agency	• Multiple complex relations in research settings among adult researchers and child participants • Power relations between child participants • Risk of domineering children's views being privileged	• Multiple points of resistance exist in research contexts
Huebner (2004)	• Involving children and youth in studying and researching life satisfaction	• Conceptual	• 'Scientific' and 'traditional' psychological discourses informing methodological approaches to life satisfaction research		• Novelty of the research field (i.e. if new, then many studies will be exploratory and appropriate methods may not yet have been refined)
Hill et al (2004)	• Multidimensional participation that enhances children's involvement in decision-making and combats social exclusion/promotes social inclusion • Key distinction drawn between participation and consultation	• Conceptual (UK-oriented)		• Effective child participation requires sustained links between research and policy domains	• Quantitative research more likely to inform policy: less capacity for child involvement?

(continued)

45

Table 2.5 (continued)

Reference (author(s)/ date)	Definition/meaning of participation taken by author(s)	Type of study: conceptual or empirical (if empirical then nature of study methodology) and scope (i.e. country coverage)	Factors mediating children's participation		
			Power as narratives/ discourses	Power as actors/networks	Power as context/ institutions
Mannion (2007)	• Participation entails discovering and understanding children's views (various rationales for this are proposed, including enlightenment, empowerment, and citizenship), and, importantly, is about child–adult relations	• Conceptual/empirical: three UK case studies (school grounds changes, arts centre, 'child-free' zones)		• Tendency to analyse children's voices in isolation from their socio-spatial contexts	• Nature of child–adult relations • Extent of intergenerational dialogues
Naker (2007)	• Drawn from Hart's ladder: The concept of child participation manifests in a variety of adult-child engagements within development practice • Power (re)distribution is key • Partnerships based on joint initiation and direction of processes	• Empirical: assessment of child participation through an investigation of a project in Uganda involving an Advisory Committee of 40 children, aged 10-17, half girls and half boys	• Understandings of the concept of participation • Adults' uncertainties about their feelings regarding sharing decision-making power with children • Scepticism among children	• Difficulties of integrating child participation into practice after years of NGOs operating in a particular way • Skills of facilitators and group leaders • Disagreements among researchers about the role of the committee	• The 'African way' of relating to children: set social hierarchies

(continued)

Reference (author(s)/ date)	Definition/meaning of participation taken by author(s)	Type of study: conceptual or empirical (if empirical then nature of study methodology) and scope (i.e. country coverage)	Factors mediating children's participation		
			Power as narratives/ discourses	Power as actors/networks	Power as context/ institutions
Powell and Smith (2009)	• If children are to be involved in research, their views must be heard and taken seriously, even (or especially) if they challenge dominant protectionist and paternalistic discourses/systems. Participation is defined as taking part and the sense of knowing that one's actions are taken note of and may be acted upon (see Boyden and Ennew, 1997, in Morrow, 1999: 149).	• Empirical : email interviews with 12 researchers working on/with children, predominantly in New Zealand	• Conceptions of children among researchers and gatekeepers • Infiltration of a protectionist discourse with regard to children • Failure to take child agency into account	• Parental consent • Gatekeepers and subsequent selection problems • Types of methods used • Communication skills of researchers; ability to build relationships • Power imbalances in research	• Choice of research topic – too sensitive to involve children? • Structural vulnerabilities
Redmond (2008)	• Children are capable social actors whose perspectives serve an important policy purpose in terms of problem and coping strategy identification	• Conceptual	• Perception among policymakers and researchers that children are passive, apolitical, and uninvolved in strategy-making • Discourses of professionalism	• Children exclude other children • Children's family environment – does it promote resilience? • Outlook and confidence of children • Do researchers create 'child-friendly' spaces? • Types of techniques used	• General social barrier separating children and adults

(continued)

Table 2.5 (continued)

Reference (author(s)/date)	Definition/meaning of participation taken by author(s)	Type of study: conceptual or empirical (if empirical then nature of study methodology) and scope (i.e. country coverage)	Factors mediating children's participation		
			Power as narratives/discourses	Power as actors/networks	Power as context/institutions
Ridge (2002)	• Children are active social agents whose views must be reflected in policy decisions that affect them • Participation is defined in contrast to social exclusion and is considered a core element of a child-centred approach to development	• Empirical: quantitative and qualitative methodology • In-depth survey conducted in 1999 of 40 children living in South-east England, and unstructured interviews that children had the opportunity to shape and define	• Embedded adult assumptions about children's lives • Perceptions that uncovered child knowledge will 'threaten' these assumptions • Children as human 'beings' or 'becomings'	• Children's backgrounds • Age of participants • Gender of participants	• Ethical and moral dilemmas surrounding research with children
Pham and Jones (2005)	• Only if children's knowledges are 'uncovered' will policies and programmes be designed in a way that is 'responsive and relevant to their concerns and needs' (Boyden and Ennew, 1997:10) • Participation must embrace the diversity of children's experiences	• Conceptual/empirical: case study material from Young Lives project in Vietnam (Children's Fora and Young Journalist Clubs)	• Dominant Western models of childhood that infiltrate policymakers' perceptions	• Presence of networks/channels linking children's knowledge generation to policymakers • Evaluations of whether outcomes of participatory initiatives influence policy-making • Is research reciprocal? • Relationships between practitioners/researchers and children and their families • Analytical and communication skills among children • Whether stakeholder 'buy-in' is secured (from the outset) • Relationships with local collaborators and project partners	• Clientalism in southern contexts. Embracing context is far more important than seeking standardised praxis or a grand theory

(continued)

Reference (author(s)/date)	Definition/meaning of participation taken by author(s)	Type of study: conceptual or empirical (if empirical then nature of study methodology) and scope (i.e. country coverage)	Factors mediating children's participation		
			Power as narratives/discourses	Power as actors/networks	Power as context/institutions
Van Blerk and Ansell (2007)	• Adults cannot presume to have insight into children's social and cultural worlds • Children are the experts in this sense and therefore have much to offer researchers in terms of knowledge generation • Participation of children in the research process results in their empowerment	• Empirical: participatory feedback and dissemination experiences in Lesotho and Malawi; participatory learning and action (PLA) workshops, dramas, community discussions, workshops with policymakers	• Perceptions of competencies of children • Views on the importance of dissemination	• Are policymakers interested in attending dissemination workshops? • Ways in which researchers involve children in dissemination processes • Understandings and utilisations of policy networks • Relationships with policymakers	• Time delays between original research and dissemination processes. • Difficulties associated with accessing street children and out-of-school children
White and Choudhury (2007)	• Ideally, participation is about raising children's voice in development matters • In reality, participation is 'produced' through the development industry via 'projectisation' of participation and promotion of agency-sponsored events and programmes	• Conceptual/empirical: case study drawn from authors' extensive experience with Amra, a children's organisation in Bangladesh • Primary data collected through intensive group and individual interviews, consultation, and field visits with various members (>100 children), in addition to interviews with parents and staff in an international agency	• Understandings of what counts as 'participation' as determined by development agency staff • Framing of the 'separate' children's world regulates what can be said by the researcher about what is taking place	• Children's agency constrained and determined by adults in development agencies (i.e. what can be said, when it should be said). • Development workers have the power to reject researchers' interpretations of child participation if they do not coincide with their own	• Participation as a new relations of power

(continued)

49

Table 2.5 (continued)

Reference (author(s)/ date)	Definition/meaning of participation taken by author(s)	Type of study: conceptual or empirical (if empirical then nature of study methodology) and scope (i.e. country coverage)	Factors mediating children's participation		
			Power as narratives/ discourses	Power as actors/networks	Power as context/ institutions
Woodhead and Faulkner (2000)	• UNCRC-based definition: entails a degree of power devolvement that goes beyond simply 'listening to children' • Children become competent through participatory research	• Conceptual	• Perceptions of children's roles and capacities • Objective and dispassionate scientific discourses that inform methodology (e.g. 'traditional' approaches to psychological research frame children as subjects rather than co-researchers)	• Power differentials and differences in status • Researchers' methodological approaches	

Notes

[1] This chapter draws on and develops ideas in Sumner and Tribe (2008). An earlier version of part of this chapter was published as Jones and Sumner (2009).

[2] The influential work of organisations such as the Cochrane Collaboration (healthcare) and the Campbell Collaboration (broader social policy, most notably criminal justice) has been key to the endorsement of quantitative and experimental techniques as the model to be followed in evidence-based policy initiatives.

[3] Commonly researched educational indicators include rates of school enrolment for girls and boys, over-age enrolment and results on standardised scholastic achievement tests.

[4] We are grateful to Laura Camfield for this observation.

[5] This section draws on Sumner and Tribe (2009: ch 5).

[6] Holland and Abeyasekera's (forthcoming) work on 'participatory numbers' presents another innovative approach to producing quantitative data from qualitative methods. See also Mayoux and Chambers (2005).

[7] Further, Brannen (2005: 14) identifies 12 specific conceivable combinations (see below). In each, there is a 'dominant' method (i.e. the method that gathers the majority of the data) and a 'non-dominant' method (i.e. the method that gathers the minority of the data). Capital letters denote the 'dominant' method (which will yield the majority of data); + denotes simultaneously occurring methods; and > denotes temporal sequencing of methods.

Simultaneous research designs:

1. QUAL + quan or
2. QUAL + QUAN
3. QUAN + quan or
4. QUAN + QUAN
5. QUAL + qual or
6. QUAL + QUAL

Sequential research designs:

1. QUAL > qual or
2. qual > QUAL or
3. QUAL > QUAL
4. QUAN > quan or

5. quan > QUAN or
6. QUAN > QUAN
7. QUAL > quan or
8. qual > QUAN or
9. QUAL > QUAN
10. QUAN > qual or
11. quan > QUAL or
12. QUAN > QUAL

[8] Holland et al (2006) provide a number of examples on school transitions, youth to work transitions, post-divorce life and so on.

THREE

Policy processes, knowledge and child well-being

3.1 Introduction

In this chapter, we extend our 3D perspective on child poverty and well-being to consider policy processes, the role of knowledge in policy processes and policy advocacy with regard to children's poverty and well-being.[1] There is a growing literature on children and policy processes. Many have defined a child-centred approach as one based on participatory decision-making with children (e.g. O'Malley, 2004). However, this is just one approach, and is no guarantee that children's voices will be heard or heard equally. A child-sensitive approach can also be achieved by ensuring that children's needs and rights are represented by children's advocates – whether service providers, advocates, bureaucrats or researchers – in policy discourse and integrated into the development of new policies and policy and programme evaluations (Jones and Sumner, 2009).

This chapter is structured as follows: Section 3.2 sets out thinking on the dynamics of policy processes. Section 3.3 then discusses types of policy change and Section 3.4 focuses on policy advocacy and knowledge–policy interaction approaches. Section 3.5 applies the preceding debates to child well-being and Section 3.6 concludes.

3.2 The dynamics of policy processes

Understanding of decision-making in public policy processes has evolved from Northern contexts since Lasswell and Lerner (1951), and particularly since the 1970s/80s (see, for example, Lindblom, 1959, 1979; Etzioni, 1967; Pressman and Wildavsky, 1973; Wildavsky, 1980; Hogwood and Gunn, 1984). Over the last two decades research has expanded to Southern contexts (see, for example, Grindle and Thomas, 1980; Walt, 1984; Thomas and Grindle, 1990; Walt and Gibson, 1994; Holmes and Scoones, 2000; Court and Young, 2003; Keeley and Scoones, 2003a, 2003b, 2003c, 2006; Brock and McGee, 2004; Leach et al, 2005). Assumptions regarding policy-making processes have been challenged, particularly in Southern contexts – notably those relating to the rationality and linearity of policy processes (see Stone Sweet et al, 2001). The net result is that there is now an array of theories and analytical frameworks of policy processes (see Box 3.1).

Box 3.1: The evolution of approaches to analysing policy processes

Approaches to understanding policy processes have evolved considerably over the last half-century. First-generation models in the 1950s/60s only took limited account of power per se in rational and linear models that largely assume a certain kind of functioning democracy. These included older rational models (e.g. Lasswell, 1951a, 1951b, 1951c, 1951d), bounded rationality models (e.g. Simon, 1957) and incrementalism and/or disjointed incrementalism models (e.g. Lindblom, 1959).

Second-generation models dealt more explicitly with power. They also expanded from considering state actors and their political or bureaucratic interests and capacities to include non-state actors and networks, and shifted from linearity and stages to iterative processes and spaces. Examples include middle-ground or mixed scanning models (e.g. Etzioni, 1967), garbage can theories (e.g. March and Olsen, 1976), interceptor/receptor models (e.g. Hanney, 2005), the three interconnecting streams model (e.g. Kingdon, 1984), the political economy approach of de Janvry and Subramanian (1993), the ladder of utilisation and receptors receptivity model (e.g. Knott and Wildavsky, 1980), the interactive or problem-solving/engineering models (e.g. Grindle and Thomas, 1980), the Research and Policy in Development (RAPID) research-into-policy model (e.g. Crewe and Young, 2002), the argumentative model (e.g. Fischer and Forester, 1993), and the structuration or KNOTS [Knowledge, Technology and Society Research Team (Institute of Development Studies)}-discourse based model (e.g. Keeley and Scoones, 2006; KNOTS, 2006).

Most recently, the 'new development anthropology' approach considers 'policy' as an organising concept that shapes how people live, think and act and seeks to not only examine the language of policy/power, but also to investigate its institutions, processes, effects and practices ethnographically – the internal dynamics of donors and 'donor land' are recent examples (see, for example, Mosse, 2004).

The stages of policy-making – agenda-setting, formation, decision-making, implementation and evaluation – are commonly used as heuristic devices to break down the complexity of policy processes, but are increasingly criticised as too linear and unrealistic (see discussion in Sabatier and Jenkins-Smith, 1993). An alternative to thinking about policy stages is the concept of 'policy spaces'. Policy spaces are moments of intervention that reconfigure relations, or bring in new ones and set the tone for a new direction. These spaces may be:

- conceptual spaces (where new ideas can be introduced into the debate and circulated through various media);
- bureaucratic spaces (formal policymaking spaces within the government bureaucracy/legal system, led by civil servants with selected inputs from external experts);
- political/electoral spaces (i.e. formal participation in elections);
- invited spaces (consultations on policy led by government agencies involving selective stakeholder participation);
- popular or claimed spaces such as protests and demonstrations that put pressure on governments (KNOTS, 2006).

Brock et al (2001), Gaventa (2006) and others have argued that spaces may be closed, invited, claimed/created, visible, hidden and/or invisible in nature. Such spaces likely differ by sector, country and time. For example, the high level of technical expertise required to engage in trade or climate change policy debates provides different policy process dynamics than do policies on social protection (e.g. Newell and Tussie, 2006; Pomares and Jones, 2009).

Different approaches to understanding the dynamics of policy processes encompass the three different conceptualisations of power noted in Chapter 1: (i) material political economy; (ii) discourse and the socio-political construction of knowledge; and (iii) power as embedded in social structures and institutions. Significantly though, there is no single approach to policy processes that explicitly accounts for these multiple (and interlinked) understandings of power. We therefore propose a synthesis approach that takes these multiple and interlocking understandings into account as follows:

- *Policy ideas and narratives:* the ways policy issues are conceptualised and how their relevance is understood with regard to policy agendas and the knowledge base that underpins them (i.e. drawing on Foucault's power as discourse);
- *Policy actors and networks:* the role of actor interests, key decision-makers and policy entrepreneurs, or networks and groups who are influential in decision-making and their political interests and incentive/disincentive structures (i.e. drawing on Marx's power as material political economy); and
- *Political contexts/institutions:* the 'hard' structures in which decisions are made and the broader 'soft' socio-economic, political and cultural

environment or rules of the game that shapes policy processes (i.e. North's [1990] understanding of power as institutions) and policy spaces – both of which provide dynamic opportunities for change.

Underlying these three domains is the assumption that there is an unclear line between those who 'make' policy and those who 'influence' policy, that policy processes are likely to be non-linear and highly iterative, and that 'evidence' used in policy processes is contestable rather than positivistic.

Because these domains are critical to our analysis in Part Two of the book, we discuss each in turn before reflecting on different types of policy change and the role that knowledge does or does not play (also see Table 3.1).

Policy ideas/narratives

Policy narratives are the 'storylines' that shape policy debates and seek to legitimise decision-making processes. We might ask what is the prevailing policy narrative? How is it framed? Whose interests does it represent? Whose interests are marginalised? It is important to ascertain, for example, the extent to which there is consensus on what should be done, the extent of influence of international domestic policy discourses, and the extent to which a policy issue is novel.

In thinking about policy narratives, it is also critical to ask about the evidence or knowledge base that supports a particular narrative. 'Evidence' is not a neutral concept (Upshur et al, 2001: 94) and some kinds are given more weight than others in the policymaking process. As noted in Chapter 2, academic rigour is often shaped by understandings of hierarchies of knowledge that privilege some methods and academic disciplines over others (e.g. quantitative methods, economics) and is a critical filter through which research evidence is consumed in policy processes. For example, indigenous, participatory or experiential 'evidence' may have lower status than mathematical modelling 'evidence'. However, the way evidence is framed so as to suit a particular political and socio-cultural context, and the credibility of the messengers who present the research findings, are also important factors and should not be underestimated.

Policy actors/networks

Although policy process analysis generally focuses on the role of politicians and government officials, policy actors are broader, including those who are formally (i.e. elected, such as legislators) and informally (non-elected, either visible or invisible/behind-the-scenes actors such as NGOs, donors, grassroots groups, the media and researchers) involved in the decision-making process.

The overall constellation of actors involved matters, but, more importantly, we need to understand what actors' respective interests are, and the formal and informal powers and capabilities available to them to realise their goals. An analysis could therefore consider such issues as the degree to which the ruling party is ideologically driven, the extent of 'special interests' (business, unions etc.), the level of civil service professionalism, the relative strength of civil society and/or the influence of donors in policy-making.

There are also various types of networks that divide and connect policymakers and non-policymakers, such as 'policy communities' (networks of policy actors from inside and outside government that are integrated with the policy-making process), 'epistemic communities' (networks of experts with recognised/'legitimised' policy-relevant knowledge) and 'advocacy coalitions' (groups of actors on an issue).

Table 3.1: Examples of determinants of policy change

Policy process dimension	Determinants of policy change
Policy ideas, narratives, and discourse(s)	• Extent to which there is consensus on the nature of the problem and appropriate responses • Extent of influence of international discourses on domestic policy • Extent to which policy issue is novel
Policy actors and networks	• Extent to which ruling party is ideologically driven • Extent of 'special interests' or range of actors – including the relative influence of service users, the private sector, unions, professional associations, civil society and donors in the policy arena • Level of bureaucracy, professionalism, and capacity to process evidence • Importance placed on evidence reviews by policymakers in power
Contexts and institutions	• Extent of democratic openness, degree of academic and media freedom, and norms of consultation and participation in policy processes • Use of multi-year development plans and other planning instruments • Level of centralisation of political decision making • Established institutional structures and policy advisory bodies • Nature of policy spaces

Source: Sumner et al (2009).

Political contexts/institutions

Institutions and political contexts are central to policy processes. Key factors to consider include: a country's political history and the extent to which some policy areas are path-dependent (largely reliant on historic policy trajectories); its level of economic and social development and the factors that underpin this (e.g. GDP level, reliance on particular economic sectors, weak governance, high levels of inequality); and the relative balance of power between political institutions (legislature, bureaucracy [and particular ministries], judiciary, political parties etc.), whether the policy process is consultative and seeks to represent the views of a broad range of stakeholders or is determined by a small technocratic group of government officials largely behind closed doors; the relative influence of external forces (e.g. global economic integration, risk of conflict) and policy actors (e.g. international financial institutions [IFIs], donors, NGOs); and which issues are politically palatable or sensitive and why.

Institutions are the formal and informal rules for interaction, presenting policy actors with a series of strategic options. We need to know what institutions prescribe, whether they enjoy legitimacy from all actors, whether their rules are effectively or selectively enforced, and whether they have stood the test of time or are vulnerable to political and economic change. For example, we could consider the degree of party competition or democratic openness, the use of multi-year development plans, the level of centralisation of political decision-making, the degree of academic and media freedom, and the presence or absence of mechanisms for public participation and consultation.

3.3 Types of policy change and the role of knowledge

In order to understand the dynamics of the knowledge–policy interface, we need to combine our 3D framework for approaching policy processes and the role of knowledge with a model that helps to capture different types of policy change. Our starting point is that a 3D well-being approach implies the need to think of policy change at multiple levels, and not only about changing policy content. We can then identify types of policy change that are linked to different and multilayered understandings of power ranging from agenda-setting and discursive shifts to procedural changes, and from changes in policy content to shifts in behaviour and popular attitudes.

Whereas 'interest group influence' theories focus on the extent to which lobbyists are able to influence electoral campaigns, key political appointments, budget decisions and legislative change (Loomis and Cigler, 2002), analysts interested in the role of ideas in policy change have highlighted the importance of adopting a broader approach that includes the capacity to set new policy agendas and shift discursive practices. Drawing on insights from Foucault's theory of knowledge as power and Lukes' (1974) observation that intangible forms of power can be strongest when it comes to shaping preferences, values and ideologies, Keck and Sikkink's (1998) work on transnational advocacy networks emphasises the centrality of information politics in policy change endeavours. They argue that the efficacy of such advocacy depends on providing alternative sources of information and filtering or interpreting these ideas through a particular set of principles or values in order to inspire political action:

> This information may seem inconsequential in the face of the economic, political, or military might of other global actors. But by overcoming the deliberate suppression of information that sustains many abuses of power, networks can help reframe international and domestic debates, changing their terms, their sites and the configuration of participants. (Keck and Sikkink, 1998: 300)

Keck and Sikkink (1998) outline five points to their approach, which are types of policy changes, as follows:

• *Framing debates and getting issues on the political agenda:* Focusing attention on new issues that were previously not part of public policy debate is one of the key levers of power that advocacy networks can exercise. Drawing on Foucauldian notions of the relationship between knowledge and power, discourse can play a powerful role in shaping which dimensions of a problem are considered or ignored, and can promote a rethinking of dominant values and policy priorities. For instance, human rights groups such as Amnesty International in the UK have sought to raise awareness of the entrenched problem of violence against women in the family by reframing it as a human rights abuse. The language of human rights abuse lends new gravity to the problem and seeks to awaken the general public to the fact that human rights concerns are not confined to developing-country contexts, but are an issue in the North too.

- *Encouraging discursive commitments from states and other policy actors:* Persuading state and non-state actors to endorse international declarations or conventions or to modify national policy positions in favour of marginalised groups can also represent an important policy-influencing step. For example, introducing the language of the MDGs into national debates puts pressure on policymakers to articulate how their country-specific plans help to reach these development targets. It also provides poor and socially excluded groups (e.g. women, children) and their advocates with a framework and with specific measurable goals against which to assess their governments' progress.

- *Promoting procedural changes at the international and domestic level:* Successful advocacy does not only involve policy outcomes, but also remoulds the process through which policy decisions are made. While procedural changes may not automatically improve policy content, they often improve dialogue processes between state and civil society actors that can lead to gradual policy reforms over time (Keck and Sikkink, 1998: 26). Here the policy spaces opened by the World Bank's and International Monetary Fund's (IMF's) PRSP initiative, which includes mandatory national grassroots consultations, constitutes a good example. Although the final content of many PRSPs has been justly criticised for not adequately recognising these multiple perspectives (e.g. Heidel, 2004; Oxfam GB, 2004), the initiative has created greater awareness among a broader array of 'counter-publics' about the importance of engaging with national development policy frameworks and provided the impetus for a range of new monitoring and evaluating endeavours.

- *Securing policy, regulatory or legislative changes:* Securing changes in policy – including budget increases, the passage of new legislation or more favourable ministerial policy positions or regulations – is most often recognised as the yardstick of effective advocacy. For example, the trial and imprisonment of military officials convicted of human rights abuses and the establishment of truth and reconciliation commissions in a number of post-conflict societies are often cited as evidence of the successful advocacy efforts of human rights organisations (e.g. Dougherty, 2004). Such policy shifts cannot be equated with policy enforcement, but their role in encouraging broader processes of cultural change should not be underestimated: 'While legal advances alone cannot eliminate discrimination … laws expanding the rights of [marginalised groups] interact with and reinforce broader processes of cultural change. The process by which de jure rights are translated into de facto rights may be frustratingly slow, but the latter is impossible without the former' (Haas, 2000: 1).

- *Influencing attitudinal and behavioural change in key actors:* Changing behaviour – at the levels of officialdom and policy implementation – is the final way of changing policy. The critical question is whether new policies are effectively implemented so as to improve people's lives? For example, are natural resource management programmes translating into less environmental degradation? Do women have better access to micro-finance? However, as the broader literature on behavioural change (especially regarding health interventions) emphasises, this complex area is difficult to evaluate as the change process is seldom linear (Gerwe, 2000).

In short, Keck and Sikkink's approach to policy change encourages a more nuanced account of the complexities of the policy process. It encompasses the full policy cycle – from expanding the policy agenda through to policy implementation. Keck and Sikkink (1998) are at pains, however, to emphasise that these are not simply different types of policy change, but are likely to represent different points of impact, which are often mutually reinforcing.

3.4 Policy advocacy and knowledge–policy interactions

Interest in the role of policy advocacy in shaping policy processes has expanded exponentially over the last three decades (Sabatier and Jenkins-Smith, 1993; Edwards and Hulme, 1996), including as part of a general trend towards democratisation in developing-country contexts (e.g. Escobar and Alvarez, 1992). Policy advocacy is the act of an individual or group seeking to influence public policy and resource allocation decisions, but not to govern (Young and Everitt, 2004). Advocacy groups, which can include social movements, NGOs, CSOs and policy networks and communities, typically engage in a range of activities to achieve their change objectives, from undertaking media campaigns and public speaking to budget analysis, lobbying elected representatives and publishing research reports and surveys. What distinguishes advocates from political parties is that they are motivated by a common set of ideas rather than by the exercise of self-interested power (Buse et al, 2005) and are pursuing a collective good framed in the public interest (Jenkins, 1978). While advocates may draw on a range of techniques, including what Keck and Sikkink (1998) have categorised as symbolic politics (using symbolic events and conferences to publicise issues and build networks), leverage politics (threatening sanctions if the gap between norms and practices remains too large) and accountability politics (whereby governments or institutions are held accountable to previous commitments and principles they have endorsed), information politics (the generation and strategic use of knowledge to enhance understanding and dramatise facts) remains one of the most powerful policy advocacy approaches. This section, focuses on this subset of advocacy, or what the literature increasingly refers to as 'research communications', 'knowledge translation', 'knowledge exchange' or 'knowledge–policy interactions'.

Knowledge translation is a term that emerged in the health sciences, and is focused on 'bridging' the divide between the policymaker and research communities (e.g. Estabrooks et al, 2006; Mitton et al, 2007). It is now widely recognised that policymakers and researchers conceptualise evidence differently, are embedded within institutions with markedly different professional incentive structures, work to very different time horizons, and that their understandings of the world are often shaped by divergent discourses and meta-narratives (e.g. Jones et al, 2009). Knowledge 'translation', therefore, entails a dynamic and iterative process involving the exchange, synthesis and application of knowledge in diverse contexts. In this system, 'knowledge brokers' are actors who negotiate and facilitate a complex system of interactions between researchers and research 'users' in order to promote greater understanding about public policy challenges and solutions (Canadian Health Services Research Foundation, 2003). It includes a range of activities that aim to present and communicate knowledge in a way that it is easily accessible and in line with users' knowledge needs. These include knowledge dissemination and communication, technology transfer, knowledge management, exchanges between researchers and those who apply knowledge, and the synthesis of results to suit a particular political or policy context. By specifying the importance of synthesis and interaction with knowledge users, the definition acknowledges the need to consider not only what knowledge should be translated, but also to which audiences, for which purpose and through which types of communication channels. In other words, this conceptualisation departs from the conventional idea that researchers are not responsible for the policy messages that are derived from their research or how they are used, but rather is informed by a commitment to consider the potential needs of knowledge users as well as their capacities to understand and make use of particular knowledge and knowledge products.

This literature also highlights the importance of 'knowledge brokers', which can play an important intermediary role between researchers, policymakers, practitioners and the citizens (e.g. Nutley et al, 2002; Lomas, 2007). Knowledge brokering is recognised as a key factor, for example, in the rapid ascent of right-wing economic and cultural thought on the American political stage in the 1980s and 1990s. Rich's (2005) comparative analysis of two leading think tanks in the USA, one progressive (the Brookings Institute) and the other conservative (the Heritage Foundation), for instance, underscores the critical role that conservative foundations placed on proactively brokering their analysis of key policy challenges. Heritage spent almost sevenfold that of Brookings on communication efforts, informed by what their former vice-president for communication described as:

> Our belief is that when the research product has been printed, then the job is only half done. That is when we start marketing it to the media.... We have as part of our charge the selling of ideas, the selling of policy proposals. We are out there actively selling these things, day after day. It's our mission. (Rich, 2005: 25)

In the same vein, the broader literature on the knowledge–policy interface includes a growing body of work on 'intermediary organisations' that seek to manage the boundary between research and policy so as to promote the credibility, salience and legitimacy of knowledge incorporated in policy (Cash et al, 2003). Key intermediary functions include: awareness-raising, leveraging access to research, signposting research and acting as a repository, synthesising and summarising research findings, capacity-building in research communication and research uptake, lobbying and advocacy for particular perspectives, and facilitating exchange and interaction among researcher and policymaker communities. The added value of intermediary organisations is their accountability to both the role of facilitating effective information flows and mediating in the case of conflict or trade-offs (Cash et al, 2003).[2]

This demand for brokering and intermediary roles notwithstanding, there is growing recognition that the terms 'knowledge translation' and 'knowledge transfer' may need to be rethought to adequately account for the complex and contested nature of applied social research (Lemieux-Charles and Champagne, 2004; Dopson and Fitzgerald, 2005). As such, a more appropriate emphasis may be on 'knowledge interaction' or 'knowledge mediation', which encompasses 'the messy nature of engagements between actors with diverse types of knowledge').As Lavis et al (2006) argue, this involves partnerships between the 'producers' and 'users' of knowledge that recognise the 'co-construction' of policy knowledge, including forging a shared understanding about what research questions to ask, how to go about answering them and how best to interpret the answers. Similar ideas have been advocated by proponents of deliberative processes that involve bringing together scientists, policymakers and citizens so as to interrogate evidence from a range of perspectives (scientific, social, cultural and ethical), and ground decisions in relevant, feasible and implementable advice (Lomas et al, 2008). In particular, such mechanisms provide opportunities for citizens to examine and challenge the positions of expert outsiders and/or domestic elites.

The term 'knowledge interaction' is also likely to be more palatable to analysts concerned about the intersection between knowledge and power (as discussed in Chapter 2) and the central role that discourse and values play in the public policy process. A growing school of thought is highly critical of the apolitical and technocratic bent of much evidence-based policy literature and is interested in addressing questions around: who decides what knowledge to translate? Who translates it? What does not get translated and why? Whose interests are served by translation and whose are excluded (e.g. Marston and Watts, 2003; Sanderson, 2004)? Drawing on the Habermasian concept of the 'argumentative turn', Fischer (2003) points out that because of the high degree of uncertainty in the physical and social worlds, analysts are regularly compelled to make interpretive judgements:

> the under-determination of the empirical world means the policy analyst has to connect data and theories through arguments rather than prove them per se.... As policy decisions have to be legitimised, the tasks of explanation, justification and persuasion play important roles in every stage of the policy cycle.... New arguments have to be constantly made to give 'the different policy components the greatest possible internal coherence and the closest fit to an ever-changing environment'. (Majone, 1989: 31, cited in Fischer, 2003: 183)

Fischer emphasises the central role of values in the policy process and the critical importance of policies and programmes tackling these directly:

> The argumentative approach recognizes that policy arguments are intimately involved with relations of power and the exercise of power. Beyond merely emphasizing efficiency and effectiveness, it calls attention to the inclusion of some concerns and the exclusion of others, the distribution of responsibility as well as causality, the assigning of praise and blame, and the employment of particular political strategies of problem framing as opposed to others. (Fischer, 2003)

Building on these insights, recent scholarship on the knowledge–policy interface has called for a shift away from models of research 'use' that assign the responsibility for knowledge 'uptake' to the individual practitioner or policymaker, and towards those that call for a shift in organisation culture that is 'research-minded'. In the latter case, research use is not only viewed as instrumental – 'what works' – but also as valuable in challenging existing paradigms and promoting new ways of conceptualising a problem. This shifts away from ideas of 'modernising' policy processes, with an emphasis on central control and rationality, and towards ideas of opening up or 'democratising' that process instead, so that a greater diversity of voices and views can be heard (Nutley et al, 2002: 259–60).

3.5 Children, policy processes and knowledge

If we seek to apply the above discussion to child poverty and well-being, evidence and policy processes, we find a relatively new but rapidly expanding array of ideas, actors and policy spaces in developing-country contexts. As Chapters 4, 5 and 6 will present more detailed discussion by region, this section sets the stage by providing a broad overview of the policy narratives, actors and contexts that constitute policy processes related to child poverty and well-being, emerging knowledge-generation efforts and the ways in which these have been reflected (or not) in advocacy and knowledge interaction endeavours.

the Committee on the Rights of the Child, including a civil society shadow reporting process, and many countries have adopted their own national plans of action for children. However, in countries facing substantial governance challenges and/or with weak legal cultures, informal rules of the game frequently override formal institutions of this nature, significantly limiting the extent to which policy decisions are informed by universal human rights considerations. Moreover, as Harper and Jones (2009) argue, a children's rights perspective is generally accorded low visibility within international donor policy agendas, thereby reinforcing weak national-level prioritisation.

Knowledge generation

Over the past 20 years, knowledge generation on childhood and child well-being in developing-country contexts has burgeoned in both academic and applied research settings. On the academic front, the discipline of childhood studies has emerged and, although scholarship remains heavily Northern in focus, there is a rapidly expanding body of knowledge related to developing-country contexts. This is exemplified by initiatives such as CHIP at the University of Manchester, Young Lives at Oxford University and Childwatch, a network of institutions focused on research on childhood in the global North and South; a growing number of childhood studies programmes at universities in the UK, the US, Europe and South Africa that include a developing-country focus; and the emergence of journals seeking to attract scholarship on children in developing-country contexts such as the *Journal of Childhood Poverty*, *Children's Geographies* and *Childhood*.

The expansion of applied and policy research on children in developing-country contexts has also been significant. Key developments have included the establishment of:

- the UNICEF Innocenti Research Centre in Florence (established in 1988), which carries out in-depth quantitative and qualitative analysis on children in developed- and developing-country contexts;
- the Child Rights Information Network (CRIN) (established in 1995), a clearing house of information on children from governmental, non-governmental, academic and donor sources;
- annual publication of UNICEF's thematic *State of the World's Children Reports*, which seek to draw attention to key issues facing children around the globe;

- UNICEF's MICS, which have been collecting quantitative household data on progress on children's rights in over 100 countries since 1995; and
- UNICEF's Global Poverty Study, which is synthesising quantitative and qualitative information on childhood poverty in developing countries and undertaking policy analysis to help explain trends in childhood poverty in different national contexts.

Policy advocacy and knowledge interaction

Evidence-informed policy advocacy on childhood poverty and well-being in developing-country contexts is newer still, dating largely from the 21st century. Not surprisingly, given the fledgling state of policy processes and knowledge-generation endeavours outlined earlier, policy advocacy and knowledge interaction efforts on child well-being are incipient and generally poorly documented. The case studies in Chapters 4, 5 and 6 seek to address this gap. Two involve champions for children – NGO- and expert-led approaches – and the third entails children's direct participation, which we also discuss later.

Evidence on children's visibility and engagement in policy processes is very recent (see Table 3.2). Perhaps unsurprisingly, when defining or outlining the meaning of 'participation', many authors either refer explicitly to Article 12 of the UNCRC, or incorporate many of the article's core concepts and ideas into their discussion. Except in cases where authors have all but eschewed any particular meaning of 'participation' (for example, Pridmore [2003: 12] conceptualises participation as 'simply a set of ideas based on a firm belief in children's agency' rather than any sort of model), understandings of the term accordingly revolve around notions of children as capable social actors, their ability to comprehend important issues and express a view on them, and their universal right to not only voice that view, but to have it listened to and incorporated into decision-making processes. In addition, many commentators categorise children's participation into further 'stages' or 'levels' depending on the type, degree and duration of the participation. For instance, a one-off, high-profile event entails a very different set of processes and outcomes than more sustained modes of participation such as the inclusion of children in local councils and assemblies (Williams, 2004). Thus, a key point is the necessity to treat 'participation' as a multidimensional and multifaceted concept as opposed to some sort of monolithic praxis. This becomes ever clearer when we recognise that at different stages of the policy process, children's participation takes on different forms that entail varying likelihoods of 'success'.

Children's participation in policy processes, like participation in knowledge generation, is mediated by a spectrum of factors across our 3D approach (see Table 3.2). As White and Choudhury (2007: 530) argue, by looking closely at the empirical realities of so-called 'genuine' or 'meaningful' participatory initiatives, a series of questions are raised that challenge the idea of an 'unmediated insertion of an authentic "child's voice" into the development arena'. Recognising that all forms of participation are circumscribed by complex power relations and located within embedded power structures – regardless of who the participants are – is a necessary step towards understanding that participation is rarely a 'neutral' and apolitical project. Many authors comment on the tension between the 'global vision' of children and their right to participate as propounded in the UNCRC, and the diverse local realities and challenges faced by practitioners around the world. As long as there are spatially and culturally contingent (contested) meanings of childhood (i.e. the 'correct' role of children in society and dominant social attitudes towards their capacities, or lack thereof), child participation will remain a fundamentally political exercise. However, this is not to say it is doomed to failure. Factors such as negative attitudes towards children and adult-oriented organisational structures, whilst clearly shaping the prospects for and processes and outcomes of children's participation in policy, do not necessarily determine these things in an absolute sense, and, further, can themselves undergo processes of transformation.

Finally, action can be taken to facilitate children's participation in policy processes. These range from training staff to better deal with child participants to utilising a variety of participatory techniques – such as drawing, role-playing and drama – in order to create child-friendly spaces and open multiple channels for expression. White and Choudhury (2007: 530) argue, however, that whilst participation is ideally about representing children's voices in development matters, in reality it is 'produced' through the 'projectisation' of participation. Drawing on primary data collected with Amra, a children's organisation in Bangladesh, they report that development-agency staff determine what counts as 'participation' and that children's agency is constrained and determined by adults in development agencies (i.e. what can be said, when it should be said). Accordingly, a number of authors call for innovative approaches that reconcile tensions between 'traditional' views and participatory initiatives (for example, through the promotion of stakeholder dialogue) and raise awareness of, in culturally sensitive ways, the potential widespread benefits of involving children in policy-making processes.

3.6 Conclusions

This chapter has sought to provide a broad overview of emerging thinking on policy processes, the role of knowledge in policy change and policy advocacy, and sought to extend the 3D approach discussed in Chapters 1 and 2. We identified a 3D approach as taking into account multiple understandings of power relations around three interlocking domains: *ideas/policy narratives, policy actors/networks* and *political contexts/ institutions*, as well as different concepts of policy change, including discursive, procedural, substantive and behavioural shifts. The discussion then turned to models of policy advocacy.

The second half of the chapter applied the theoretical literature to policy processes concerned with childhood well-being and poverty in developing-country contexts, arguing that the constellation of actors and institutions involved are especially complex given the particular voicelessness of children in many contexts and their exclusion from conventional policy spaces. Nevertheless, there is scope for optimism within a growing array of child participation initiatives taking place at multiple policy levels (international, national and sub-national) in a variety of policy sectors that the chapter briefly reviewed. This said, direct participation approaches to policy advocacy and knowledge interaction continue to face a number of challenges, including tokenism, inadequate resources to overcome structural inequalities and difficulties moving away from projectising children's right to participation, and towards embedding children's involvement in policy processes. These challenges are unlikely to be quickly or comprehensively addressed, and it is therefore important that participatory approaches are complemented and developed in synergy with other approaches that involve experts and NGOs.

Table 3.2: Factors mediating children's direct participation in policy processes

Reference – author(s)/date	Definition/meaning of participation taken by author(s)	Factors mediating children's participation			
		Policy ideas and power as narratives/discourses	Policy interests and power as actors/networks	Policy institutions and power as context/institutions	
Adolescent Development and Participation Unit, UNICEF 2009	• Involvement in (national) policy planning and development processes (e.g. through consultations).		• Very few countries have set up nationwide youth consultations (i.e. poor government commitment to child participation in PRSPs) • UNICEF's weak capacity	• Economic agendas and outcomes have been promoted over social ones	
African Child Policy Forum (2006)	• Active and democratic involvement of youth in programme decisions, design and implementation through relationships with adults based on mutual respect and understanding.	• Youth cynicism about politics • 'Adultism'	• Lack of access to education and training • Limited roles in collecting information and lack of constructive outlets (and expression) for young people	• HIV/AIDS • Discrimination against girls • Organisational culture and institutional resistance	
Afini (2006)	• People (children) taking active roles in shaping the circumstances of their own lives. Participatory processes enable stakeholders to identify, develop, and express their own interests and ideas and influence decisions. Multidimensional and occurs in various forms and settings.	• Utilitarian (involving children as a means to something/ or rights-based approach • Prevalence of participation discourse in the development industry – encourages agencies to 'produce' participation	• Adult initiatives – motivations and aims of adults • Issues of control • Type of environment created by practitioners • Practitioners'/agencies' transparency and accountability • Children's characteristics – information, physical strength, access to transport	• Stage at which children are involved in the policy process • Issues of selection • Dangers of creating an elite group of participating children • Location/site of participatory exercise	

(continued)

Reference – author(s)/date	Definition/meaning of participation taken by author(s)	Factors mediating children's participation		
		Policy ideas and power as narratives/discourses	Policy interests and power as actors/networks	Policy institutions and power as context/institutions
Bessell (2009)	• Ideas about child participation informed by world views (i.e. universality of human rights, citizen participation, UNCRC), principled beliefs (i.e. social justice based on equality and respect for all citizens), and causal beliefs (i.e. children's involvement leads to better policy outcomes). The study is, in part, about defining child participation – it is reported that in the Filipino context there is a lack of definitional clarity and poor understanding of the concept.	• Widespread view of children as developing, passive, subordinate, and incompetent • Fears that participation has a negative educational impact	• Government initiatives that promote child participation (e.g. *Katipunan ng Kabataan* – youth assemblies)	• Lack of definitional clarity of child participation
Black (2004)	• UNCRC definition – creating spaces and opportunities in civic society for children to contribute, exchange ideas with other social actors, and be consulted on matters that concern them. Key distinction drawn between genuine child participation and children as project beneficiaries.	• Dominant negative community attitudes towards children's participation (i.e. children seen as subservient, particularly in South Asia)	• NGOs' and workers' (un)familiarity with participatory methods • Degree of facilitative adult support • Bureaucratic obstruction	• Children in 'hidden occupations' less likely to have their voices heard
Brady (2007)	• Children have a voice in matters that affect them, and their views are given due weight in accordance with their age and maturity. Children should be treated as autonomous human *beings* with legal rights.		• Selection of participants (e.g. only those children with access to local youth groups could be selected) • Limited capacity of child participants • Degree of adult support and skills of facilitators	• Timeframe of project • Funding – consistent/inconsistent?

(continued)

Table 3.2 (continued)

Reference – author(s)/date	Definition/meaning of participation taken by author(s)	Factors mediating children's participation		
		Policy ideas and power as narratives/discourses	Policy interests and power as actors/networks	Policy institutions and power as context/institutions
Fanelli et al (2007)	• UNCRC definition – children who have the capacity to form a viewpoint have the right to express their views in all matters affecting them, and due weight will be afforded those views in accordance with age and maturity.	• 'Traditional' views towards role and position of the child in Zimbabwean society	• Lack of understanding among facilitators of what constitutes child participation (e.g. sometimes seen as when children are targeted by programmes)	• Resources to support child participation in organisations, e.g. funds, training of adults
Hart (2008)	• Participation serves to 'ensure the "transformation" of existing development practice and, more radically, the social relations, institutional practices and capacity gaps which cause social exclusion' (Hickey and Mohan, 2005: 13).	• The 'localisation' of participation which constructs the 'local' as separate and isolated from wider (global) structures – depoliticises the local	• Development agencies might hijack concept of child participation and adopt the associated rhetoric in order to appear responsible	• Broader and deeper structural change necessary for genuine social transformation to take place • Constraints imposed by neoliberal institutions/structures
Heidel (2004)	• Extensive participation of children and young people (and their organisations) in the development, implementation, and monitoring of PRSPs. Key involvement in decision-making processes – not just being heard.	• Scepticism among child rights organisations towards PRSPs	• Unsatisfactory child poverty analysis and inadequacy of planned projects • Little effort made by civil society organisations to embed child rights perspective in PRSP (Ethiopia)	• Lack of structural cooperation between governments and child rights organisations • Too much PRSP focus on economic aspects

(continued)

			Factors mediating children's participation		
Reference – author(s)/date	Definition/meaning of participation taken by author(s)	Policy ideas and power as narratives/discourses	Policy interests and power as actors/networks	Policy institutions and power as context/institutions	
Hill et al (2004)	• Multidimensional participation that enhances children's involvement in decision-making and combats social exclusion/promotes social inclusion. Key distinction drawn between participation and consultation.	• Perceptions of children's capabilities • View that children's rights undermine adults' authority and rights • Lack of the authentic voice of children in public discourses about childhood	• 'Adult-oriented' participatory project models are susceptible to manipulation by adults • 'Elected' children on, say, a council, may not be representative • Effective child participation requires sustained links between research and policy • Intergenerational networks, relations, and transactions • Lack of confidence and skills among child participants	• Diversity among children • Children excluded from adult life • Lack of funding • Pressures of performance indicators • Lack of appropriate staff training	
Hinton (2008)	• Children's views inform the allocation of resources used in their name.	• Dominant conceptualisations of children and childhood (i.e. children are conventionally located in the private sphere and deemed to be passive recipients of care) • Dominant models of age-based developmental stages that promote a 'competence bias' – examples of agency overlooked	• Greater understanding of policy networks and governance is required for policymakers to take seriously ideas of children as active social agents	• Schools and health centres often used as interfaces to access children, thereby further excluding the most isolated and vulnerable children from participatory programmes • Policy context rarely enables prolonged access to listen to children	
Invernizzi and Milne (2002)	• Incorporating children's specific needs and views into decision making processes within the context of what is possible institutionally and culturally (Ennew, 1998: xvii).	• The way participation is defined has 'by far' the greatest influence on participatory processes • Discourses surrounding child exploitation • Views on children's involvement in politics more generally • Tension between 'universal' and local views	• Selection and presentation of particular types of children by NGOs • Degree of consultation before conferences with children • Degree of understanding of the issues by children	• Adult-initiated and adult-run campaigns might only use tokenistic participation • Local differences and complexities • Lack of overall consensus on what constitutes meaningful participation	

(continued)

Table 3.2 (continued)

Reference – author(s)/date	Definition/meaning of participation taken by author(s)	Factors mediating children's participation		
		Policy ideas and power as narratives/discourses	Policy interests and power as actors/networks	Policy institutions and power as context/institutions
Lansdown (2001)	• UNCRC definition	• Perception among parents, teachers and NGO workers that greater child involvement will result in a loss of power • Generally negative attitudes towards children	• Types of methods and techniques employed by practitioners/researchers • Three 'meaningful' approaches: consultative processes, participative initiatives, and promotion of self-advocacy	• Likelihood of children's views achieving any real impact on particular decisions
Lansdown (2006)	• Linked closely to children's evolving capacities (Article 5 of the UNCRC): as children acquire greater capacities, there should be a gradual transfer of power to children themselves, enabling them to make decisions about matters that affect them.		• Training of adult staff and facilitators • (Lack of) Access to networks of people with power	• Environment in which participation takes place (i.e. conducive and child-friendly? Is there enough potential to build relationships?) • Scope and quality of participation • Structuring of legal and political conditions
Lund (2007)	• Multilayered and multifaceted. Generally voluntary involvement in projects and decision making processes. Can be understood as a way to sensitise people about issues that need action, as a way to actively take part in development processes, as a way to foster dialogue, and as a right to influence policymaking.	• The way participation is conceived and framed (i.e. as a means or an end) • How the 'participating child' is understood in development and child research • Perceptions of children as passive recipients of change	• Children's organising powers • Constraints imposed by family and local community members: marginalisation, fear, violence	• Economic restructuring (globalisation) • Whether participation is accompanied by wider structural and political reforms • Type of 'place' in which participation occurs ('right' or 'wrong' places) • Cultural factors

(continued)

Reference – author(s)/date	Definition/meaning of participation taken by author(s)	Factors mediating children's participation		
		Policy ideas and power as narratives/discourses	Policy interests and power as actors/networks	Policy institutions and power as context/institutions
Mannion (2007)	• Participation entails discovering and understanding children's views (various rationales for this are proposed, including enlightenment, empowerment, and citizenship), and, importantly, is about child–adult relations.	• Tendency to analyse children's voices in isolation from their socio-spatial contexts	• Nature of child–adult relations • Extent of intergenerational dialogues	
Mayo (2001)	• Hart's ladder. Participation may be concerned with individual decision-making, participation in service development and provision, participation in research, participation in communities, and participation in influencing policies.	• Policymakers' attitudes towards children • Scepticism among child participants and practitioners	• Nature of relationship between practitioners and youth • Relationships between children (e.g. importance of child-to-child approaches)	• Whether children's voices are genuinely listened to – is participation rhetoric or reality?
Mniki and Rosa (2007)	• Child participation occurs in everyday life situations, with or without adult facilitation. 'Natural' exercising of child agency.	• Conceptualisations of childhood	• Adults' support and creation of appropriate spaces for children's participation	• Children's access to information, tools, and resources to enable them to achieve change • Level at which they participate – some settings not appropriate (e.g. negotiating law-making processes) • Time and financial resources • Presence of other developmental priorities (particularly in developing countries)

(continued)

Table 3.2 (continued)

Reference – author(s)/date	Definition/meaning of participation taken by author(s)	Factors mediating children's participation		
		Policy ideas and power as narratives/discourses	Policy interests and power as actors/networks	Policy institutions and power as context/institutions
Pham and Jones (2005)	• Only if children's knowledges are 'uncovered' will policies and programmes be designed in a way that is 'responsive and relevant to their concerns and needs' (Boyden and Ennew, 1997:10). Participation must embrace the diversity of children's experiences.	• Dominant Western models of childhood infiltrate policymakers' perceptions	• Presence of networks/channels linking children's knowledge generation to policymakers • Evaluations of whether outcomes of participatory initiatives influence policymaking • Is research reciprocal? • Relationships between practitioners/ researchers and children and their families • Analytical and communication skills among children • Whether stakeholder 'buy-in' is secured (from the outset) • Relationships with local collaborators and project partners	• Clientalism in southern contexts • Embracing context is far more important than seeking standardised praxis or a grand theory
Pinkerton (2004)	• Public consultation as a necessary part of policy-making and strategy development.		• Power relations • Adult-child relations	• Quantity and types of channels for expression available • Effective evaluation of mechanisms overseeing children's participation
Pridmore (2003)	• Children's participation is a dynamic, constructive process embedded within a complex network of political, economic, social, cultural, and linguistic factors. There is no single model, but simply a set of ideas based on a firm belief in children's agency.	• Conceptualisations of the roles of children and young people	• Degree of dialogue between policymakers, parents and community leaders	• Specific factors associated with community contexts • Historical experiences of popular (non-)participation • Entrenched social hierarchies • Levels of education

(continued)

		Factors mediating children's participation		
Reference – author(s)/date	Definition/meaning of participation taken by author(s)	Policy ideas and power as narratives/discourses	Policy interests and power as actors/networks	Policy institutions and power as context/institutions
Prout (2003)	• Children and adults bound by mutual interdependence: without the active participation of children, there will be no social future. Therefore, children's participation is a process of citizenship.	• Dominant social attitudes towards children's capacities, competencies, responsibilities and aspirations (i.e. 'little angels' versus 'little devils')		• Institutional arrangements and presence or lack of spaces for children's participation
Ray and Carter (2007)	• Child rights-based approach – children should be provided with opportunities to participate in policy discussions at all levels. Children's participation in governance.	• Discriminatory attitudes towards children and their capacities	• Willingness of different stakeholders to take responsibility for children and their families • Activities and priorities of community-based organisations • Extent of participatory assessments – do they go deep enough? • Presence of children's clubs	• Appropriate mechanisms for children's involvement available • Selection bias involved with identifying youth representatives • Physical distance from and therefore lack of access to sites where participatory initiatives take place • Language barriers • Working children less likely to participate
Save the Children (2005)	• The opportunity to express a view, influence decision-making, and achieve change. Informed and willing involvement of children in any matter concerning them directly or indirectly.	• Assumptions about what children can and cannot do	• Degree of adult facilitators' training, skills, and confidence • Quality of relationships built • Children's access to information • Types of participatory methods employed by organisations • Degree of support from parents, guardians, and teachers • Children's other time commitments • Level of protection afforded to those participating • Whether evaluation exercises are conducted	• Stage at which children are involved in the participatory process • Local and 'traditional' knowledge and practice • (In)equality of selection

(continued)

Table 3.2 (continued)

Reference – author(s)/date	Definition/meaning of participation taken by author(s)	Policy ideas and power as narratives/discourses	Policy interests and power as actors/networks	Policy institutions and power as context/institutions
			Factors mediating children's participation	
Shier (2001)	• There are five levels of participation, ranging from 'children are listened to' to 'children share power and responsibility for decision-making', and three stages of commitment on the part of organisations relating to openings, opportunities, and obligations.	• Belief that children are not interested in having a say in decisions	• Actions and structuring of organisations involved in child participation • Support from adult facilitators • Low self-esteem, shyness, previous experience of not being listened to among children	• No historical culture of participation • Language barriers • Availability of opportunities • How child-friendly organisational procedures are
Sinclair (2004)	• Children and young people should be more involved in making decisions that affect them. Multidimensional with four key elements: level of participation, focus of decision-making, nature of participation activity, and children involved.	• Attitudinal barriers • Conceptualisations of participation as a passive ('listening to') or active (empowerment) process	• Practitioners' clarity (or lack thereof) of purpose • Motivations of adult workers • Willingness to work in partnership and to recognise validity of child's agenda • Accuracy of adults' interpretations of what children are saying • Consultation fatigue	• Presence of overarching strategies for children in government planning • Selection/representativeness of issues • Lack of evidence regarding whether child participation has any impact on major policy decisions • Level of integration of child participation into organisational structures for decision-makers
Skelton (2007)	• Participation is embedded within the UNCRC: children who are capable of forming their own views should have the right to freedom of expression and access to information. However, Skelton is critical of what participation actually means, and subsequently ambivalent towards the universal view of it.	• Conceptualisation of children as 'adults in waiting' ('human becomings') • Children as future citizens • Romanticisation of child agency	• Suppression of children's views when they are critical of particular institutions • Organisations can establish from the outset what can and cannot be said	

(continued)

		Factors mediating children's participation		
Reference – author(s)/date	Definition/meaning of participation taken by author(s)	Policy ideas and power as narratives/discourses	Policy interests and power as actors/networks	Policy institutions and power as context/institutions
Tisdall (2008)	• In order for children's participation to influence public decision-making, practitioners need to go beyond simply listening to children's views, and consider the various relations between children and broader institutional contexts, other stakeholders, and communities of interest. Participation should entail a more routine involvement of children. Participation is multidimensional.	• Ideas about what constitutes 'legitimate' forms of participation • Exclusion of children who do not fit dominant views of how participating children should be	• The role of participation facilitators: if an 'invisible' facilitative role is adopted, a disincentive for further funding may be inadvertently created • External donors' influence over activities • Pressure on children to present the views of children in general	
UNICEF (2009)	• UNCRC definition. Children as young citizens, therefore involvement encouraged at all levels.	• Negative ('traditional') attitudes towards children and their capacities • Conceptualisations of participation that inform approaches (e.g. narrow or holistic approaches)	• Adults can be reluctant to engage in dialogue with children • Whether all stakeholders are involved or some are left out	• Current or recent political contexts – some more conducive to child participation than others (e.g. less conducive under authoritarian regimes) • Rigid organisational structures • Widespread lack of data and expertise in working with children • Lack of frameworks – unaligned interventions • Difficult to ensure equitable participation of girls • Duration of projects
Van Blerk and Ansell (2007)	• Adults cannot presume to have insight into children's social and cultural worlds. Children are the experts in this sense and therefore have much to offer researchers in terms of knowledge generation. Participation of children in the research process results in their empowerment.	• Perceptions of competencies of children • Views on the importance of dissemination	• Are policymakers interested in attending dissemination workshops? • Ways in which researchers involve children in dissemination processes • Understandings and utilisations of policy networks • Relationships with policymakers	• Time delays between original research and dissemination processes • Difficulties associated with accessing street children and out-of-school children

(continued)

Table 3.2 (continued)

Reference – author(s)/date	Definition/meaning of participation taken by author(s)	Factors mediating children's participation		
		Policy ideas and power as narratives/discourses	Policy interests and power as actors/networks	Policy institutions and power as context/institutions
White (2002)	• A child-centred perspective on participation privileges the child and recognises the importance of their views, but should also situate the child in relation to his/her family and community. Thus, participation is a fundamentally relational concept.	• Attitudes towards children (from the savage pre-social to the innocent and pure) • Conceptualisations of 'adult' and 'child' categories – parallel or sequential? • Children often conceptualised within development practice as categories rather than persons	• Power relations between children and adults • The relatively short timescale of children's critical developing years	
White and Choudhury (2007)	• Ideally, participation is about raising children's voice in development matters. In reality, participation is 'produced' through the development industry – projectisation' of participation and promotion of agency-sponsored events and programmes.	• Perceptions that when a grassroots children's organisation, or at least its core members, become incorporated into the development industry, that particular organisation becomes dissociated from the majority of children it purports to represent • Understandings of what counts as 'participation' as determined by development agency staff	• Children's agency constrained and determined by adults in development agencies (i.e. what can be said, when it should be said) • Development agencies' bias towards attractive, articulate, middle-class participants • Complexities of power relations	• Nature of a large part of the mainstream development industry: operational shifts from action to advocacy and promotion of individualist over collectivist orientations (in terms of a particular 'core' of children being required to participate in international events, and benefiting from the associated material enrichment) • Participation as a new power relationship • The element of 'show'

(continued)

Reference – author(s)/date	Definition/meaning of participation taken by author(s)	Policy ideas and power as narratives/discourses	Factors mediating children's participation		
			Policy interests and power as actors/networks	Policy institutions and power as context/institutions	

Reference – author(s)/date	Definition/meaning of participation taken by author(s)	Policy ideas and power as narratives/discourses	Policy interests and power as actors/networks	Policy institutions and power as context/institutions
Williams (2004)	• Affording decision-making power to less powerful stakeholders. 'An ongoing process of children's involvement in decision-making ...in matters that concern them.... Genuine participation gives children the power to shape both the process and outcome' (O'Kane, 2003). Varying levels of participation – Hart's ladder.	• Attitudes towards children, their capacities, and their role/place in society	• Type of participation as decided by practitioners (one-off and high-profile or sustained, local-level activity) • Motivations and aims of practitioners • Interventions of the 'development industry' – inviting children to high-profile events impacts on their organisations' work on the ground • Do children's organisations exist to serve adult organisations?	• Wider political structures – any single policy is part of a broader framework of ideas, therefore child participation attempts to challenge larger structures • Level (i.e. local, sub-national, national) at which participation takes place/intends to impact upon • Stage of the policy process being targeted
Williams (2005)	• UNCRC definition. Children's views influence agenda-setting, policy formulation, policy implementation and/or policy monitoring/evaluation.	• Perceptions of children as passive recipients of services or recognition of the value of their participation	• Understanding on the part of practitioners/researchers of how to ensure children's views effect change • Difficulties associated with opening up and sustaining spaces for policy influences • Policymakers' awareness of child rights and agency • Importance of advocacy work	• When participation targets or becomes involved with legal institutions/spaces, efforts are likely to be made to reduce children's influence (i.e. preventing the challenging of the status quo)

Notes

[1] This chapter draws on and develops ideas in Sumner and Jones (2010), Sumner and Harpham (2008) and Sumner and Tiwari (2010).

[2] A recent global survey found strong consensus among Southern scientists on the need for intermediary organisations to serve as knowledge-brokers and capacity-builders for both researchers and policymakers. There is, however, only limited agreement on the role that such intermediaries should play, exacerbated by a dearth of empirical investigation into the practicalities of managing the role of intermediaries (see Jones et al, 2008).

Part Two

Child poverty, evidence and policy: regional perspectives and case studies

FOUR

Child poverty, knowledge and policy in Africa

4.1 Introduction

This chapter is about children and the knowledge–policy interface in sub-Saharan Africa, and is structured as follows: Section 4.1 briefly outlines the extent and nature of child poverty and well-being across Africa using the 3D approach. Section 4.2 reflects on the characteristics of the knowledge-generation process in Africa. Section 4.3 discusses the knowledge–policy interface surrounding child well-being in Africa. Section 4.4 focuses on a case study of evidence-informed policy change in the context of an expert-led initiative to promote a more child-sensitive PRSP during the revision process of Ethiopia's second-generation PRSP[1] and Section 4.5 concludes.

4.2 Child poverty and well-being in Africa

In this section we provide an overview of the extent and nature of child poverty and well-being in Africa across material, relational and subjective dimensions.

Material child well-being

To recap Chapter 1, the material dimension of child well-being concerns practical welfare and standards of living and the objectively observable outcomes that children and adults are able to achieve, for example, income, wealth and assets; employment and livelihood activities; education and skills; physical health and (dis)ability; access to services and amenities; and environmental quality. A brief overview of child nutrition, child education and child health using the MDGs as a barometer reveals an uneven picture of children's material well-being in Africa.

The child-relevant MDGs – 1 (underweight children) and 4 (under-five mortality) – are unlikely to be met in sub-Saharan Africa. The proportion of underweight children at birth is currently 28% in sub-Saharan Africa, and is expected to fall to 26% in 2015 compared

Table 4.2: Africa: Levels and trends in MDG 4 – under-five mortality, 1990–2008 (mortality rate per 1,000 live births)

	1990	2000	2005	2008	Decrease 1990–2008 (%)	Average annual rate of reduction 1990–2008 (%)
Africa	168	152	139	132	21	1.3
Sub-Saharan Africa	184	165	152	144	22	1.4
Eastern and Southern Africa	167	146	129	119	29	1.9
West and Central Africa	206	188	176	169	18	1.1
Middle East and North Africa	77	56	47	43	44	3.2

Source: You et al (2009:1–2).

Relational child well-being

To recap Chapter 1, the relational dimension of child well-being concerns the extent to which children and adults are able to engage with others in order to achieve their particular needs and goals. This includes, for example, relations of love and care (networks of support and obligation) and relations with the state (law, politics, welfare, social, political and cultural identities and inequalities; violence, conflict and (in)security; and scope for personal and collective action and influence).

Figure 4.4: MDG 3 – gender equality in primary education in sub-Saharan Africa

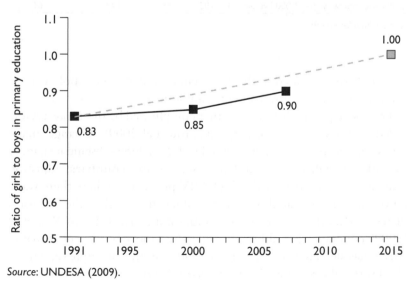

Source: UNDESA (2009).

Figure 4.5: MDG 5 – maternal mortality ratio in sub-Saharan Africa

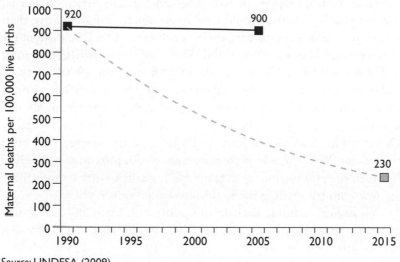

Source: UNDESA (2009).

Such relational well-being data is difficult to find for Africa, Asia and Latin America, but there are growing data-collection efforts.

First, relational well-being indicators are evident in a crude sense in the MDG indicators that relate to children and inequality such as gender (in)equality in education, inequality in under-five mortality and maternal mortality.[3] A quick review of these, again, suggests a very mixed picture in Africa.

At 90%, MDG 3 (gender equality in education) is almost on track in sub-Saharan Africa, and is estimated to reach 96% in 2015 compared with the target of 100%. However, at 900, MDG 5 (maternal mortality) is very badly off track, and is estimated to reach 887 in 2015 compared to a target of 230.

Hogan et al (2010) recently re-estimated maternal mortality data in *The Lancet* using all available data for maternal mortality from 1980 to

Table 4.3: Children in sub-Saharan Africa: selected relational well-being indicators

MDG	1990	2005–08	2015 estimate on current trend	MDG target
Gender equality in education (%)	83	90	96	100
Maternal mortality (per 100,000 live births)	920	900	887	230

Source: UNDESA (2009).

2008 for 181 countries (from registration data, censuses, surveys and verbal autopsy studies – see Table 4.4). Hogan et al argue that in the absence of HIV, progress in reducing sub-Saharan Africa's maternal mortality ratio (MMR) would have been much more extensive than was recorded.[4] Their estimates are lower than the UN Department for Economic and Social Affairs (UNDESA) but show MMR increasing in Southern, East and West sub-Saharan Africa in the 1990s.

An important part of relational well-being is inequality. The poorest children are considerably poorer than the average, and trends are not good for the poorest children. If we take the under-five mortality Demographic and Health Survey (DHS) country average (not even the richest 20%), there is often a difference of approximately 20–30% between the poorest and the average for a country. Furthermore, there are few countries where the trend is towards convergence.

We can also examine data on the poorest children and under-five mortality rates (see Tables 4.5 and 4.6). The World Bank's DHS provides

Table 4.4: MMR per 100,000 live births by region, sub-Saharan Africa

	1980	1990	2000	2008
North Africa/Middle East	299	183	111	76
Sub-Saharan Africa, Central	711	732	770	586
Sub-Saharan Africa, East	707	690	776	508
Sub-Saharan Africa, Southern	242	171	373	381
Sub-Saharan Africa, West	683	582	742	629

Source: Hogan et al (2010).

Table 4.5: Under-five mortality rates: average versus poorest quintiles in selected sub-Saharan African countries

	Average 2000–05 (year)	Poorest 20% 2000–05 (year)	Poorest as % of average
Benin (2001)	156	198	127
Burkina Faso (2003)	190	206	108
Ethiopia (2005)	130	130	100
Ghana (2003)	108	128	119
Kenya (2003)	110	149	135
Malawi	156 (2004)	184 (2004)	118
Mali	233 (2001)	248 (2001)	106
Mozambique	172 (2003)	196 (2003)	11
Tanzania	130 (2004)	137 (2004)	105
Uganda	146 (2006)	172 (2006)	118

Source: Vandemoortele and Delamonica (2010), based on DHS.

Table 4.6: Under-five mortality rates: trend data of average versus poorest quintiles in selected sub-Saharan African countries

	Average		Poorest 20%	
	1995–2000 (year)	2000–05 (year)	1995–2000 (year)	2000–05 (year)
Benin (1996–2001)	179	156	208	198
Burkina Faso (1998/99–2003)	219	190	239	206
Ethiopia (2000–05)	187	130	159	130
Ghana (1998–2003)	105	108	139	128
Kenya (1998–2003)	101	110	136	149
Malawi (2000–04)	200	156	231	184
Mali (1995/96–2001)	249	233	298	248
Mozambique (1997–2003)	208	172	278	196
Tanzania (1999–2004)	160	130	160	137
Uganda (2000/01–2006)	154	146	192	172

Source: Vandemoortele and Delamonica (2010), based on DHS.

strong and reliable data for the poorest 20% of the population because they have data-by-wealth quintiles (i.e. fifths of the population) for numerous countries.[5] The poorest 20% are generally worse off but the degree varies considerably across countries: Ethiopia, Tanzania and Mali have smaller differences; Benin, Ghana, Kenya, Malawi, Mozambique and Uganda have differences in the range of 20–30% or more.

The UNICEF-supported MICS data set contains a limited number of indicators that relate to children's relational well-being, albeit for a limited number of sub-Saharan African countries. The indicators include birth registration; the prevalence of orphans, children with inadequate care and vulnerable children; whether young women have comprehensive knowledge about HIV prevention and transmission; rates of marriage for young adolescents and all adolescents; and the rate of female genital mutilation/cutting (FGM/C).[6] In Africa, as Table 4.7 below illustrates, a variety of patterns emerge.

While the percentage of births registered varies widely, from a low of 3% in Somalia to a high of nearly 80% in Togo, overall only one in two African children is registered at birth. Children remain highly vulnerable, regardless of whether they are orphans. In Togo, nearly one in three children is without adequate care, while nearly one fifth of children are orphans in Burundi and are judged to be vulnerable in Sierra Leone. Regionally, approximately 10% of all children have lost their parents.

Table 4.7: Selected sub-Saharan African countries and relational well-being data in UNICEF MICS

	Marriage before age 15 among women (%)	Marriage before age 18 among women (%)	Preva-lence of orphans (%)	Children left with inade-quate care (%)	Preva-lence of FGM/C (%)	Preva-lence of vulner-able children (%)
Burkina Faso (2006)	3.9	52.0	7.4	n/a	72.5	9.0
Burundi (2005)	2.8	20.4	19.3	n/a	n/a	n/a
Gambia (2005–06)	9.9	48.7	8.7	17.4	78.3	4.4
Guinea Bissau (2006)	7.3	27.3	11.3	n/a	44.5	10.0
Malawi (2006)	10.3	49.6	12.4	n/a	n/a	7.4
Sierra Leone (2005)	27.2	62.0	11.3	20.7	94.0	18.2
Somalia (2006)	7.7	46.0	9.5	n/a	97.9	n/a
Togo (2006)	5.2	27.9	9.9	30.2	5.8	9.2

Source: UNICEF MICS3 downloaded from www.micscompiler.org.MICS.html.

The incidence of adolescent marriage, while dropping, remains alarmingly high in some countries. In Sierra Leone, for example, over one quarter of all girls are married before the age of 15 and nearly two thirds by the age of 18. In Burundi, on the other hand, marriage in early adolescence is extremely rare, at less than 3%, and only 20% of women had married before the age of 18. Overall, approximately one in two African women married as an adolescent. The prevalence of FGM/C also shows extreme variation, from nearly 100% in Sierra Leone and Somalia to less than 5% in Togo. Burkina Faso and Gambia also had high rates of FGM.

Children and subjective well-being

To recap Chapter 1, the subjective dimension of child well-being concerns meanings that children and adults give to the goals they achieve and the processes in which they engage. For example, understandings of the sacred and the moral order, self-concept and personality, hopes, fears and aspirations, sense of meaning/ meaninglessness, levels of (dis) satisfaction, and trust and confidence. Such subjective well-being data are difficult to find for Africa, Asia and Latin America. However, a relatively small number of studies have asked children in Africa about their perceptions of poverty and well-being, as shown in Table 4.8.

Overall, these studies suggest that children view poverty not only in terms of material deprivation, but also in terms of social marginalisation, insecurity, vulnerability and distress. Bethlehem et al (2009), for instance,

Table 4.8: Children in sub-Saharan Africa: selected subjective well-being studies of children's perceptions of poverty and well-being

Country and reference	Findings
Ethiopia Bethlehem et al (2009)	This article draws on a small field study to discuss the advantages and disadvantages of using qualitative methods to ascertain poor children's perspectives on their own well-being. The author used diaries, drawings, and interviews to identify what children saw as threats to and positive influences on themselves. For example, children reported that it made them happy to play football or jump rope with their friends and to be in a clean environment. They reported that teachers who hit, being sent on errands at night, and the school toilet were things that they did not like.
South Africa Bonn et al (1999)	This interview-based study of rural and urban children found that children's environment was instrumental in forming their beliefs about poverty and unemployment. Children with regular exposure to unemployment, for example, believed it to be linked to poverty. Age and developmental stage, however, were more important than environment in terms of children processing causality.
Ethiopia Camfield and Tafere (2009)	Using qualitative data from Young Lives, this study explores what children perceive to be 'the good life' – and how to get it. The study also addresses how these perceptions vary by the child's place in social relationships.
Ethiopia Camfield (2010)	Using mixed-methods data from Young Lives, the author found that even young children were able to identify poverty indicators. Personal appearance, clothing, education, food, and housing were salient markers of poverty. Children reported shame and stigma as the result of poverty.
Ethiopia, Peru, Vietnam and India Crivello et al (2009)	This article reviews Young Lives' work on developing child-focused, participatory, qualitative methods that capture what children understand vis-à-vis their own well-being and how that understanding changes over time. These methods, which included timelines and body mapping, allow research to move beyond simple quantitative measures of child poverty. They also showed that, despite the fact that family well-being was crucial to child well-being, children had unique perspectives that needed to stand on their own. Children, for example, wanted playtime, which adults rarely saw as important. They also wanted to focus on their education, which adults often considered secondary to work. Furthermore, children simply saw the world through a different lens. For example, in India adults saw sickness and dirty appearance as two key indicators of child ill-being. Children, on the other hand, chose 'plays in drainage ditch' and 'kills birds' as their top indicators.
Uganda Whitter and Bukokhe (2004)	This field study asked Ugandan children about their experiences of poverty and their opinions about the government's policies addressing it. It found that adults and children have different perspectives on poverty, that children see a positive role for themselves in terms of mitigating poverty and that they are highly critical of the governmental response.

Table 4.9 (continued)

Name	Home location	Affiliations and partnerships	Thematic focus
Child and Youth Research and Training Programme, University of the Western Cape	Cape Town, South Africa	Childwatch partner	The Child and Youth Research and Training Centre operates out of the Faculty of Community and Health Sciences. The centre's primary research areas are aligned with strategic social policy concerns for children and youth within the transformation and development agenda of post-apartheid South Africa.
The Children's Institute	Cape Town, South Africa	Childwatch partner; publishes the South African Child Gauge and manages the Children Count website (http://www.childrencount.ci.org.za/)	The Children's Institute aims to bring research to bear on the development of laws, policies, programmes, and service interventions for children across a number of disciplines. Key focus areas are in line with major issues that impact on children's lives significantly, namely poverty and HIV/AIDS. These are addressed within a rights-based framework underpinned by the UNCRC and the Bill of Rights in the South African Constitution. http://www.ci.org.za/
National Research Foundation Unit for Child Development	Pieter-marizburg, South Africa	Housed at the University of KwaZulu Natal	The unit works to build scientific knowledge relevant to children in South Africa. Its aim is to produce practical benefits for disadvantaged and underserved children around the country. http://www.psychology.unp.ac.za/nrfunit.htm
Institute for Childhood Education	Soweto, South Africa	Housed at the University of Johannesburg	Launched in 2010, the institute is dedicated to finding out what promotes or hinders the attainment of educational skills in young grade school children. http://www.uj.ac.za/en/faculties/edu/centresandinstitutes/ujice/pages/home.aspx
Children's Rights Project	Western Cape, South Africa	Based at the University of the Western Cape	The project researches children's rights and works towards their recognition and protection. http://www.communitylawcentre.org.za/clc-projects/childrens-rights/

However, as Table 4.10 highlights, while most European and North American governmental donor agencies are heavily involved in development initiatives on the African continent, investment in child well–being-related research is limited. Partial exceptions include several large, multi-year, DFID-funded projects – the Young Lives project on childhood poverty includes Ethiopia as one of four focus countries globally; the CHIP initiative on children and chronic poverty, which carried out research in Tanzania; and the Consortium for Research on Educational Access, Transitions and Equity (CREATE), which

Table 4.10: International donor agencies and investment in research on child poverty and well-being

Name of agency	Investment in children's research over time	Focus of children's research	Geographical focus
Austrian Development Cooperation (ADC)	The systematic protection of the rights of the child is explicitly stated in the Austrian Development Cooperation (ADC) Act, and is reiterated in Austria's 2006–08 Three-year Development Policy Programme.	While the collection of child-sensitive information, its analysis and assessment of the consequences is one of the six key principles that underpin work for and with children in the ADC guidelines, evidence suggests that it is a weak cornerstone. Child rights issues may be included on a case-by-case basis if relevant or requested by the Austrian government or an NGO, but there is no broader systematic approach to the generation and management of knowledge about children's rights.	Programmes and projects are largely located in Nicaragua, Bhutan, Cape Verde, Burkina Faso, Uganda, Ethiopia, Mozambique, the Palestinian Territories, Albania, Bosnia and Herzegovina, Macedonia, Montenegro, Kosovo, Serbia, and Moldova.
Directorate-General for Development Cooperation and Belgian Technical Cooperation (BTC)	Child rights became a cross-cutting theme for the ministry in 2005, and in 2008 a formal document was issued conceptualising child rights.	At present, child rights issues do not appear to be the subject of the ministry's research agenda. No evaluations have been carried out on programmes that target children, hence there is no knowledge management system based around these issues.	Since 2003, Belgium has concentrated its governmental cooperation on 18 countries: Algeria, Benin, Bolivia, Burundi, the Democratic Republic of Congo (DRC), Ecuador, Mali, Morocco, Mozambique, Niger, the Palestinian Territories, Peru, Rwanda, Senegal, South Africa, Tanzania, Uganda and Vietnam.
Canadian International Development Agency (CIDA)	CIDA had a strong research team from 2001 to 2007, but today its research capacity is precarious. There has been little substantive effort to reinvigorate research into child protection and rights, and key findings have not been effectively disseminated throughout the agency.	The research team historically focused on child protection and rights, but since 2007 this work has been largely discontinued.	Policies and services specifically directed towards child well-being and child rights outcomes were visible in plans for Colombia, Haiti, Mali, Burkina Faso, and Côte d'Ivoire. CIDA also works in Bolivia, Honduras, Peru, Afghanistan, Bangladesh, Indonesia, Pakistan, Vietnam, Ethiopia, Ghana, Mozambique, Senegal, Sudan, and Tanzania.
German Development Cooperation (GTZ)	A specific focus on how children's rights are unique compared to those of other social groups is largely missing from the 2008–10 Human Rights Action Plan.	There is no specific research strategy on children and key informants within the Federal Ministry for Economic Cooperation and Development (BMZ) and the GTZ. Instead, children and youth remain seen as 'just another target group' and a 'soft issue'. Nonetheless, considerable priority has been accorded to documentation of good practice in child and youth rights programming and practice.	GTZ works worldwide, serving 16 countries in Asia, 41 countries in sub-Saharan Africa, and 19 countries in Latin America.

(continued)

Table 4.10 (continued)

Name of agency	Investment in children's research over time	Focus of children's research	Geographical focus
Swedish International Development Cooperation Agency (Sida) and Ministry for Foreign Affairs	As early as 1998, Sida produced a handbook on integrating child rights into diverse policy and programming areas. Swedish development assistance has an explicit commitment to child rights, as laid out in a 2001 Government Communication on the Rights of the Child as a Perspective in Development Cooperation.	The child rights team does not manage a portfolio of child-focused research or policy analysis, and was unaware of country offices undertaking similar work. The team has limited contact with the Sida Research Department. Furthermore, with the exception of a 2005 report, no systematic lesson learning initiative has been undertaken on child rights programming.	Sida works worldwide, serving 19 countries in sub-Saharan Africa, 10 countries in Asia, and four countries in Latin America.
UK Department for International Development (DFID)	In 2007, a substantial (30-day) review of DFID policy and practice on child rights was commissioned by NGOs and paid for by DFID (Maguire, 2007). DFID recognised its programming was not especially oriented to child rights, but in subscribing to the research it was responding to both an external demand for clarity and an internal desire to envision a sharper focus.	The organisational imperative to address children's well-being is thus oriented to the delivery of the MDGs, with children's well-being achieved as an indirect outcome of good governance, economic growth, trade, and access to services. While DFID has a strong research programme, children, rights and child rights are not specifically mentioned as core themes in its 2008–13 research strategy. However, DFID has funded research on childhood and rights, in particular Young Lives, CHIP and CREATE. Child-related DFID research outputs include projects on HIV/AIDS and malaria. DFID also co-funds with Nike the Girl Hub.	DFID works worldwide, with programmes in five countries in Latin America and the Caribbean, 23 countries in sub-Saharan Africa, and 14 countries in Asia (DFID's bilateral and multilateral aid programmes are under review as of 2010).
European Union (EU)	A Special Place for Children in EU External Action (2008 communication) represents a significant EU policy document on children. It sets out EU policy for incorporating children into its external policies – its political dialogue, development, and humanitarian programming.	The EU's research agenda includes children, but there is no clear focus. The first edition of the European Report on Development, a joint initiative between a variety of European research centres and several EU member states, was published in 2009. A report on mid-term progress towards the MDGs, many of which are focused on child-related indicators, was launched in 2008.	The Directorate-General for Development is in charge of policy and relations with African, Caribbean and Pacific (ACP) countries. The Crisis Section of the Directorate-General Relex works across Asia and Africa.

Source: Harper et al (forthcoming).

has partner institutions in Ghana and South Africa – and German Development Cooperation's (GTZ) documentation of good practices for working with children and youth.

In 2007, the Overseas Development Institute (ODI) undertook a DFID-funded review of the top-20 international research donors. On the basis of existing but limited data on research funding, this study found that issues related to rights and social justice, including on children and youth-related issues, tended to be priorities for smaller bilateral donors (especially Scandinavia, but also Germany) and some private foundations (Ford, the Rockefeller Centre, the Open Society Institute and the Leverhulme Trust) (Jones and Young, 2007).

On a more positive note, however, UNICEF and the World Bank are increasingly carrying out important research into childhood poverty and well-being in Africa. UNICEF country and subregional offices on the African continent have partnered with a range of research institutions (e.g. Institute for Development Studies [IDS], Maastricht University [ODI], Oxford Policy Management [OPM] and the University of Bristol's Townsend Centre) to undertake research on children and PRSPs, children and social protection, children and public finance management, and multidimensional poverty and deprivation. In addition, there are two major international data-collection initiatives funded and implemented by UNICEF in partnership with governmental statistical offices and local research institutes: the MICS and the Global Childhood Poverty Study, both of which include a significant number of African country cases. As we note in more detail later, many of these research initiatives have led to major policy advocacy and influencing efforts at the national and regional levels. The World Bank has also developed its own website on children and youth, providing a range of publications on children and young people, especially related to early childhood education, child nutrition and youth employment and vocational training.[7]

Finally, there is a growing, albeit still fledgling, body of research about children covering a small subset of African countries that involves children's participation (see Table 4.11).[8] This work highlights the necessity of considering context-specific dynamics such as age hierarchies, social stigma and the location of research interactions in order to effectively involve children in research about sensitive issues in their lives and to employ innovative methodological approaches to recognise children's voices. It also underscores new perspectives that children may bring to development initiatives – for instance, children pointed to unrecognised hazards in a transport planning initiative in Ghana (Porter and Albane, 2008), prioritised a school over a planned youth centre in a refugee camp (Guyot, 2007) and highlighted school violence and inadequate toilets as key education-related concerns (Bethlehem et al, 2009).

Table 4.11: Selected research in peer-reviewed journals about participatory research with children in Africa

Reference	Subject	Country	Key findings
Abebe (2009)	Children's participation	Ethiopia	This article uses two field studies with disadvantaged children in Ethiopia to discuss the methods and ethics of participatory research with children. It argues that notions of research ethics formed in the 'global North' are difficult to apply in other contexts. For example, parental consent is difficult when a child has no clear guardian; privacy is impossible in the context of communal living spaces in which children occupy subordinate positions (adults often interrupted to clarify children's positions); and children often mentioned involvement in dangerous activities, such as selling or using drugs, which raised confidentiality issues. The article concludes that it is vital for researchers to recognise the complexity of children's lives.
Bethlehem et al (2009)	Use of qualitative methods in research with children	Ethiopia	This article draws on a small field study to discuss the advantages and disadvantages of using qualitative methods to ascertain poor children's perspectives on their own well-being. The author used diaries, drawings, and interviews to identify what children saw as threats to and positive influences on themselves. For example, children reported that it made them happy to play football or jump rope with their friends and to be in a clean environment. They reported teachers who hit, being sent on errands at night, and the school toilet as things that they did not like. While all methods produced valuable data, the cultural context of oral tradition led to some challenges.
Camfield and Tafere (2009)	Children's perceptions of poverty	Ethiopia	Using qualitative data from Young Lives, this study explores what children perceive to be 'the good life' – and how to get it. The study also addresses how these perceptions vary based on the child's place in social relationships.
Clacherty and Donald (2007)	Ethical considerations of research with children	Africa	This article highlights the ethical challenges that underlie work with children, all of which fundamentally stem from the unequal positions of power occupied by children and adults. Care needs to be taken in understanding context for participation – for example, in Africa strong cultural norms of obedience to adults often preclude children speaking their minds. Furthermore, children need to be treated as experts on their own lives and given the space to explain their own data. Finally, care needs to be taken around the issues of consent and confidentiality. This is particularly tricky in the context of extremely rural homes, often migratory parents, and the pervasive stigma of HIV. For example, researchers should take pains to ensure that neither they nor their vehicles are in any way marked with symbols or words that would cause neighbours to think that HIV is a research focus. Furthermore, allowing children to tell stories without naming names (using silhouette cut outs for example) allows them the distance they need to talk.
Cooper (2007)	Refugee youth participation	Kenya	This article presents a case study in which participatory action research methods were used with long-term youth refugees in Kenya. It found that, despite the top-down nature of the setting, the project engendered new capacity and psychological growth in the teens. They reported learning new skills, such as listening without leading, and finding new areas of expertise in their own lives – one young woman became a spokesperson against forced marriage.
Guyot (2007)	Refugee youth participation	Africa	This article proposes asking child refugees what they think they need. Covering literature from several disciplines, the author tells of one humanitarian organisation that came to build a youth centre in a camp. Upon hearing that a school was actually preferred, they were unable to shift set and accommodate the children's wishes. The author speculates that in refugee situations, where traditions have been fractured and customs abandoned, it may be easier to work with the idea of children's voice.

(continued)

Reference	Subject	Country	Key findings
Keenan (2007)	Children's participation	Tanzania	This study used participatory methods to ascertain whether youth participation in urban agriculture projects contributed to their own development and that of their communities. The youths in question were former street children who were now living in centres. It found that the children were proud of their work and felt connected through it to their rural home communities. They felt the skills they learned were vital to their futures – both in terms of farming and speaking for themselves.
Naker (2007)	Children's participation	Uganda	Drawing on a field study in Uganda on violence against children, the author discusses complications inherent in representing children's perspectives. These include raising children's expectations and a need to account for the heterogeneous nature of children's experiences, which vary by age, gender, and school enrolment, for example. Care needs to be taken to allow time for trust to develop. Location may also have different meanings for children. For example, the researcher found that meeting with children in a school building was not nearly as productive as meeting with them at a playground. Moving beyond rhetoric to genuine inclusiveness requires a fundamental power shift that may threaten cultural norms, which in Africa often make it difficult for even practitioners to release power to children.
Porter and Albane (2008)	Child-led research	Ghana	This article discusses the differences between child-focused and child-centred research, and lays out the evolution of, and concerns inherent to, truly child-led research. Children have never been included in transport planning before, and this pilot demonstrated that they were capable contributors bringing new perspectives to the project. For example, children saw open drains beside roads, which they could be forced into when cars attempted to pass one another; as a significant risk. Lack of street lights, danger crossing the road, and molestation by taxi drivers were all seen as issues by children but not adults. The author notes that a risk that must be addressed is the possibility that addressing children as agents could increase conflict by undermining local customs.
Robson et al (2009)	Children's participation	Malawi	This article discusses ethical issues surrounding a child-led transport study. The children's research included many spaces that made them afraid, such as graveyards, bushy places, and bridge underpasses. They were also afraid of dangerous animals and people. The article concludes that while children's perspectives are vitally important and often different from those of adults, it is also important to understand that child researchers do not necessarily represent all children. Differences in age, class, gender, education and religion make the complexity of childhood difficult to understand – even for children.
Twum-Danso (2009)	Cultural impact on the ethics of child participation	Ghana	This discussion of cultural impact on children's participation raises questions about the balance of power between children and adults, informed consent, and volunteerism. Children, for example, are used to saying what they believe adults want to hear, regardless of whether it is what they believe. Adults, on the other hand, even those who work with children, are used to believing that children either do not know what they need or that they should not ask for it. Balancing the cultural realities of 'Southern' children's lives with the 'North's' need to ensure methodological and ethical correctness is difficult.
Young and Barrett (2001)	Children's participation in research	Uganda	This review of four visual methods of encouraging children's participation found that all had positive effects. Photographs, drawings, maps, and daily timelines all allowed for a multiplicity of life experiences and permitted children to be active researchers of their own lives. It was found, for example, that older children used more 'space' in the city than did younger children; that leisure, work, eating, and stealing were important daily activities; and that survival is always at the front of street children's minds.

4.4 Knowledge–policy interactions in Africa

As discussed in Chapter 3, the ways in which knowledge can influence the policy process are complex and context-dependent. Sub-Saharan Africa is obviously a very diverse continent with considerable variation in terms of types and quality of governance, the nature of state–civil society interactions, levels of economic development, social policy regimes and so on. By the same token, the opportunities and challenges for engaging in evidence-informed policy influencing in the region are also quite distinct from those in the North, as well as in other developing world regions (see also Chapters 5 and 6). Therefore, this section provides a brief overview of some of the key contours that shape the knowledge–policy interface in the sub-Saharan African region.

First, it is important to consider the nature of interaction between the state and civil society – is it one of opposition and confrontation, critical engagement or co-optation? Is there an open exchange of knowledge or is access to knowledge and its expression restricted? The existence of modern civil society in Africa can be traced back to political movements that rallied against the colonial powers for independence, but it is largely in the past 20 years that CSOs have been able to participate openly in political and development processes. The transition of many African countries to multiparty systems in the 1990s meant that CSOs were afforded a larger platform and accorded more legitimacy by ruling governments (e.g. Makumbe, 1998). In this environment, CSOs, including research-oriented organisations such as the Civil Society for Poverty Reduction in Zambia, the Malawi Economic Justice Network in Malawi, Research on Poverty Alleviation (REPOA) in Tanzania and the Ghana Centre for Democratic Development burgeoned and began participating in the policy process at a number of different levels.

The efficacy of African CSOs' involvement in the policy process is, however, highly contested (Jones and Tembo, 2008). Concerns include the strong influence that donors have played in shaping civil society formation at the potential expense of independence and longer-term sustainability (Mamdani, 1996; Buhler, 2002); insufficient coordination and funding (Fatton, 1995, 1999); and inadequate linkages with governmental or CSO actors to develop credible policy alternatives (Nasong'o, 2007). Admittedly, this pattern has changed somewhat over the past decade, due in part to several cycles of multiparty elections and rapid growth in CSO activities. Some CSOs in newly democratising and post-conflict states have sought to establish a set of minimum 'engagements' between civil society and executive and legislative branch actors, promoting government transparency and respect for human rights (Amundsen and Abreu, 2006). Nevertheless, the relationship remains uneasy in many contexts in the region, as is highlighted by a recent trend towards tighter regulation of NGOs' roles in policy advocacy (for example, Ethiopia's recent NGO law – see discussion later this chapter).[9]

Another key challenge faced at the knowledge–policy interface in the region is widespread neglect of investment in higher education (Bloom et al, 2005). In 2000, sub-Saharan Africa's higher education Gross Enrolment Rate was just 3.5% (Varghese, 2004). Contributing factors include resource-constrained governments, low prioritisation of education spending (until recently), donor focus on primary education and stringent structural adjustment policies in the 1980s/90s that further curtailed social sector spending. Moreover, with the exceptions of Sida and the International Development Research Centre (IDRC), very few donors have invested in long-term research capacity, limiting the efficacy of investment in Southern research capacities (Jones et al, 2007). This underinvestment is particularly pronounced in the case of social sciences, with the exception of economics (Jones et al, 2007). As a result, both the quantity and research capacities of local researchers have been seriously impacted (Sawyerr, 2004).

These effects have not been limited to the research community, but have spilled over into the research literacy, or research uptake capacities, of policymakers. Many government officials have limited research knowledge and, in particular, limited ability to interpret research findings, especially qualitative research (Chowdhury et al, 2006). These challenges have been exacerbated by weak knowledge management practices and extractive models of research undertaken by Northern researchers (Touré, quoted in Jones et al, 2007).

Finally, evidence-informed policy advocacy initiatives are often constrained by a dearth of well-positioned intermediaries to facilitate the uptake of new knowledge in policy debates. As Table 4.12 highlights, there are very few communities of practice concerned with child well-being in sub-Saharan Africa that have either a regional or national focus, and are able to straddle research, policy and practitioner communities. While international initiatives such as the MDGs and the Education for All Campaign have had an important impact on children's access to health and education services (Sumner and Melamed, 2010), local champions of children's rights to protection from abuse, neglect and violence and participation in decision-making are less prominent and lack resources (see, for instance, the Inter-African Committee on Traditional Practices, the African Network for the Prevention and Protection against Child Abuse and Neglect [ANPPCAN] and

Table 4.12: Selected communities of practice on child well-being in Africa

Name	Time frame	Objectives	Examples of policy impact
Inter-African Committee on Traditional Practices (IAC) http://www.iac-ciaf.net/		The IAC is a membership organisation with national committees in 28 African countries working to eliminate FGM and other harmful traditional practices, including child marriage, abduction, nutritional taboos, widow inheritance, wife sharing, practices associated with childbirth, and skin-cutting practices like scarification and tattooing. These not only constitute serious health risks but also violate the basic human rights of women and girls.	The IAC educates and empowers women and girls, undertakes research on FGM and advocates and lobbies for an end to the practice. The IAC has had a variety of policy impacts, including: • inclusion of FGM in the Maputo Protocol; • networking with Solidarity for African Women's Rights (SOAWR) for ratification of the Maputo Protocol (currently there are 45 signatories and 26 ratifications in force); • declaration on gender equality by African heads of state; • declaration of 6 February as the International Day of Zero Tolerance to FGM; • adoption of Common Agenda for Action to eliminate FGM, with emphasis on integrated approach.
The African Network for the Prevention and Protection against Child Abuse and Neglect (ANPPCAN) http://www.childtraffickinginafrica.org/	2007	Based in Kenya, the network works in partnership with other organisations against child maltreatment in Africa, and has undertaken a limited number of research-based reports to raise awareness of child trafficking.	ANPPCAN's anti-trafficking programme aims to raise awareness and build capacity for service providers towards eliminating child trafficking in Ethiopia, Kenya, Tanzania, and Uganda.
African Child Policy Forum (ACPF) http://www.africanchildforum.org/site	2003	A pan-African policy advocacy centre based in Addis Ababa, the forum aims to put African children on the public agenda by providing a forum for dialogue, improving knowledge of African children, and promoting African action to develop and implement effective policies and programmes.	The Forum runs the African Child Observatory and the African Child Information Hub (http://www.africanchildinfo.net/site/). It also publishes a variety of reports, including the African Report on Child Well-being (http://www.africanchildinfo.net/africanreport08/index.php), which is groundbreaking in that it scores the performance of African government efforts to improve child well-being. Governments are ranked as 'most child friendly' (e.g. Namibia, Tunisia, South Africa), 'child-friendly', 'fairly child-friendly', 'less child-friendly' and 'least child-friendly' (including Chad, Liberia, Eritrea). The report also stresses the dissonance between countries' formal acceptance of an international treaty and practice, while decreasing government budgetary commitments

(continued)

Name	Time frame	Objectives	Examples of policy impact
Southern African Network to End Corporal and Humiliating Punishment of Children http://www.rapcan. org.za/sanchpc/ default.asp	2001	The network is an alliance of Southern African organisations working independently in their own countries to prevent and address child abuse and neglect and ensure the protection of the rights of children.	The network brings together interested and committed organisations in Southern Africa to work towards prohibiting corporal punishment through capacity building, information dissemination, and joint regional advocacy initiatives.
Committee for Liaison between Social Organisations for the Defence of Child Rights (CLOSE), Benin	1998	CLOSE is a network of more than 30 NGOs in Benin concerned with protecting children from sexual abuse and commercial sexual exploitation.	CLOSE is involved in the implementation of a bilateral agreement with Nigeria to combat trafficking.
Child Protection Alliance (CPA), Gambia http://www. cpagambia.gm/	2001	CPA has 63 member organisations. Its objectives include: raising awareness of child abuse and exploitation; building national and institutional capacity to prevent child abuse and exploitation and protect victims; promoting networking and alliance building; and empowering children.	CPA runs sensitisation workshops for teachers, religious and community leaders, parents, protection service providers, and security officers. It also produces quarterly newsletters and position papers on child protection issues and promotes research on children's issues.
Ghana NGO Coalition on the Rights of the Child (GNCRC) http://www. smeghana.com/ mysite/index. cfm?CompanyID=147	1996	The GNCRC is an umbrella organisation that aims to: build capacity on good models of law enforcement practice to prevent the commercial sexual exploitation of children; build the capacity of local youth groups, the media, and lobbyists; raise awareness and provide training on children and young people's participation for groups; and identify areas for regional collaboration.	The GNCRC collaborates with ministries and agencies, including the Ministry for Women and Children Affairs, lobbies government to establish temporary shelters for victims in each region, and ensures implementation of the make-IT-safe campaign. It also develops structures to protect child welfare (foster homes, hospitals, etc), collects data, develops child-friendly material, and disseminates information across regions to strengthen networks.

(continued)

Table 4.12 (continued)

Name	Time frame	Objectives	Examples of policy impact
Uganda Child Rights NGO Network (UCRNN) http://www.ucrnn.net/ucrnn/index.php	1997	UCRNN is a network of more than 60 child-focused organisations that engage in direct programme implementation and service delivery throughout Uganda.	UCRNN is engaged in promoting and popularising national, regional, and international instruments on the rights of children; monitoring the implementation of the UNCRC and its optional protocols; carrying out national level advocacy on key child rights issues; engaging in policy development and review processes; facilitating information sharing through networking; researching key child rights issues; capacity building with member organisations and other actors; and piloting initiatives to increase access to services for vulnerable children.
End Child Prostitution, Child Pornography, Child Trafficking for Sexual Purposes (ECPAT) Uganda http://www.ecpatuganda.net/index.php	2002	ECPAT Uganda is a six-member coalition working to create vigilant communities and stakeholders who safeguard children from trafficking and sexual exploitation.	ECPAT undertakes research on commercial sexual exploitation of children (CSEC) to provide up-to-date information on its nature and magnitude. It lobbies and runs media awareness campaigns, networks with other actors, and works with children. It is also working to strengthen legal and policy frameworks to ensure better and sustainable protection mechanisms for children.
Child Welfare South Africa (CWSA) http://www.childwelfaresa.org.za/	1924	CWSA has 263 member organisations and is the largest non-profit, non-governmental, and volunteer-driven organisation providing child protection services in the country. CWSA works to prevent child abuse, serve orphans and vulnerable children (OVC) – including those made vulnerable by HIV/AIDS, build organisational capacity, and advocate for children on a national and regional level.	CWSA develops forums to create awareness of the specialised services needed for child victims of trafficking and commercial exploitation; runs workshops and training sessions countrywide; ensures that legislation is in place to protect children; and forges national and international linkages that develop Codes of Conduct and a good practice model for children affected by violence.
Children in Need Network (CHIN), Zambia http://www.chin.org.zm/	1993	CHIN is a consortium of over 240 organisations working to promote the rights and welfare of children in Zambia, including child protection and resource tracking with regard to orphans.	CHIN's activities include awareness-raising, such as consensus-building workshops to identify issues and strategies, community meetings, group discussions, drama performances, and film screenings. It has recently undertaken research to ascertain the prevalence of CSEC in Zambia, and is now undertaking an awareness raising campaign on national TV highlighting issues of child trafficking, pornography, prostitution and child sex tourism (CST).

the Southern African Network to End Corporal and Humiliating Punishment of Children in Table 4.12). Moreover, these communities have generally had greater success in agenda-setting and securing discursive commitments from governments than in impacting on substantive policy change and influencing behavioural shifts.

International agencies such as Save the Children, Plan, World Vision and UNICEF are all helping to plug this gap, as their work increasingly shifts away from direct service delivery, and towards evidence-based policy advocacy (see Table 4.13 for examples). However, they still face considerable challenges in establishing dialogue with policy actors outside ministries with child-related mandates (i.e. ministries of children and youth, health, education) and with International Financial Institutions (IFIs).

Table 4.13: Selected examples of evidence-informed policy influencing child well-being in Africa by international agencies

Agency	Year	Theme	Evidence base	Policy outcomes
UNICEF West and Central Africa and ODI	2007–09	Child-sensitive social protection	• Assessments of social protection systems in Congo (Brazzaville), Equatorial Guinea, Ghana, Mali, Senegal • Thematic reports on social health insurance, social protection systems, social protection financing, social protection, and child protection linkages www.odi.org.uk/projects/details.asp?id=665&title=social-protection-children-west-central-africa	• Contributed to the development of a five-year social protection plan in Mali • Initiated a national cash transfer programme in Senegal • Secured formal commitments to invest in social protection for children in Equatorial Guinea (the Malabo Declaration) and in Congo (adoption of a White Paper on social protection) • Changed UNICEF's historic support for the Bamako Initiative, which endorses user fees for health care
Save the Children UK, Help Age International, and IDS	2005	Cash transfers to promote human development	Report called 'Making Cash Count: Lessons from Cash Transfer Schemes in East and Southern Africa for Supporting the Most Vulnerable Children and Households' www.ids.ac.uk/go/idsproject/making-cash-count	Invested in cash transfer programmes by international agencies and governments in the region
World Vision and Johns Hopkins University Centre for Refugee and Disaster Response	2001	Children's post-conflict mental health	Impact evaluation on mental health programme in refugee camps in northern Uganda http://www.certi.org/publications/policy/ugandafinahreport.htm	Contributed to successful fund-raising to undertake similar work in other contexts on the basis of the rigorous evidence base developed (Jones et al, 2008)

(continued)

Table 4.13 (continued)

Agency	Year	Theme	Evidence base	Policy outcomes
Plan, ODI, and the International Observatory on Violence in Schools	2007–08	School-based violence	Reports on the prevalence of and underlying causes of school-based violence in developing and OECD countries http://plan-international.org/learnwithoutfear/resources/publications/campaign-report	This research underpinned Plan's Learn Without Fear Campaign. Initial outcomes in Africa include: contribution to UNICEF and World Health Organization (WHO) complementary initiatives for developing health-related and behavioural indicators to improve international violence against children monitoring and evaluation standards; the adoption of the Togolese Children's Code and community training on the UNCRC and its child protection-related provisions; and the establishment of a free 24-hour telephone helpline facilitating preventive and support services through referrals and school outreach services

4.5 Case study: children, expert-led policy advocacy and the Ethiopian PRSP

> As the central, country-led strategy for achieving the Millennium Development Goals, PRSPs must include a strong focus on children's rights. The Committee urges governments, donors and civil society to ensure that children are a prominent priority in the development of PRSPs (Committee on the Rights of the Child, 2003, p 14, para 62)

Background

We now turn to a case study on evidence-informed policy advocacy efforts in Ethiopia, a country that shares many of the broader knowledge–policy–practice characteristics outlined in the previous sections. The case study concerns an initiative led by an academic–NGO partnership to mainstream a child-sensitive perspective into Ethiopia's second PRSP and provides a useful lens for exploring linkages between knowledge on child poverty and policy change in sub-Saharan Africa.[10]

Policy change objective(s) and children's 3D well-being

The Ethiopia children and PRSP project – an IDRC-funded policy research initiative involving a North–South academic consortium and an NGO, Save the Children UK – sought to examine the impacts of Ethiopia's first PRSP (2002–05) on children's experiences of poverty and well-being, and to draw lessons for the formulation of its second PRSP, the 2006–10 Plan for Accelerated and Sustained Development to End Poverty (PASDEP). Given that the first-generation PRSP did not include a specific analysis of childhood poverty and vulnerability, had limited child-related policy commitments (only those related to the MDG commitments on child survival, health and education) and had even fewer measurable indicators (Heidel, 2005), the aim of the project was to explore the national poverty-reduction strategy's broader impacts on children's multidimensional well-being and to raise awareness among civil society and state actors in order to influence the second-generation PRSP revision process. The aim was thus to challenge the normalisation of the exclusion of children and children's rights from mainstream policy processes, and to enhance the visibility of children's well-being not only in policy sectors that are child-focused but also in other areas of development that may have important intended or unintended impacts on children.

In response to growing criticism of the top-down, technocratic approach of structural adjustment programmes of the late 1980s/early 1990s, public participation and consultation were introduced as defining characteristics of the PRSP process in the late 1990s/early 2000s (Piron and Evans, 2004). The recognition that civil society groups (from peasant associations to women's groups and labour unions to traditional authorities and religious groups) had important insights to offer on poverty and vulnerability marked a critical departure from prior international development community thinking (McGee, 2004). The integration of a child rights perspective, however, proved more challenging. Especially in the interim and first-generation PRSPs, children and young people were routinely excluded from civic consultation processes, and civil society umbrella organisations were often equally remiss at including child rights issues in their recommendations papers (e.g. Marcus and Wilkinson, 2002; Jones et al, 2005).

Moreover, where child rights issues were incorporated, this tended to be in terms of child-targeted programmes in traditional social policy areas such as education and health. While important, this approach overlooked a growing body of evidence regarding the ways in which children living in poverty may also be deeply affected by broader economic development and poverty-reduction policies (Marcus and Wilkinson, 2002). In addition, data constraints hampered situational analyses and the development of measurable child-sensitive indicators, while officials' and donors' lack of awareness of the importance of including children in policy processes limited uptake of the knowledge generated by children's participatory poverty assessments (PPAs). Recognition of the multidimensional nature of child poverty and well-being and the ways social and power relations often perpetuate children's vulnerability to exploitation, abuse and neglect were also overlooked (Harper et al, 2009).

3D evidence generation on 3D child well-being

In order to overcome some of these political and data constraints, the case study project sought to generate evidence on childhood poverty and well-being and its reflection in poverty-reduction frameworks in Ethiopia. A mixed-methods approach was employed, focusing on: (i) a child-focused content analysis of the first-generation PRSP and related sector policy frameworks; (ii) a review of child-related indicators in select international PRSPs identified as child-friendly by a 2002 comparative review (see Marcus and Wilkinson, 2002); and (iii) primary research on children's time use, education experiences and nutritional health over the course of the implementation of the first PRSP. There was thus a mix of primary and secondary research using both qualitative and quantitative approaches that included children's own vision of their poverty experiences.

The project was embedded within the broader Young Lives research programme, a multi-year UK DFID-funded project on childhood poverty over the course of the MDGs, and was thus able to draw on the Young Lives data set, which involves a relatively large (3,000 households) sample spanning five of the most populated regions of the country. The project combined quantitative analysis of this survey data with community dialogues, focus group discussions and semi-structured interviews undertaken with government officials, caregivers and children. The latter allowed for greater insight into causal processes and the complex dynamics behind quantitative findings.

Equally importantly, the project's research team combined multiple academic disciplines: economics, political science, public health, sociology and gender studies. Although doubtless more time- and labour-intensive than mono-discipline research, the combined perspectives facilitated an analytical approach that was convincing for multiple audiences. Econometric analysis provided currency in the language of power: not only are economists highly respected in Ethiopian society, but they also constitute the majority of officials in the Ministry of Finance and Economics and were key players in the donor community. Meanwhile, contextual sociological analysis and in-depth case studies and participatory approaches allowed technical analysis to be translated into a compelling, human-centred narrative about the implications of the PRSP on child well-being, and broadened the project's reach to diverse civil society and public audiences. Moreover, where possible, resulting policy recommendations were informed by international good practice, especially with regard to progress indicators (see Jones et al, 2005).

3D approaches to knowledge–policy interaction

The project's approach to knowledge–policy interaction was embedded within the project design from the outset. It included a multi-pronged dissemination and communications strategy that sought to engage with the dynamics of policy narratives/messages, actors/networks and context/institutions.

In terms of actors and networks, seminars with key policy and academic stakeholders were held to discuss working paper findings, the development of video documentary and photography projects to raise awareness of the urgency of tackling childhood poverty, and capacity-building workshops with national- and state-level officials and civil society practitioners to foster a better understanding of linkages between child well-being and macro-level poverty and economic development policies.

The political context and analysis of it formed the rationale for this choice of approach (see Jones et al, 2008), which, as Piron and Evans (2004: 10) argue, cannot be underestimated in PRSP processes:

> The process interacts with institutional constraints, in particular those which originate from the nature of the state, its historical antecedents, and the way its power is exercised. Formal aspects of the political system matter as well as the informal rules by which they operate…. The PRSPs are significantly affected by the degree to which poverty is politically salient and to which there is 'political capital' to be derived from poverty reduction efforts. This is affected in turn by the nature of the nation-building project and associated political ideologies.

In this case, a situation analysis underscored the Ministry of Finance and Economy's (MOFED's) dominant role in shaping the PRSP formulation process, supported by a select group of academic and IFI consultants and advisors. By contrast, civil society engagement with the first-generation PRSP process had been relatively superficial and restricted, with more substantive negotiations taking place between the donor community (responsible for significant aid flows) and MOFED (Tefera, 2003). In order to manoeuvre within this complex constellation of actors and institutions, it would therefore be important to liaise closely with MOFED officials and their networks on a formal and informal basis to understand their knowledge demands and constraints, but also to keep civil society actors abreast of emerging evidence on child-specific PRSP outcomes. Given Ethiopia's federal political structure, it would also be necessary to ensure that policy-influencing efforts were directed at both the national and sub-national regional state levels.

The accumulated learning by researchers and activists alike has shown that a sense of government and community 'ownership' of a research project is likely to facilitate the acceptance and recognition of research findings (e.g. Pham, 2003). Accordingly, one of the central aims of the project was to promote government buy-in to the research objectives from the outset. An important component of this strategy involved building strong relationships with key government champions – this involved housing the research component of the project within the Ethiopian Development Research Institute (EDRI), which was headed by the Prime Minister's Chief Economic Advisor; securing approval from the Disaster Prevention and Preparedness Committee for the dissemination and advocacy components carried out by Save the Children; and forming a project advisory panel comprised of key sector ministry officials and donor and international organisation representatives. In addition, while structuring seminars with donors and government officials where project research findings were launched, key players in the PRSP development process were invited to give presentations on how they were seeking to incorporate children's rights. In this regard, rather than seeking to criticise existing government policies or to embarrass prominent officials into action, the format provided space for officials (from EDRI, MOFED and the Ministry of Labour and Social Affairs) to reflect on the relationship between broad development strategies and children's rights, and to develop an approach to strengthen these linkages.

The project's relationship with civil society actors was less clear-cut. Although project members enjoyed links with the two major civil society umbrella groups, the Christian Relief Development Agency (CRDA) and the Poverty Action Network Ethiopia (PANE), closer networking with MOFED suggested that government officials were somewhat wary of these groups. The roles of these umbrella bodies had not been clearly communicated to the PRSP committee, and there were questions about the rigour of their analysis and evidence base. Somewhat disappointingly, opportunities for alliances with child rights-focused organisations also proved limited as their organisational strategies were sector-focused and had minimal space for engaging with broader macroeconomic issues. This experience, therefore, underscored the need for partnership projects of this nature to be cognisant of and flexible regarding who delivers policy research messages. As Start and Hovland (2004) argue, the messenger matters in facilitating the translation of ideas into policy action.

Finally, in terms of policy ideas/narratives, message-framing was also of critical importance. Given limited awareness about the nature, severity and underlying causes of childhood poverty, the construction of policy narratives that drew the attention of donor, civil society and government audiences ordinarily unfamiliar with child rights issues was a critical part of the project's knowledge interaction endeavour. Framing policy messages requires a mixture of skills, including the use of culturally and audience-appropriate discourses, the construction of pithy narratives that do not unnecessarily 'dumb down' what are often complex messages, and the development of specific concrete policy recommendations. As Tarrow (1995) argues, collective action does not result from a simple conversion of objective socio-economic conditions into demands for change, but rather depends on subjective perceptions of injustice and how political discourses are framed in culturally resonant ways.

Two examples suffice to illustrate this point. First, while international conventions and standards hold some sway at least in part because of Ethiopia's heavy reliance on international aid, there is simultaneously a strand of political culture that is weary of accepting international norms without first assessing their feasibility in a low-income, multi-ethnic society with a recent history of political turmoil. Accordingly, there tends to be a strong emphasis on ensuring that international frameworks are 'localised': for example, rather than speak of the UNCRC, officials often prefer to look towards the 'National Action Plan for Ethiopian Children'. In this vein, the project's partnership with Southern institutions, which are more attuned to such cultural sensitivities, was a key ingredient of successful message-framing.

King et al (2005) argue that 'skilful narratives' and 'pithy summaries' are needed to encapsulate the key elements of research conclusions. Given the public's and, in particular, the media's penchant for messages in sound-bite format, there is a frequent danger that the impact of findings will be diluted or even misinterpreted if they are stripped of context. Mindful of these considerations, the project sought to reframe common assumptions about the nature and causes of childhood poverty. Findings were presented around a core message that children are not only impacted by education and health sector policies, but that their well-being may be critically shaped by broader development and poverty-reduction policies. As such, children's rights need to be 'mainstreamed' into national development and economic policy frameworks. By adapting the language of gender mainstreaming, which has been widely adopted throughout development circles in the country, the project sought to highlight that all sectoral ministries need to consider the direct and indirect impact of their policies on children and that policymakers need to pay attention to the potential synergies or contradictions among policies on child outcomes. For example, research on the impacts of the core economic pillar of Ethiopia's first PRSP – agricultural-led industrial development – on child well-being highlighted unintended negative spillover impacts on children. The PRSP's agricultural extension policy's heavy reliance on subsistence agriculture had increased child involvement in work activities, particularly animal herding, to the detriment of their school attendance and/or time available to invest in homework and study (Woldehanna et al, 2005a). Similarly, food or cash for work programmes in the absence of affordable and available childcare services had been found to encourage women and children's participation in public work activities at the cost of caring time for children and/or children's education (Woldehanna et al, 2005b). In other words, household-level poverty-reduction strategies risked indirectly undermining education sector initiatives to increase child enrolment and, as such, threatened achievement of the MDG for Universal Education for All. A more child-sensitive approach to poverty-alleviation policies was therefore needed, including piloting alternative policy measures such as community childcare mechanisms and communal grazing policies.

Outcomes of a 3D approach

In what way – if at all – did the 3D approach to knowledge–policy interaction shape child well-being outcomes? It is exceedingly difficult to measure the impact of research knowledge on policy change, especially given the multiplicity of factors that shape policy processes and the potential for research to directly and indirectly affect actors involved in the knowledge–policy interface (see Chapter 3 for further discussion of this issue). In this case, given the project's close links to officials drafting the second PRSP, we can surmise that the project's research findings did contribute to greater visibility of children's well-being in policy circles as reflected in the inclusion of a specific section on children's poverty and well-being in the PRSP's vulnerability analysis. The section explicitly mentioned that the PRSP should be implemented in such a way as to be compatible with the National Action Plan for Ethiopian Children, which incorporates a strong child rights perspective. Accordingly, there was a window through which recommendations related to children's multidimensional rights could subsequently be taken up. However, while this marked an important advance vis-à-vis the country's first-generation PRSP, the analysis was relatively brief and lacked specific recognition of children's rights to protection from violence and abuse, including exposure to harmful forms of child labour, which had been a key recommendation. Progress indicators against which governments are held responsible by donors were also not expanded to include many of the child-sensitive indicators that the project had recommended based on lessons learned from other low-income contexts.

To understand the broader context in which the PRSP revision process took place, it is also important to be mindful of the dramatic shift the May 2005 national elections represented in Ethiopian politics. Prior to the elections, Ethiopia was generally perceived to be on a positive development trajectory, with stable economic growth and a pro-poor development agenda, the cessation of conflict with its neighbour Eritrea, and improving governance conditions, including growing openness to civil society engagement in policy debates. Indeed, President Zenawi Meles had been heralded by Tony Blair as emblematic of the 'New Africa'. Accordingly, few analysts predicted the speed with which the political context would shift. Unexpectedly high voter turnout and a surprisingly strong showing by the new coalition of opposition forces had two major implications: (i) discussions about (and media coverage of) the PRSP and general development issues were overshadowed by highly charged debates about the election, election fraud and violent unrest in Addis Ababa; and (ii) the credibility of the CRDA, the main civil society umbrella group, was eroded in the eyes of the government due to its alleged link to the opposition. Overall, this resulted in the demise of an already fragile (but previously thawing) relationship between civil society and the ruling party/government, with the latter conceding little political space. It is perhaps not surprising, then, that the eventual outcome of the PRSP revision process was limited in scope as more pressing political–economy dynamics came to dominate the political stage.

4.6 Conclusions

Three general insights emerge from the discussion on child well-being, the regional overview of knowledge and policy actors and processes working on policy change to improve child well-being, and the empirical study of knowledge–policy interactions in one context in Africa.

Policy ideas and narratives

First, research needs to be credible and framed around narratives that are culturally resonant. Owing to what Ahmed (2005: 767) calls the 'multiplier effect', research is likely to prove more persuasive to a broader audience if it includes interdisciplinary perspectives and mixed methodologies. For example, econometric analysis can be powerful in persuading poverty-reduction strategists of the importance of incorporating children's rights into national development strategies as it resonates with the disciplinary perspective of officials in ministries of economics and finance and IFIs. But equally importantly, in-depth qualitative findings can enable research about child well-being to be framed in human terms and to make sense of sometimes seemingly counter-intuitive survey findings. This is critical in reaching broader civil society and sub-national-level audiences.

Framing messages in succinct, easily remembered and culturally resonant ways provides a linguistic bridge between often complex academic texts and policy action. Such packaging needs to take into account politico-cultural and ideological sensitivities, and for this the insights from Southern partners are essential. Reference to best practices elsewhere can also strengthen policy recommendations, but only if care is taken to ensure that ideas are adapted to the local context.

Policy actors and networks

Second, the importance of securing strong relationships with key players or policy entrepreneurs – many of whom may be outside child-focused ministries or agencies – cannot be overestimated. Such links provide vital information on officials' knowledge demands, decision-making hierarchies, processes and timelines. Moreover, research findings are unlikely to be accorded the necessary credibility if stakeholder support for a project's objectives has not been previously established, and this is arguably particularly the case with many child-related issues that have yet to be mainstreamed. In some political contexts, policy entrepreneurship may also entail investing significant energy and resources in forging strategic partnerships. For instance, locating a research project within a government-affiliated agency may be critical to promote buy-in. In short, the credibility of the 'messenger' needs to be taken as seriously as the development of the actual messages.

Policy context and institutions

Third, there are ways of approaching policy advocacy that are more likely to lead to policy change. Given the complexities of the policy process and the role of knowledge in shaping policy trajectories, intent to shape policy change is significant.

Although research-based knowledge may have an impact on policy practitioners' thinking and practice through the process of 'knowledge creep', whereby ideas gradually filter through to a broader array of policy stakeholders (Crewe et al, 2005), there is growing consensus that research explicitly designed to influence policy has a better chance of success than research that relies on chance or accident to shape policy (Saxena, 2005). Policymakers' demands for research findings to be translated into specific, context-appropriate indicators and policy recommendations means that if policy influencing is not an explicit aim, it is unlikely that the effort required for this interpretive task will be taken. For example, the effort required to package an academic-style research paper into readily accessible policy-relevant messages is considerable and cannot be left to chance. Not only do research outputs have to be produced under tight and changing deadlines to meet governmental drafting deadlines and to hold stakeholder workshops, but there often has to be considerable flexibility in approaching the way in which research findings are framed and communicated over the course of a project as politico-institutional contexts change. In light of this fluidity, a dual strategy of engagement may be most conducive to ensuring social change whereby independent dialogue with officials is balanced with networking and awareness-raising with civil society coalitions in order to develop a broader support base.

Notes

[1] This section draws on Jones et al (2008).

[2] In response to the need to generate accurate estimates for under-five mortality (due to the challenge posed by lack of data in developing countries), experts at UNICEF, WHO, the World Bank, the United Nations Population Division (UNPD) and members of the academic community formed the Inter-agency Group for Child Mortality Estimation (IGME). The group aims to source and share data on child mortality, to improve and harmonise estimation methods across partners, and to produce consistent estimates on the levels and trends in child mortality worldwide. It does this by compiling national-level estimates, including data from vital-registration systems, population censuses and household surveys. A regression curve is then fitted to these points and extrapolated to a common reference year. In addition, to increase the transparency of the estimation process, the IGME developed a publicly accessible database containing full details of country-specific estimates and their underlying source data.

[3] We include maternal mortality here because a high number of maternal deaths are suffered by girls. Adolescents aged 15 through 19 are twice as likely to die during pregnancy or childbirth as those aged over 20, and girls under 15 are five times more likely to die (WHO and UNFPA, 2006). The foundations for maternal risk are often laid in girlhood. Girls and women whose growth has been stunted by chronic malnutrition are vulnerable to obstructed labour. Anaemia predisposes women to haemorrhage and sepsis during delivery and has been implicated in at least 20% of post-partum maternal deaths in Africa and Asia. The risk of childbirth is even greater for girls and women who have undergone female genital mutilation (FGM) – there are an estimated two million girls each year who are subject to this procedure. Child marriage is another important risk factor – young women report being less able to discuss contraceptive use with their husband, and thus child marriage is associated with higher prevalence of early childbearing. Early marriage also puts young women at greater risk of HIV (ICRW, 2006). In addition, at least two million young women in developing countries undergo unsafe abortions, which can have devastating health consequences (ICRW, 2006). Indeed, in Nigeria, abortion complications account for 72% of all deaths in women under the age of 19 and 50% of all maternal deaths among Nigerian adolescents (Airede and Ekele, 2003). See also: http://www.childinfo. org/maternal_mortality.html

[4] The new study narrows the uncertainty around global and national MMR estimates compared to previous assessments. The improved accuracy is a result of an extensive database coupled with the use of analytical methods with increased explanatory power and improved out-of-sample predictive validity.

[5] This is more reliable than income or consumption inequality survey data because it is based on household assets that can be readily observed – such as the possession of a bicycle or a radio, electricity or water connections, and the size and construction quality of a dwelling (Filmer and Pritchett, 2001). Country differences are much clearer based on this criteria. Bolivia and Namibia have similar under-five mortality, but children in the bottom quintile in Bolivia are considerably worse off than what the national under-five mortality rate statistic suggests. Children in the top quintile in Bolivia, on the other hand, face a much smaller risk of premature death than their counterparts in Namibia. Vandemootele and Delamonica (2010) also note that of the 63 countries in their under-five mortality sample, 46 present trend data – of those, the majority display either widening disparities over time or no consistent trend. Only two countries (Bolivia and Ghana) show a distinct tendency towards less inequity (see Vandemoortele and Delamonica, 2010, Table 4).

[6] Note that these indicators are only currently available for the MICS 3 data set.

[7] See: http://web.worldbank.org/wbsite/external/topics/extcy/0,,me nuPK:396467~pagePK:162100~piPK:212344~theSitePK:396445,00. html

[8] Note that there is some overlap with Table 4.8, which focuses on children's perceptions of poverty and generally employed participatory methods.

[9] This law was passed ahead of the 2010 elections and prohibits NGOs that receive more than 10% of their funding externally from participating in policy debates on a far-reaching list of thematic areas, including governance, rights and gender equality.

[10] This case study draws on Jones et al (2008).

FIVE

Child poverty, knowledge and policy in Asia

5.1 Introduction

This chapter is about children and the knowledge–policy interface in Asia, and is structured as follows: Section 2 briefly outlines the extent and nature of child poverty and well-being across Asia using the 3D well-being approach and reflects on the characteristics of the knowledge-generation process in this region. Section 3 discusses opportunities and challenges involved in the knowledge–policy interface surrounding child well-being in Asia, paying particular attention to the significant decentralisation trend many countries in the region have undergone and the implications for evidence-informed policy-influencing initiatives. Section 4 focuses on a case study of evidence-informed policy change in the context of a citizen monitoring initiative of child educational and nutritional services in rural Andhra Pradesh, India.[1] Finally, Section 5 concludes.

5.2 Children and 3D well-being in Asia

In this section we provide an overview of the extent and nature of child poverty and well-being in Asia across material, relational and subjective dimensions.

Material child well-being

To recap, the material dimension of child well-being concerns practical welfare and standards of living and the objectively observable outcomes that people – children and adults – are able to achieve. In terms of aspects of material well-being, a quick review of child nutrition, child education and child health using the MDGs as a barometer reveals a mixed picture in Asia.

The story these graphs tell is different in different parts of Asia (also see Table 5.1). Child MDG 1 (underweight children) is on track in Eastern and South-eastern Asia, not far off track in Western Asia, but significantly off track in Southern Asia. In contrast, MDG 2 (primary

Figure 5.1: MDG 1 – underweight children in Asia

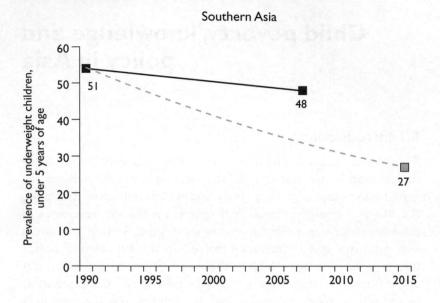

Southern Asia

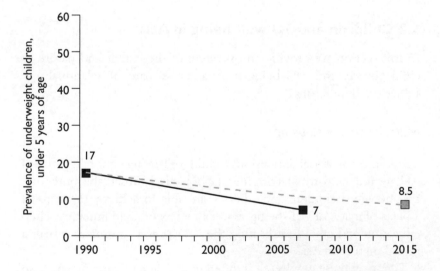

Eastern Asia

(continued)

Figure 5.1 (continued)

Western Asia

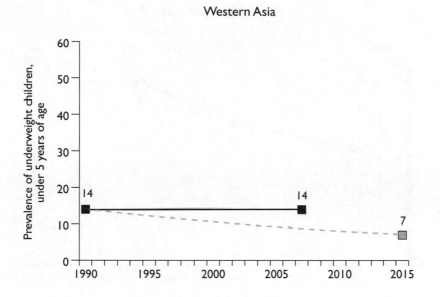

South-eastern Asia

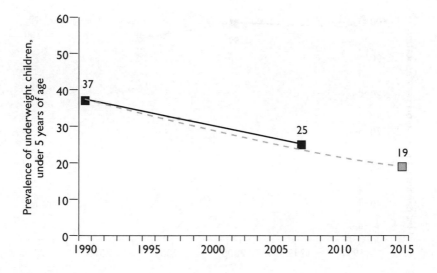

Source: UNDESA (2009).

Figure 5.2: MDG 2 – net primary enrolment in Asia

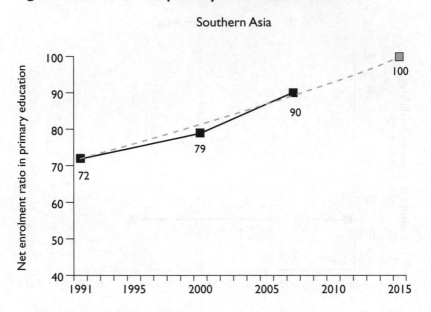

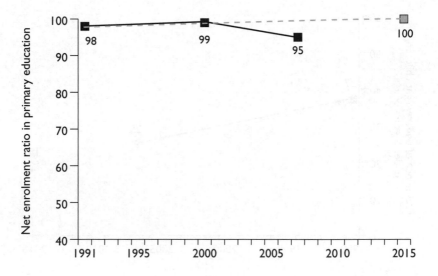

(continued)

Figure 5.2 (continued)

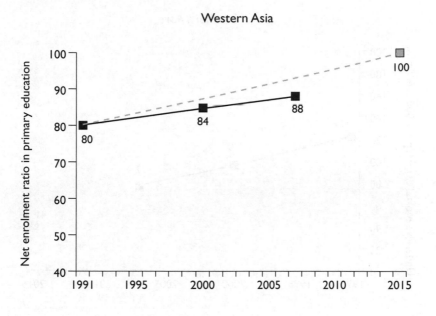

Western Asia

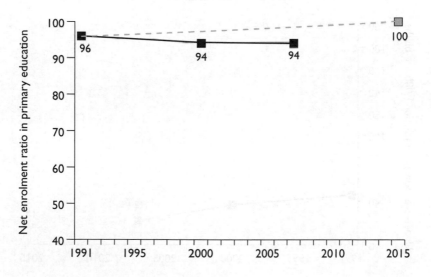

South-eastern Asia

Source: UNDESA (2009).

Figure 5.3: MDG 4 – under-five mortality in Asia

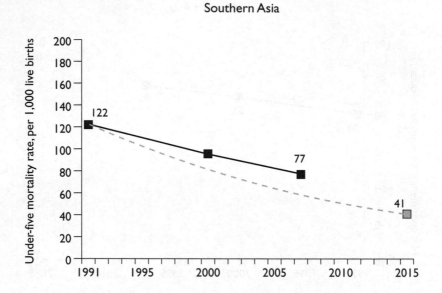

Southern Asia

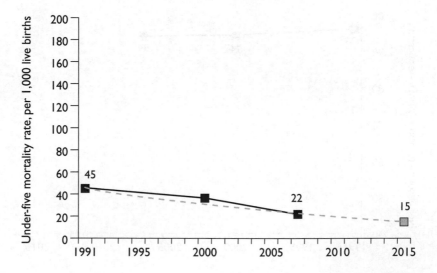

Eastern Asia

(continued)

Figure 5.3 (continued)

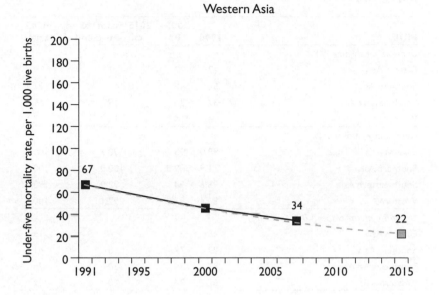

Western Asia

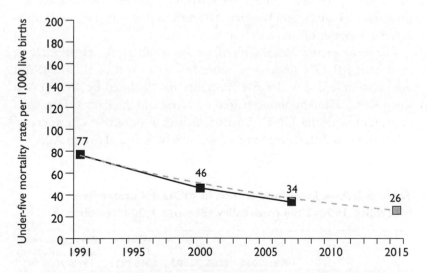

South-eastern Asia

Source: UNDESA (2009).

Table 5.1: Children in Asia: selected material well-being indicators

MDG	1990	2005–08	2015 estimate on current trend	MDG target
Underweight children (%)				
Eastern Asia	17	7	1	9
Southern Asia	54	48	45	27
South-eastern Asia	37	25	19	19
Western Asia	14	14	14	7
Net primary enrolment (%)				
Eastern Asia	98.0	95.2	90.7	100
Southern Asia	71.9	89.8	100.0	100
South-eastern Asia	95.6	94.1	93.9	100
Western Asia	80.4	88.2	92.1	100
Under-five mortality (per 1,000 live births)				
Eastern Asia	45	22	6	15
Southern Asia	122	77	56	41
South-eastern Asia	77	34	20	26
Western Asia	67	34	20	22

Source: UNDESA (2009).

education) is on track in 100% of Southern Asia, but slightly off track in all other parts of Asia at 91–94%. MDG 4 (under-five mortality) is on track in Eastern and Western Asia and slightly off track in South-eastern Asia, but off track in Southern Asia.

The above picture has, as with Africa, been complicated by the *Lancet* review of MDG 4 under-five mortality data (You et al, 2009). You et al conclude that under-five mortality has declined by 38% in Asia since 1990, falling by almost half in East Asia and the Pacific. However, consistent with the UNDESA data, You et al note that considerable intra-regional differences exist between East Asia and South Asia.

Table 5.2: Asia: levels and trends in MDG 4 – under-five mortality, 1990–2008 (mortality rate per 1,000 live births)

	1990	2000	2005	2008	Decrease 1990–2008 (%)	Average annual rate of reduction 1990–2008 (%)
Asia	87	71	60	54	38	2.6
South Asia	124	99	83	76	39	2.7
East Asia and the Pacific	54	41	32	28	48	3.6

Source: You et al (2009: 1–2).

Relational child well-being

As with other developing-country regions, relational well-being data is difficult to find for Asia, but there are growing efforts to collect data. First, relational well-being indicators are evident in a crude sense in the MDG indicators that relate to children and inequality such as gender (in)equality in education, inequality in under-five mortality and maternal mortality. A brief overview of these suggests a mixed picture in Asia again.

Figure 5.4: MDG 3 – gender equality in education in Asia

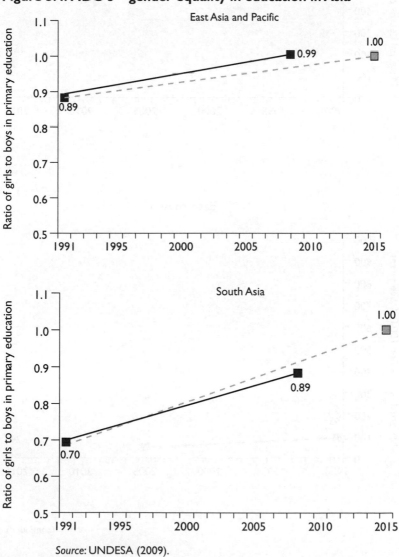

Source: UNDESA (2009).

Figure 5.5: MDG 5 – maternal mortality ratio in Asia

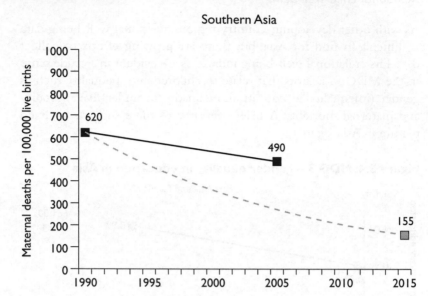

Southern Asia

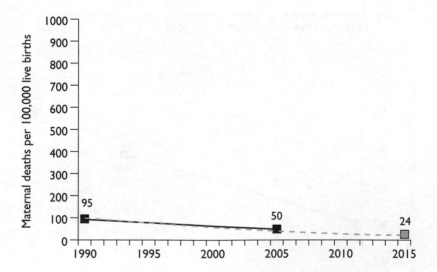

Eastern Asia

(continued)

Figure 5.5 (continued)

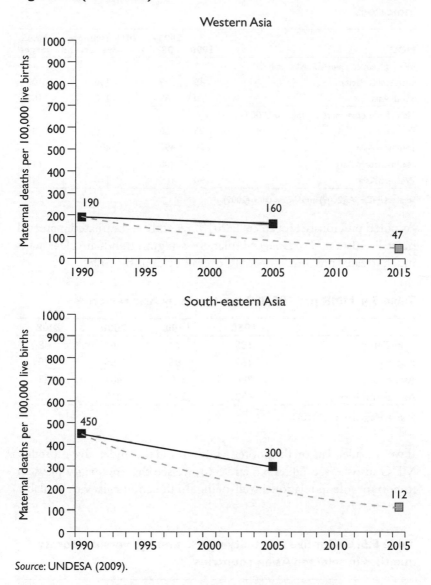

Source: UNDESA (2009).

The story these graphs tell is also mixed (also see Table 5.3). MDG 3 (gender equality in education) is more positive with East Asia already achieving equality in education and South Asia on target for parity. However, MDG 5 (maternal mortality) is off track in much of Asia, with Eastern Asia being the exception. Maternal Mortality Ratio (MMR) estimates for 2015 in Asia range from 403 in Southern Asia to 20 in Eastern Asia.

Table 5.3: Children in Asia: selected relational well-being indicators

MDG	1990	2005–08	2015 estimate on current trend	MDG target
MDG 3 Gender equality in education (%)				
East Asia & Pacific	89	99	100	100
South Asia	70	89	100	100
MDG 5 Maternal mortality (per 100,000 live births)				
Eastern Asia	95	50	20	24
Southern Asia	620	490	403	155
South-eastern Asia	450	300	200	113
Western Asia	190	160	140	48

Source: UNDESA (2009) and World Bank (2009).

As noted previously, Hogan et al (2010) recently re-estimated maternal mortality data in *The Lancet*. Similar cross-region trends are clear, with much greater progress on MMR overall evident by 2008.

Table 5.4: MMR per 100,000 live births by Asia region

	1980	1990	2000	2008
Asia, Central	105	72	60	48
Asia, East	162	86	55	40
Asia, South	788	560	402	323
Asia, South-east	438	248	212	152

Source: Hogan et al (2010).

If we consider data on the poorest children and the under-five mortality MDG in Asia (see Tables 5.5 and 5.6), we see that inequality plays an important role in relational well-being. In the countries with available

Table 5.5: Under-five mortality rates: average versus poorest quintiles in selected Asian countries

	Average 2000–05 (year)	Poorest 20% 2000–05 (year)	Poorest as % of average
Bangladesh (2004)	94	121	128
Cambodia (2005)	101	127	126
Indonesia (2002–03)	53	77	145
Nepal (2001)	105	130	124
Vietnam (2002)	31	53	171

Source: Vandemoortele and Delamonica (2010) based on DHS.

Table 5.6: Under-five mortality rates: trend data of average versus poorest quintiles in selected Asian countries

	Average		Poorest 20%	
	1995–2000 (year)	2000–05 (year)	1995–2000 (year)	2000–05 (year)
Bangladesh (1996/97–2004)	124	94	141	121
Cambodia (2000–05)	117	101	155	127
Indonesia (1997–2002/03)	67	53	109	77
Nepal (1996–2001)	135	105	156	130
Vietnam	44 (1997)	31 (2002)	63 (1997)	53 (2002)

Source: Vandemoortele and Delamonica (2010), IDS Bulletin based on DHS.

data, the poorest quintiles are generally worse off and by a considerable extent.

Second, for a very limited set of countries, there are also a number of indicators from the MICS data set that relate to Asian children's relational well-being. The indicators include birth registration; the prevalence of orphans and children with inadequate care; whether young women have comprehensive knowledge about HIV prevention and transmission; and rates of marriage for both young adolescents and all adolescents.[2]

Due to the fact that there are only three countries for which data are available, it is not possible to extrapolate regional trends. Birth registration is quite uncommon in Bangladesh and quite common in Mongolia and Vietnam. While few of the region's children, unlike sub-Saharan Africa's, are orphaned, nearly one in five Vietnamese children lacks adequate care. Furthermore, approximately only half of all women understand mother-to-child HIV transmission mechancisms, and rates for HIV prevention knowledge are even lower. Adolescent marriage is

Table 5.7: Selected Asian countries and relational well-being data in UNICEF MICS

	Marriage before age 15 among women (%)	Marriage before age 18 among women (%)	Preva-lence of orphans (%)	Children left with inade-quate care (%)	Preva-lence of FGM/ Cutting (%)	Preva-lence of vulnerable children (%)
Bangladesh (2006)	33.1	74.0	5.8	n/a	n/a	n/a
Mongolia (2005)	0.3	7.7	7.9	13.1	n/a	n/a
Vietnam (2006)	0.7	13.1	3.8	18.8	n/a	n/a

Source: UNICEF MICS.

very uncommon in Mongolia and very common in Bangladesh, where nearly three quarters of all girls are married before their 18th birthdays.

Children and subjective well-being

To recap Chapter 1, the subjective dimension of child well-being concerns meanings that children and adults give to the goals they achieve and the processes in which they engage. Subjective well-being data on impoverished Asian children are almost non-existent. However, a trio of studies have each found that poverty contributes to children's and teens' sense of ill-being in one way or another (Harpham et al, 2005; Crivello et al, 2009; Halik and Webley, 2009). Halik and Webley found that as children age they gain increasingly complex understanding of the causality of poverty, seeing both structural and individual causes. However, there is evidence that despite their sophisticated thinking, they still feel the stigma associated with poverty deeply enough that they need to see others as 'more poor' than themselves. Harpham et al (2005) found that even young children feel great shame about being poor. For example, they report that having to borrow textbooks, tend animals and watch television at a neighbour's house rather than at home is distressing. While these poverty indicators are familiar to us as adults, Crivello et al (2009), drawing on Young Lives data from India, found that poor children often have other, less obvious, ways of understanding poverty. They, for example, saw playing in drainage ditches and killing birds as indicators of child ill-being.

Table 5.8: Children in Asia: selected subjective well-being studies of children's perceptions of poverty and well-being

Country and reference	Key findings
India, Vietnam, Peru and Ethiopia Crivello et al (2009).	This article reviews Young Lives' work on developing child-focused, participatory, qualitative methods capturing what children understand about their own well-being and how that understanding changes over time. These methods, which included timelines and body mapping, allow research to move beyond simple quantitative measures of child poverty. They also showed that, despite the fact that family well-being was crucial to child well-being, children had unique perspectives that needed to stand on their own. Children, for example, wanted playtime, which adults rarely saw as important. They also wanted to focus on their education, which adults often saw as secondary to work. Furthermore, children simply saw the world through a different lens. For example, in India adults saw sickness and dirty appearance as two key indicators of child ill-being. Children, on the other hand, chose 'plays in drainage ditch' and 'kills birds' as their top indicators.

(continued)

Table 5.8 (continued)

Country and reference	Key findings
Vietnam Harpham et al (2005)	Using PPA methods with both children and adults, the study identified that the two groups had markedly different views about the nature of child poverty. Adults, for example, saw lack of access to clean water as a key distinguishing feature of poverty; children, on the other hand, mentioned shame, labour requirements, and a lack of assets such as toys or a television.
Malaysia Halik and Webley (2009)	This study of Malay teens found that older adolescents were likely to see a multifaceted causality of poverty that included both individualistic and structural causes. Rural teens were more likely to identify themselves as poor, while poor urban teens were more likely to conclude that there were others with worse conditions than their own. This may be to avoid stigma. Rural teens were more likely to be downcast about their poverty. All teens saw education as a way to ensure a more positive future.

5.3 Knowledge generation and child well-being in Asia

As with Africa, the generation of research-based knowledge on child poverty and well-being is a relatively new phenomenon in Asia. Wells (2009: 11), in her discussion of the history of childhood, notes that, 'Presenting a coherent historiography of childhood for Asia is more difficult than for the Americas or Europe or Africa because of the extraordinary diversity of this region', and only provides a brief discussion on understandings of child well-being and childhood in China. This limited knowledge base persists, as reflected in the limited number of institutions or research programmes focusing on child poverty and well-being in Asian contexts (see Table 5.9).[3] Indeed, as Table 5.9 highlights, there are no pan-Asian initiatives to monitor and evaluate progress in children's rights to well-being, and only a small number of organisations with a dedicated research focus on children (see the Philippines' Psychological Support and Children's Rights Resource Centre and Thailand's National Institute on the Child and Family Development). The remaining institutions, predominantly based in South Asia, include a stream of work on children as part of their broader research portfolios. Their thematic foci include children and social justice, children and legal rights, child labour, children and emergencies, children's education and health, and violence against children.

Given the high level of international aid to the South Asian region, and, to a lesser extent, South-east Asia, it seems this knowledge gap would be partially filled by donor agencies. However, as discussed in Chapter 4, donor investment in research related to child well-being is

Table 5.9: Selected institutions with a research focus on child poverty and well-being in Asia

Name	Home location	Affiliations and partnerships	Thematic focus
Collaborative Research and Dissemination (CORD)	New Delhi, India	RECOUP[4] partner	CORD is an independent research group seeking to articulate the problems of the disadvantaged through field-based research. CORD endeavours to influence policy and public opinion by making its research findings accessible to the public. http://www.cordindia.com/
Tata Institute for Social Sciences (TISS)	Mumbai, India	Childwatch[5] partner	TISS is a university that makes a decisive difference in achieving equity and justice in many spheres via research, teaching, hands-on work, and influencing people-centred policies. http://www.tiss.edu/
Centre for the Study of Developing Societies (CSDS)	Delhi, India		The centre is one of India's premier institutes of social sciences and humanities. It provides a unique institutional space that seeks to nurture intellectual interests outside the entrenched boundaries of academic disciplines, and currently has faculty serving on the board of the journal *Childhood*. http://www.csds.in/
Child Workers in Nepal Concerned Centre (CWIN)	Kathmandu, Nepal		CWIN provides research, education, legal representation, and lobbying on areas involving children's rights. CWIN's main areas of concern are child labour, street children, child marriage, bonded labour, trafficking of children, children in conflict with laws and CSEC. www.cwin-nepal.org
Mahbub ul Haq Human Development Centre	Islamabad, Pakistan	RECOUP partner	The Mahbub ul Haq Human Development Centre is a policy research institute and think tank committed to organising professional research in the area of human development and promoting the human development paradigm as a powerful tool for informing people-centred development policy. http://www.mhhdc.org/html/objectives.htm
Psychosocial Support and Children's Rights Resource Centre (PST CRRC)	Quezon City, Philippines		PST CRRC's focus is research for, about, and with children in the Philippines and South-east Asia. Its aim is to provide a better understanding of children and childhood through research on issues ranging from child labour to the impact of natural disasters on children. http://www.pstcrrc.org/
National Education Research and Evaluation Centre (NEREC)	Colombo, Sri Lanka	Childwatch partner	NEREC works to develop and disseminate knowledge to educators around Sri Lanka. http://www.cmb.ac.lk/academic/edu/nerec/objectives.htm
National Institute for the Child and Family Development	Bangkok, Thailand	Childwatch partner	The institute is a central academic organisation playing a key role in child and family research and teaching. It also gathers data related to child behaviour and development and provides advice and policy recommendations to government and social movement agencies. www.cf.mahidol.ac.th/
Vietnamese Academy of Social Sciences, Institute of Family and Gender Studies	Hanoi, Vietnam		The institute is involved in research on education, child labour, violence against children, HIV/AIDS, and adolescent reproductive health. http://hurights.pbworks.com/Vietnam+Centers#InstituteforFamilyandGenderStudiesIFGS

generally limited. Partial exceptions include several large multi-year projects funded by DFID – the Young Lives project on childhood poverty, which covers Andhra Pradesh State in India, and five provinces in Vietnam; the CHIP initiative on children and chronic poverty, which carried out research in India and Mongolia; and CREATE, which includes partner institutions in Bangladesh and India.

On a more positive note, UNICEF and the World Bank are increasingly researching childhood poverty and well-being in Asia. UNICEF country and sub-regional offices in the region have partnered with a range of institutions (e.g. IDS, ODI and the Townsend Centre at the University of Bristol) to undertake research on, for instance, children and the economic crisis, children and social protection, and multidimensional poverty and deprivation. In addition, as discussed in Chapter 4, the UNICEF MICS and Global Childhood Poverty Study are generating important data and analysis on childhood poverty and well-being in the region, while the World Bank is supporting a range of impact evaluations on child-related services, especially education and nutrition programmes (Saroj, 2009) and mother and child health services (e.g. World Bank, 2005).

Finally, there is a growing, albeit fledgling, body of research into children's participation, predominantly from South Asia and Vietnam (see Table 5.10). This work highlights the importance of children's gendered experiences of poverty (Chakraborty, 2009), the way in which age mediates children's understandings of risk and care-seeking behaviour (Baker, 1996), the distinctive meanings children attach to poverty (e.g. while adults identified the absence of clean water as a key concern children focused on experiences of shame) (Harpham et al, 2005; Lolichen et al, 2006), and the value of employing interactive research methodologies (such as photography, daily diaries, mobility maps and drawings) to draw out children's views (Sapkota and Sharma, 1996; Theis, 1996).

5.4 Knowledge–policy interactions in Asia

Asia is an exceedingly diverse continent, with particularly stark differences between South and East Asia. In the brief discussion of political context characteristics that follows, however, we focus on two dimensions that have some resonance across the region: a trend towards political and fiscal decentralisation with important implications for the knowledge–policy interface on child well-being, and the strong role of governments in knowledge-production processes.

Table 5.10: Research about children involving children's participation in Asia

Reference	Subject	Country	Key findings
Ahsan (2009).	Children's participation	Bangladesh	This article argues that researchers must recognise the social dimensions of children's participation in research. The author found that attempting to obtain children's consent was difficult because in Bangladesh children are relatively powerless and thus unable to exercise their judgement without the influence of adults in their environments. Some teachers, for example, chose who would and would not be allowed to participate. One international NGO refused access to 'its' children, fearing government reprisals. The power dynamics that relegate girls to lower social positions made it even more difficult for them to participate; girls were particularly concerned about privacy issues.
Baker (1996)	Street children	Nepal	This small study, which focused on the feasibility and methods of doing participatory research with children, collected qualitative and quantitative data on health issues faced by street children and how they responded to them. Older children and those living with their families were more likely to understand risks and seek appropriate care. Younger children, for example, do not appear to prioritise drinking clean water, using soap, or wearing shoes while rag picking in the same way that older adolescents do. They are also possibly less likely to seek care unless they are totally incapacitated.
Chakraborty (2009)	Participation and identity in Muslim girls	India	This study addresses what it means to young women living in the slums of Kolkata to be a 'good Muslim girl'. Using photographs and focusing primarily on clothing, the study examines ways girls challenge what it means to be 'good'. While the girls' photos began with simple shots of home life and consumer goods, as mutual trust developed they moved to shots of themselves in Western clothing or at 'bad' locations, such as malls. The girls' experiences were positive: it was a chance to escape the 'daily grind' of schoolwork and chores. The author points out that 'fun' should be a relevant outcome for academics.
Hastadewi (2009)	Child participation	Indonesia	This article focuses on a UNICEF study in Indonesia and the '12-step' method that was used to involve children in research about child labour. Researchers found that information gathered from community sources about where to find child workers was often incorrect. They were told, for example, that many children made tempeh or worked in the fish market, but actually the tourist sector and farming were found to employ most of them. Body maps were a very useful tool; they enabled children to show which parts of their bodies had been injured at work. Adults were often inquisitive and wanted to be involved; researchers found that it was best to distract them by giving them separate activities. Another difficulty was the degree to which researchers came to be emotionally involved with the children, which was very stressful.

(continued)

Reference	Subject	Country	Key findings
Harpham et al (2005)	Child participation	Vietnam	Using PPA methods with both children and adults, the study identified that the two groups had markedly different views about the nature of child poverty. Adults, for example, saw lack of access to clean water as a key distinguishing feature of poverty; children, on the other hand, mentioned shame and lack of assets, such as toys or television.
Jabeen (2009)	Child participation	Pakistan	This article compares two studies with children in Pakistan – one quantitative and one qualitative. The former, a study on missing children, lent itself to mapping the scope of the problem while the latter, on the experiences of street children, offered the children genuine voice. Particularly in Pakistan, where rigid hierarchies typically preclude children's autonomy, qualitative research enabled the children to express their own beliefs, which they preferred to do verbally, as most had never been to school. Over time, as they learned to trust the researcher, they disclosed more than they would have under more typical research conditions, including their participation in sex work and drug use.
Lolichen et al (2006)	Child-led research	India	This field study highlighted the methods and findings of the Concerned for Working Children's (CWC's) participatory project with children in Kundapur Taluk, India. CWC left the project's design and choice of tools, as well as data collection and interpretation, entirely in the hands of children. Over 300 children, the majority of whom were in school, participated in mapping what they perceived as community needs and ascertaining how to address them. For example, children who walked long distances to school during the rainy season often arrived at school muddy from the splashing of passing cars. Other children were concerned about an abandoned dry well, used as a dump, located near a playground. The repair of one bridge ranked high for children, who were forced to walk miles out of their way to school and for chores. The article concludes that the process of involving children is far more important than the product and can lead to genuine change.
Sapkota and Sharma (1996)	Children's participation in research	Nepal	This small study, which used drawings, diaries, mobility maps, and interviews, attempted to ascertain the usefulness of participatory methods for children. The key finding was that triangulation was vital to data collection: multiple modes of data collection increased reliability. For example, drawings showed what children did when they were not in school, mobility maps showed where they did it, and interviews allowed them to explain what was important.
Theis (1996)	Children's participation in research	Vietnam	This article reviews the Save the Children Fund's efforts in Vietnam to use participatory methods with children in an attempt to ascertain whether development projects were genuinely meeting their needs as social actors in their own right. Key findings included that it is far more important that the whole process be participatory than it is that each method be so, that choosing the correct facilitators is vital to encouraging children's participation, and that intermediate media (such as drawings) often elicit better responses. One child, for example, refused to respond to questions, but happily filled out her daily schedule on paper.

Decentralisation and implications for child well-being

The last two decades have seen a widespread trend towards decentralisation, with a range of innovative approaches undertaken throughout Asia to reform the role and nature of the state as an agent of development and to deepen democracy (Crook and Manor, 1998; Agrawal and Ribot, 1999; Gaventa, 2006; Mehotra, 2006). As Westcott and Porter (2005: 1) note:

> Across Asia Pacific, and most marked in East Asia, one common feature of the policy and institutional package applied by governments keen to foster growth alongside poverty reduction has been to assign state powers, responsibilities and resources to sub-national authorities and to private and civil society agencies under various forms of contract, partnership or principal–agent relationship. Decentralization has become the catch-all term for what proves in practice to be a highly differentiated, and differently motivated, range of practices and institutional forms.

By creating institutional arrangements to strengthen the relationship between citizens and the state, decentralisation aims to combat the inefficiencies of centralised bureaucracies and promote policies and programmes that are informed by local knowledge and better reflect people's real needs, especially the poor. In theory, decentralisation increases the capacity of the citizenry to impose sanctions on non-performing local authorities – especially in terms of public service delivery – through voting and recourse to higher-level authorities (Johnson, 2003). Evidence to date, however, suggests that decentralisation does not always generate positive outcomes for the poor (Ahmad et al, 2005). The multiple reasons for this include: entrenched patron–client relationships rather than rights-based citizenship; weak information systems and knowledge-sharing between national and local government institutions; lack of transparent decision-making and use of funds; low capacity levels among local functionaries; weak accountability mechanisms; minimal opportunities for meaningful civic participation in policy processes; and inadequate data for monitoring purposes (Bardhan, 2002). Analysts are increasingly realising that decentralised governance is not a quick fix, and in particular that promoting inclusive and effective participation in local-level decision-making is a complex and often long-term challenge (e.g. Crook and Sverrisson, 2001).

In particular, initiatives to open policy spaces to promote greater participation in local institutions have shown that new institutional arrangements often replicate existing patterns of power and exclusion. An emphasis on the ideal of 'community empowerment' risks overlooking power differentials and oppressive social norms within groups (Cornwall, 2002; Williams, 2004) such as informal power structures and norms (e.g. gender and caste inequalities), which often determine who is able to attend meetings or to speak up, and even the type of issues that are raised (e.g. Goetz, 2004).[6] Indeed, a growing body of evidence suggests that decentralisation alone is insufficient to mitigate inequality and social exclusion if it is not accompanied by deliberate, systematic initiatives to ensure that marginalised groups are able to access these new policy debate and decision-making spaces (e.g. Mukhopadhyay, 2005).

Issues of power relations are even more complex in the case of child-related service delivery, as children are largely excluded from the policy process and their voices are seldom heard in the Asian context (e.g. Theis, 1996). This is due to age-based notions of citizenship (informed by Confucian hierarchies in East Asia, for instance) and questions about children's evolving capacities over the course of childhood and the appropriateness of their direct participation in the policy arena, particularly in the case of pre-adolescents (e.g. Ansell, 2005; Pham and Jones, 2005; also see discussion in Chapter 3).

In order to address these challenges, Lockheed's (2006) work on education outlines four preconditions for effective decentralisation of child-related services: a national consensus on goals,[7] a supporting legal framework, well-defined financial flow mechanisms and training to cope with new responsibilities at the sub-national level. In practice, however, despite appropriate policy frameworks being in place at the national level in much of Asia, the delivery of child-related services is too often fragmented and under-resourced. This is in large part due to the tendency for governmental children's agencies to be among the most marginalised (Harper, 2004), and thus unable to secure sufficient funding for child-related services and programmes due to competing demands for scarce sub-national government resources. These resource challenges are often compounded by a dearth of specialised children's agencies and issue champions, limited age-disaggregated data[8] and/ or parents' lack of sufficient knowledge and awareness to effectively champion child-sensitive service provision at the local government level (e.g. Akehurst and Cardona, 1994).[9]

The state and knowledge intermediaries

A second important dynamic in the region is the growing prevalence of think tanks – institutions engaged in the business of evidence-informed policy influencing – in policy processes in the region (McGann with Johnson, 2005). Alongside generally substantial investments in the higher education sector,[10] a recent analysis of the evolution of think tanks in developing-country contexts by Datta et al (2010) highlights the role the state has played in supporting the establishment of think tanks in many Asian countries. The first think tanks in the North-east and South-east Asian sub-regions were established by state bodies to inform development plans, promote economic growth and support public policy formulation, and have been complemented by the emergence of independent think tanks amid growing political liberalisation in much of the region since the 1990s (Stone and Denham, 2004). While the latter group produces research that is critical of the state to varying extents, many governments also continue to rely on research evidence from state- or party-affiliated think tanks. A not dissimilar trend has been seen in South Asia. For example, since independence in 1947, India has had a think tank tradition in which successive governments have invested substantially in think tanks and have largely tolerated their critiques of public policy. However, the weakening of the dominant Congress party, an increasingly partisan political culture, the rising influence of IFIs and popular mobilisations around human rights have created space for further growth of non-governmental think tanks. Established government-funded think tanks, which tend to provide national and state governments with most, if not all, of the policymaking evidence they require, are diversifying their funding sources to include foreign and private-sector donors, while relatively new think tanks are almost totally dependent on foreign funding. These foreign-funded think tanks often channel their research through influential academics and activist/advocacy-oriented NGOs. In short, there is a reasonable degree of openness towards evidence-informed policy dialogue in the region, albeit with the government playing a relatively strong role in producing and filtering the knowledge that is taken up.

In terms of knowledge intermediaries focusing on child well-being, the field is more limited, as Table 5.11 illustrates, with only a small number of communities of practice concerned with child well-being, especially at the regional level, but also at the national and sub-national levels. Partial exceptions include communities focused on the prevention of child trafficking and sexual exploitation and the eradication of child labour (see, for example, Asia Against Child Trafficking [AACT], End

Table 5.11: Selected communities of practice on child well-being in Asia

Name	Time frame	Objectives	Type of policy impact
Regional focus			
Asia Against Child Trafficking (AACT) http://www.cridoc.net/asia_acts.php http://www.humantrafficking.org/countries/philippines/resources	2002	Part of the International Campaign against Child Trafficking, AACT works as a regional campaign to fight child trafficking in Brunei Darussalam, Myanmar, Cambodia, Indonesia, Lao People's Democratic Republic, the Philippines, Thailand, and Vietnam.	AACT lobbies governments and authorities to implement human rights standards for trafficked children (through national legislation, the creation of regional protection mechanisms, cooperation, support for victims, and prosecution of offenders).
Southeast Asia Coalition to Stop the Use of Child Soldiers (SEASUCS) http://www.facebook.com/pages/Southeast-Asia-Coalition-to-Stop-the-Use-of-Child-Soldiers/100393233757?v=info	2002	SEASUCS is a network of national and regional human rights and child-focused organisations working in Burma, Indonesia, and the Philippines. SEASUCS advocates for the protection of children involved in armed conflicts in the South-east Asian region.	SEASUCS advocates for the universal ratification of the Optional Protocol to the Convention on the Rights of the Child on the Involvement of Children in Armed Conflict (OPCRC-AC), raises awareness, and promotes respect for children's rights by conducting peace and human rights education among non-state armed groups and civil society; develops capacities of partner organisations in advocating for the implementation of programmes for children involved in armed conflict; and monitors compliance by governments and non-state armed groups.
Campaign Against Sex Selective Abortion (CASSA) http://cassa.in/index.html	1998	CASSA is a campaign consisting of social action groups, women's organisations, human rights groups, advocates, educators, research institutions and professionals working to stop the misuse of sex-selection technologies.	The campaign carries out educational programmes for healthcare professionals, NGOs, and adolescents. It also monitors and reports violations.

(continued)

Table 5.10 (continued)

Name	Time frame	Objectives	Type of policy impact
National focus			
End Child Prostitution Abuse and Trafficking (ECPAT) in Cambodia http://www.ecpatcambodia.org/ index.php?menuid=2	1995	ECPAT Cambodia is a network of 26 national and international organisations and institutions working to combat CSEC. It mobilises key stakeholders and promotes coordinated action for the elimination of child prostitution, child pornography and trafficking in children for sexual purposes.	The group's activities include: conducting CST workshops training tourism industry personnel to prevent child abuse in tourist destinations; capacity-building workshops on care and protection for coalition members who provide direct services to victims; and the production of awareness-raising and informational materials on trafficking of children for sexual purposes. ECPAT Cambodia works closely with a variety of Cambodian government ministries.
Network Against Trafficking and Sexual Exploitation in Andhra Pradesh (NATSAP) http://traffickinginap.com/ profile.html#	2000	NATSAP is a coalition of 50 NGOs working in Andhra Pradesh, India, to prevent trafficking and exploitation of children and women.	NATSAP undertakes research on the issue of child trafficking. It serves on governmental committees in Andhra Pradesh and serves as a unified force in lobbying efforts to end the practice.
India Alliance for Child Rights (IACR)	2001	The IACR represents a countrywide alliance of networks, NGOs, think tanks, activists, academia, and concerned individuals working for the realisation of the rights of children.	The IACR lobbies governments and the UN and monitors the UNCRC. It produces supplementary shadow reports on India's progress vis-à-vis the UNCRC.
Campaign Against Child Labour (CACL)	1992	A network of over 6,000 anti-child labour groups spread over 21 states in India, the CACL is committed to eradicating child labour through building public opinion, investigating abuse, advocacy, and monitoring national and international development plans. It undertakes research on child rights and legal casework on behalf of children and works with the media and press. In 2000 it published *An Alternate Report on the Status of Child Labour In India.*	The CACL lobbies state and national governments and the UN to improve the realisation of children's rights and to eradicate child labour.

(continued)

Name	Time frame	Objectives	Type of policy impact
National Alliance for the Fundamental Right to Education (NAFRE), India	1998	The alliance is composed of groups in India united by the belief that children have a fundamental right to education. Its aims are: • to act as a platform to voice various opinions about specific issues so that people who normally do not hear such debates learn about them and participate in creating a broader consensus; • to work with all levels of government, parliament, citizenry, the media and industry/business to make the fundamental right to education and related matters a national priority; • to monitor the status of education while encouraging, creating and catalysing large-scale replicable models realising the fundamental right; • to work to gather and disseminate factual information about education to opinion-makers, policymakers and the parents of the children whose future is at stake.	The alliance was instrumental in the 2009 passage of the Right of Children to Free and Compulsory Education Act. The Act guarantees free education for all children up to the age of 14 and specifically focuses on the education of girls and minorities.
National Coalition for the Elimination of Commercial Sexual Exploitation of Children, Indonesia http://www.eska.or.id/en/index. php?option=com_content&view w=article&id=51&Itemid=58	2000	The National Coalition has 17 members located in 11 provinces, including NGOs, law experts, and a university. It has implemented a series of programmes designed to eliminate child prostitution, child pornography, and child trafficking for sexual purposes, and to push community members and government to ensure that every child gets their fundamental rights and is protected from any form of commercial sexual exploitation.	Recent coalition activities include formulating a strategic plan for legal reform on CSEC in Indonesia; mapping stakeholders to implement CSEC programmes in Indonesia; producing a directory of CSEC stakeholders in Indonesia; documenting experiences in handling CSEC cases; drafting and disseminating articles on CSEC; analysing incidences of CSEC in selected provinces in Indonesia; and advocating for the central and provincial governments to strengthen the plan of action for the elimination of CSEC.

(continued)

Table 5.11 (continued)

Name	Time frame	Objectives	Type of policy impact
Network of Indonesian Child Labor NGOs (Jarak)		Jarak is a strategy-focused network of national NGOs promoting the elimination of the worst forms of child labour in Indonesia. Jarak supervises and assists with the implementation of member activities and coordinates regional efforts.	Jarak works to change public opinion by conducting training and studies, providing funding for programming and promoting information access. Jarak also consults with the Indonesian government and law enforcement on changing public policy.
Coalition to Fight Against Child Exploitation (FACE)	1995	FACE operates at both the policy and the grassroots levels in Thailand. Members include the Centre for the Protection of Children's Rights, Development & Education Programmes for Daughters and Communities, Friends of Thai Women Workers in Asia, and Child Workers in Asia	FACE began with the aim of monitoring Thailand's justice system (assisting in obtaining evidence from victimised children and accompanying them to court) and is now also active lobbying local and international NGOs for laws, raising awareness through education and mass media, and cooperating to prosecute offenders.

Child Prostitution, Child Pornography, Child Trafficking for Sexual Purposes [ECPAT] in Cambodia, and the Campaign Against Child Labour [CACL]). India also appears to have a relatively more active community of child-focused organisations involved at the knowledge–policy interface level. Overall, however, the communities of practice identified have generally had greater success in agenda-setting and securing discursive commitments from governments than in achieving substantive policy change and influencing behavioural shifts.

Finally, as discussed in Chapter 4, international agencies such as Save the Children, Plan, World Vision and UNICEF are all helping to plug this knowledge–policy interface lacuna, as their work increasingly shifts towards evidence-based policy advocacy. However, as international donors and agencies have limited influence in many parts of Asia, their stature at the policy dialogue table is often modest, especially in contexts such as India, China or Vietnam.

5.5 Case study: children, citizen-led policy advocacy and the delivery of child-focused services in India

Background

We now turn to a case study of policy-influencing efforts to strengthen the quality of education and health services for children in Andhra Pradesh State, India. As the preceding sections highlighted, Asia's diversity makes it difficult to identify particular characteristics of the region's knowledge–policy interface. However, there is a regional tendency for knowledge-production processes to be heavily shaped by the state, and even India, the region's oldest democracy, shares this tendency. Thus, this case study provides a useful lens for exploring linkages between knowledge on childhood poverty and policy change in Asia. We begin by outlining the policy change objective of this citizen-led policy-influencing endeavour, then discuss how evidence was generated and utilised in an attempt to shape policy debates and eventual policy change outcomes.

Policy change objective and children's 3D well-being

Our case study focuses on a UNICEF-funded policy research initiative to assess civic monitoring of children's education and nutritional health services in Andhra Pradesh, one of India's middle-income states (see Box 5.1) in 2005–07. The initiative sought to raise awareness about the strengths and weaknesses of decentralised approaches to social policy delivery for children and to identify areas for improving child well-being outcomes.

Box 5.1: User committees focused on basic services for children

Mothers' committees were established to improve Integrated Child Development Services (ICDS) or *anganwadi* services (child and maternal health and referral services, supplementary nutrition, immunisations, health and nutrition education, and preschool education). Their responsibilities include expanding the reach of and monitoring *anganwadi* services and government health campaigns (e.g. Pulse Polio). Membership tenure is formally two years and contingent upon regular participation in weekly/bi-weekly meetings.

School education committees were established to improve local school management, but were largely discontinued following state elections in 2005. Comprising four members selected from among parents whose children attend the local government school, education committees' formal responsibilities included monitoring teacher attendance and performance; hiring local teachers; promoting student enrolment, attendance, retention and scholastic achievement; managing the funding and construction of school facilities (infrastructure, equipment and health programmes); and promoting parental commitment to children's schooling. The education committee chairperson, elected from among committee members, worked closely with the school principal to facilitate these activities.

There is growing recognition that India needs to take decisive action to enhance the well-being of millions of poor children. Despite strong economic growth and its emergence as an increasingly respected economic powerhouse, India continues to face significant challenges to improving human development indicators. The UNICEF (2007) MDG Progress Report revealed that India making insufficient or no progress on most goals, with the exceptions of eliminating gender disparities in primary education and the provision of safe drinking water. Andhra Pradesh is similarly off track in achieving the child-related MDGs.[11] Approximately 32%[12] of the state's 76 million residents are aged 14 or under, many of whom live in rural areas with high levels of poverty.

There are encouraging signs of progress, however, in the Union Government's Tenth and Eleventh National Five-Year Plans (2002–07, 2007–12), which provide clear child-related targets that are closely aligned with the MDGs. The mid-term evaluation of the Tenth Plan further emphasised the critical role of state governments in supporting these efforts by providing additional resources and ensuring that state-level agencies are in charge of child-focused policies. The extent to which such decentralisation initiatives are making a difference in children's lives, nevertheless, remains under-researched. In Andhra Pradesh, parental user committees were established to hold service providers accountable to the community for providing quality service to poor children (see Box 5.2 for further discussion on Andhra Pradesh's decentralisation dynamics). These grassroots committees aim to correct the high level of centralisation in Indian service delivery,[13] and have a mandate to monitor the delivery of maternal and child health and nutritional services and primary and secondary schools.[14] Understanding the extent to which this model is empowering communities, improving service delivery and meeting national- and state-level child rights commitments is therefore of considerable policy importance.

Box 5.2: Decentralisation in Andhra Pradesh

In Andhra Pradesh, participatory user committees were established by the Chandhra Babu Naidu government (1995–2004) to promote greater citizen involvement in natural resource management and service delivery. These user committees, or parallel institutions, were conceptualised as a mechanism for direct participation in local government structures (e.g. Reddy et al, 2006) and as a means to reduce elite capture and political interference (Manor, 2004). The user committee initiative has, however, proved controversial. Although providing additional channels for the poor to voice their demands for improved services, critics claim that they, at best, cause confusion and replicate established local government structures and, at worst, weaken local democracy by diverting funds and responsibilities to committees easily controlled by the ruling party bureaucracy (Powis, 2003). Moreover, this 'second wave of decentralisation' has increasingly meant that service users are required to bear part of the costs of social services by contributing in kind or in cash (Brock et al, 2001).

3D evidence generation on 3D child well-being

Although natural resource-related user committees have sparked vigorous academic debate, the evidence base on the impacts of education and mothers' committees on child well-being is thin. Here we focus on a partnership between Save the Children UK and the Hyderabad-based Centre for Economic and Social Studies, a state-affiliated research institute, which explored the extent to which participatory policy spaces introduced as part of the state's decentralisation process were enhancing child well-being outcomes, especially educational attainment, nutritional health and protection from harmful forms of child labour. A mixed-methods approach was employed, combining quantitative survey data and in-depth qualitative research involving repeat visits with committee members and programme implementers over the course of a year to a subsample of sites covering the state's three main regions (Telangana, Rayalseema and Coastal Andhra). A detailed budget analysis was also undertaken[15] despite considerable data constraints.[16] To compensate, the project also collected information on policy, planning and budgeting processes to gain insights into local governance dynamics, including the spaces created by local governments for civic participation and grassroots implementation of policies and programmes (see Pereznieto et al, 2007).

Overall, the research findings painted a mixed picture of the impact of inclusive and meaningful participation in mothers' and education user committees on service delivery. While parental involvement in monitoring service delivery processes appeared to be an important first step, programme design and implementation processes had to pay careful attention to minimising existing power relations if child well-being outcomes were to be realised. On the one hand, key informants and committee members agreed that committees enabled a broader cross-section of villagers to participate in public affairs than is the case with other governance institutions. Some members also felt that participation in education committees gave them a sense of entitlement and the right to question school authorities and even, potentially, government officials. Indeed, in several cases there were reports that education committee members continued to monitor education service delivery and interact with school personnel even after the committees were dissolved in 2005. Research also found positive accounts of improved interaction between mothers and *anganwadi* service providers in a number of communities.

On the other hand, however, a number of factors limiting the effectiveness of user committees as mechanisms to participate in service delivery decision-making and monitoring practices also emerged. Participation opportunities were significantly shaped by socio-economic, caste and gender power relations. The education committee chairmanship, for instance, emerged as a valued position for aspiring local party cadres, as it represented not only a potential stepping-stone to a career in politics, but also access to considerable funds for infrastructure development, and, hence, decision-making leverage. By contrast, parents who were wage labourers were less interested and less involved in committee activities as participation came at the cost of their daily wage, and was thus deemed less important. There were also limited tangible incentives to be actively involved in mothers' committees, which accorded members little prestige on account of the generally low priority placed on child and maternal health issues in village politics.[17]

Gender differences were also found to affect participation levels. Education committees were typically male-dominated, and, in cases where women were involved, their participation was more likely to be limited (especially if they were uneducated), with their husbands handling their responsibilities. Indeed, education levels – also mediated through class and caste positioning – played a key role in how involved members were in committee activities:

> Women and lower-caste people have never been courageous enough to raise their voice against the upper castes. Elected leaders want to help their followers and are not interested in the marginalized or children.... When it comes to the backward classes, although they may be appointed sarpanch (village head), the vice chairman is typically a forward caste person who does all the work. So, the reservations are for namesake only. (Programme manager, Amrabad Mandal, interview, 2006)

In this regard, effective monitoring of teachers and *anganwadi* workers proved a demanding task, as many committee members felt unable to challenge front-line service providers, considering the latter to be socially and professionally superior.

Not surprisingly, given these structural power imbalances, the ambitious goals the government set for these committees, ranging from financial management and infrastructure development to greater parental involvement and responsibility for their children's human capital development and monitoring of service provider standards, were only partially met. For instance, in committees with active members and/or support from proactive service providers, there was general consensus that local public health and education service outreach had improved. In the case of education committees, many respondents talked about efforts to persuade parents to monitor their children's school enrolment and attendance, to allow drop-outs to re-enrol and to allocate time for children to do their homework. Several informants mentioned the important role that education committees played in addressing problems of child labour, child marriage and child trafficking, as well as HIV/AIDS prevention. However, little demand was generated in committees where members were illiterate and/or poorly informed about their roles and responsibilities, unless their inactivity was compensated for by activist-oriented leaders or *anganwadi* workers.

Another important weakness identified was a strong bias towards infrastructure investment. Given that an important function of education committees was to oversee school development budgets together with school principals, many respondents focused on building repairs, constructing classrooms and toilets, whitewashing classroom walls, and purchasing gifts at national holidays. Although committee members also talked about their role in ensuring teacher attendance and teaching quality, such activities have fewer concrete outcomes, and success was therefore viewed as more difficult to demonstrate to the wider community and consequently less rewarding.

3D approaches to knowledge–policy interaction

The project's approach to knowledge–policy interaction was embedded within the project design, including careful attention to the dynamics of policy narratives/messages, actors/networks and context/institutions.

Knowledge–policy interaction initiatives are especially complex when engaging with issues of decentralised service provision as multiple and interacting political-institutional contexts need to be taken into consideration. The project therefore sought to understand the political economy of decision-making around decentralisation at the national and state levels, including concerns about good governance and accountability, as well as the realities of decentralisation of social services in practice at the sub-state and local levels, including capacity deficits and elite capture of local decision-making authorities.

The multi-context focus in turn resulted in a multiplicity with whom to engage. These ranged from national-level officials and international agency staff to state and sub-state civil servants, and from programme implementers and service providers to committee participants. On account of their diverse vantage points and policy priorities, developing compelling policy narratives had to be approached creatively and avoid the temptation of 'one message suits all'.

Accordingly, at the national and state levels, the strategy entailed the publication of high-level UNICEF reports disseminated at policy stakeholder seminars in Hyderabad and Delhi. These events aimed to highlight strengths and weaknesses of decentralisation efforts, and to discuss possible responses and approaches to support citizen-led monitoring efforts. In particular, national- and state-level policy narratives were framed so as to support UNICEF to identify potentially transferable lessons across states and potentially across the South Asian region. For instance, at the national level, findings were framed within a broader debate about the value of decentralised service provision models, but introduced a cautionary note regarding the importance of ensuring that parents from low socio-economic strata are supported to develop the requisite capacities to monitor service quality. At the state level, the focus was somewhat distinct, drawing upon the positive developments that committees had contributed to local communities in an effort to encourage stakeholders to not dismiss the potential of parental user committees despite the problems related to their politicisation in the Andhra Pradesh context (see Jones et al, 2007a, 2007b).

At the district and sub-district (*mandal*) levels, policy-influencing efforts focused on developing tailored policy briefs drawing on locale-specific findings for follow-up discussions with local stakeholders, and disseminating cartoon-based brochures for community feedback sessions. The latter were deemed critical in order to communicate to a largely illiterate or semi-literate population who had contributed time and insights during key informant interviews and focus group discussions. It was also seen as a mechanism for honouring a project commitment to the principle of community reciprocity and more equal exchange of information. Policy narratives were kept simple, focusing on the benefits of engagement in service monitoring committees, and opportunities for strengthening knowledge and skills about existing policies and services for child well-being.

Finally, at the international level, the results were presented at international conferences on governance (in the US) and on child rights and policy processes (in Norway). Here the narrative employed highlighted the importance of more careful empirical work on decentralised social policy budget provisions and delivery to plug important knowledge gaps and to strengthen evidence-informed policy and programme development.

Outcomes of a 3D approach

This evidence-informed policy-influencing initiative had mixed outcomes for child well-being. On the positive side, after close dialogue with UNICEF Hyderabad and the Andhra Pradesh Department of Women and Children, the project team was invited to help formulate a State Action Plan for Children and draw on insights from the project's evidence base. Although this role did not involve the development of detailed policy prescriptions relating to the parental user committees per se, it represented an important opportunity to contribute directly to policy development on child well-being. More generally, the project's evidence-generation process helped strengthen awareness among UNICEF, researchers at the Centre for Economic and Social Studies and officials with child-related mandates about the specific challenges involved in monitoring decentralised service delivery. It especially highlighted the shortcomings of budgetary data-collection efforts in the area of child service delivery, and the need for child well-being advocates to think strategically about how best to capitalise upon the new window represented by the 2005 Right to Information Act.

Equally importantly, the process of interacting with user committee members over the course of a year facilitated some participants' unprecedented reflection on the potential of their role. As one education committee member from Kataram *mandal* reflected:

> We now realise that the absence of the committees will be an advantage for teachers. An EC [education committee] chairman can question teachers as a representative of parents of 400 children. If we ask about teachers' attendance individually, they used to dismiss our queries. If the committee is not there, they won't listen to anybody. Even the headmaster, they pressure him through the [teachers'] union. But they cannot do it to us. (Interview, 2006)

However, the project's knowledge interaction efforts also highlighted important limitations. First, there was a dearth of local champions for children's rights with whom to partner. A common thread across the project's research sites was the extent to which child well-being is marginalised in policy and programming debates at the local level. Despite less than satisfactory child well-being indicators in Andhra Pradesh and significant disparities in district performance, there seemed to be little interest in investing in children beyond state-contributed resources. One of the main reasons for the invisibility of children revealed by interviews was the fact that political leaders are interested in popular programmes that will translate into political support. Given that children are not seen as 'vote banks', political platforms do not focus on child-related issues:

> During the last two years none of the local council members ever discussed issues related to woman and children. Nobody in the *zilla parishad* [district council], either councillors or

MPs, raised such issues. But if our children get educated and our women's health progresses, then we can have a good district, good *mandal* and good village. We need to do more to make this happen. (Chairman *zilla parishad*, Mahboobnagar district, interview, 2006)

In this regard, the project's findings endorsed the view that user committees were functioning as parallel institutions weakly connected to local political structures. This distance tended to be exacerbated by the capacity deficits of many committee members, who were often inexperienced vis-à-vis policy processes and were generally offered few opportunities to develop their capacities through the user committee programme.

Second, while education and mothers' committees were set up to improve user participation in public services, there were very limited provisions for children's voices to be taken into account in service delivery or for their interests to be represented on committees. Indeed, not only did the project find an absence of children's participation across the research sites, but there was little support for such an initiative. This was particularly evident in the case of education committee chairs. Concerned with securing future political advancement, their incentives lay in promoting activities popular with the voting public, for example, investing in visible examples of infrastructure development such as the construction of compound walls or new school buildings, rather than actions that prioritised children's concerns about the content of the school curricula or bullying. As such, a key project conclusion was the importance of identifying and supporting adult champions of children's rights without which demand for integrating a child-sensitive perspective into local decision-making is likely to remain weak. Ideally knowledge interaction efforts would include working alongside local actors to strengthen such capacities, but this requires mid- to long-term project funding, which is unfortunately rare.

A third key challenge the project encountered was the difficulty of liaising with poorly coordinated government agencies with child-related mandates. A prime consideration in assessing any decentralised policy initiative is the extent to which responsible government agencies have an institutional presence at the sub-national level and, if so, the relative efficacy of mechanisms to facilitate joined-up child-focused service provision. In theory at least, India's ICDS offers a compelling institutional structure, as it is nationally coordinated and funded; has offices and staff at the state, district and *mandal* levels; and seeks to address children's educational, health and nutritional needs. However, although

ICDS coverage in Andhra Pradesh is relatively high,[18] it has not been as effective as its design would suggest due to underfunding, inadequate staff training and often poor infrastructure. ICDS programmes also only target children aged six and under, leaving a pronounced gap in services to address the needs of older children at the village and municipal levels.[19] Furthermore, in most cases state-planned child-related programmes lack local-level government officials to implement them. For example, no one is directly responsible for implementing child protection programmes, and project directors/officers from the Department for Women and Children tasked with running ICDS centres have little clout. Thus, they can do little to ensure that other, more powerful, local government officials push for the implementation of child protection schemes, including eliminating child abuse and harmful forms of child labour, resulting in limited government action on these key issues.

Finally, the project's budget monitoring work found that at the district and *mandal* levels decisions about budget planning and spending remained centralised at the state level, indicating a disjuncture between political and administrative decentralisation in Andhra Pradesh (Pereznieto et al, 2007). Only in cases of emergency, such as drought or epidemic outbreaks, are district budgets given additional resources and the flexibility to tackle specific problems. By contrast, funds to address child welfare problems such as higher-than-average child labour or infant mortality rates were not available (Pereznieto et al, 2007). The findings further indicated weak linkage between departments and sectors at the state and local levels. Sectoral linkages were only vertical, with the transfer of funds from state line departments flowing to administrators at the implementation points, and district governments playing no role. As such, interviews with local government officials in charge of implementing sectoral schemes were unaware of child-focused programmes in other sectors that could be implemented in a more coordinated manner (Pereznieto et al, 2007). This lack of horizontal linkages hinders the identification and realisation of potential policy and budget synergies to address the interlinked causes of childhood poverty holistically (Harper, 2004).

5.6 Conclusions

Three general insights emerge from the discussion on child well-being, the regional overview of knowledge and policy actors and processes working on policy change to improve child well-being, and the empirical study of knowledge–policy interactions in India. This chapter has paid particular attention to the complex challenges involved in research-informed policy engagement work around decentralised policy processes for children, and identified a number of key areas that urgently need to be addressed if decentralisation is to fulfil its potential to promote the achievement of the child-related MDGs and childhood poverty reduction more broadly.

Policy ideas and narratives

As decentralisation is a relatively new and evolving process in many developing-country contexts, a key policy concern entails addressing knowledge gaps about policy and programme impacts on child well-being over time. The robustness of any child-focused policy- and budget-monitoring effort depends on the availability of age- (and gender-)disaggregated programme and budgetary data down to the lowest tiers of government, and corresponding child well-being indicators. Accordingly, promoting the collection, reporting and use of age-disaggregated data at the sub-national level needs to be urgently prioritised. Too often data-collection investments are made at the national or state levels, but not below, thereby risking overlooking the importance of spatial patterning of poverty and vulnerability.

Investing in a systematic mapping of policies, from the national level down, is also an important prerequisite for policy engagement efforts around decentralised policy issues as it can help identify entry and veto points in local-level policy and programming. Given the differing governance dynamics and dominant policy narratives at play at the sub-national level, it is also critical that policy-mapping of this nature be understood vis-à-vis specific local political contexts – an endeavour that is often more time-consuming than similar national-level analysis due to less readily available materials.

Policy actors and networks

One of the main constraints to adequate service delivery in the context of decentralisation is the capacity gaps faced by local government officials and civil society actors. Therefore, an important component of any policy research endeavour in this area is to assess the capacity-building mechanisms being put in place in accordance with the responsibilities being devolved and the existing capacity constraints. If local participatory spaces for planning and monitoring are to be used effectively to improve governance and pursue locally identified needs, specific mechanisms need to be put in place to encourage such participation by parents and children irrespective of caste, class or gender. Incentives for participation appear to be a particularly important consideration in the area of childhood well-being, which typically attracts little attention from officials and mainstream civil society practitioners. Practical livelihood barriers for the poorest also need to be overcome, as do social exclusion practices through longer-term empowerment initiatives so that women and lower-caste groups are encouraged to participate in local policy processes.

Policy context and institutions

Finally, given that national-level policy frameworks (often informed by international commitments) and local development plans coexist and guide the actions of stakeholders at different levels of government, it is important to ensure institutionalised dialogue among these levels. Monitoring mechanisms are needed to ensure that minimum national standards and targets are met and also to serve as a check and balance against the dominance of local elites. At the same time, incomplete devolution of responsibilities and budgets from central to local governments may hinder effective coordination and roll-out of child-sensitive policy initiatives. In such cases, without greater national government commitment to genuine decentralisation, the ability of new policy pronouncements to tackle childhood poverty are likely to be limited. Knowledge–policy interaction efforts around decentralised policy issues must therefore balance communication and interaction with state- and local-level actors, with policy advocacy efforts that reach national and international audiences in order to contribute to such synergies.

Notes

[1] This chapter draws on and develops ideas from Jones et al (2007a, 2007b) and Pereznieto et al (2007).

[2] Note that these indicators are only currently available in the MICS3 data set.

[3] Note that there is no central database of such institutions and this table is the authors' own compilation.

[4] RECOUP is a research partnership of seven institutions in the UK, Africa and South Asia funded by DFID and led by the University of Cambridge. RECOUP examines the impact of education on the lives and livelihoods of people in developing countries, particularly those

living in poorer areas and from poorer households. See http://recoup. educ.cam.ac.uk//

[5] The Childwatch International Research Network is a global network of institutions collaborating on child research for the purpose of promoting child rights and improving children's well-being around the world. See http://www.childwatch.uio.no/

[6] Although there was considerable optimism that local governance would increase women's access to political power, quantitative evidence suggests that it has actually been more difficult for women to gain political office at the sub-national level, except where gender quota systems are in place (Mukhopadhyay, 2005). Moreover, contrary to the view that participation at the local level may serve as a springboard to national politics, local government is often more hierarchical and embedded in local social structures than national government, making it difficult for women to introduce gender equality measures (e.g. Jones, 2006). Where decentralisation has facilitated better gender justice outcomes, it has been supported by complementary policies to address gender inequality – such as capacity-building initiatives for women elected to local government bodies, the introduction of gender audits and/or gender budgeting mechanisms, and the organisation of women's constituencies – and concerted civil society organising (Cos-Montiel, 2005).

[7] As responsibilities and funding are devolved to local bodies, national governments still have two important roles to play: i) ensuring equitable financing across sub-national regions; and ii) maintaining quality control of standards.

[8] Often comparative data are only involved at the national or state level, but not at more decentralised levels, making it difficult to tailor policy measures and related monitoring and evaluation mechanisms. This is particularly problematic when it comes to budgetary data. While there is increasing recognition of good practice examples from Latin America of children's participation in local council budget monitoring activities (especially the now famous case of a children's municipal council in Barra Mansa, Brazil, where children actively contribute to municipal planning, see Guerra, 2002), such examples have tended to be pilots that have seldom been scaled up. As such, the availability of budget data that can be easily disaggregated to track spending on child-related services over time remains a major challenge to implementing the UNCRC commitment to progressive realisation of rights (Pereznieto et al, 2007).

[9] The 'Plan of Action' adopted at the 1990 World Summit for Children recognised the importance of grassroots initiatives for children at the provincial level. In many countries, this call for 'decentralisation' has triggered the beginnings of an unprecedented process.

[10] Varghese (2004) points out that East Asian countries saw rapid expansion of higher education enrolment rates between 1970 (5.1%) and 2000 (24.6%).

[11] According to a Centre for Economic and Social Studies (Dev, 2007) report, Andhra Pradesh is off track in halving the proportion of underweight children; in achieving universal primary education, especially for girls; and in reducing child mortality by two thirds.

[12] Andhra Pradesh census data (Census of India 2001[2006]).

[13] This need was particularly pressing in the case of maternal and child health and early child development services, which are the responsibility of the ICDS, a programme funded and managed by the Union of India federal government. Education services are largely funded by a nationwide programme, Sarva Shiksha Abhiyan, with some state-level input into education policy development.

[14] There is a more substantial literature analysing the strengths and weaknesses of the natural resource management user committees (e.g. Manor, 2004).

[15] See Jones et al (2007a) and Pereznieto et al (2007).

[16] Problems included the lack of budget-related data collection by some local governments; the absence of state government records on public expenditure data per district or sub-district unit; and/or reluctance on the part of some officials to share such information, the 2005 Right to Information Act notwithstanding. The project also sought to obtain child well-being indicators corresponding to the districts and sub-districts (*mandals*) where data was collected to draw out linkages between outlays and outcomes, but, again, indicators at this level are not available in official statistics (Pereznieto et al, 2007).

[17] There was more enthusiasm in sites where members had received training on health and nutrition issues and recognised the value of this knowledge to improve their own and their families' health.

[18] ICDS covered 7,742,986 children in 2007/08 aged six years and under in Andhra Pradesh. See http://wdcw.ap.nic.in/icds/html

[19] For middle childhood and adolescence, the range of departments involved in providing specific children's services is broad and includes the Departments of Women and Children; Education; Health and Family Welfare; and Social Welfare and Labour. Yet according to key state government officials, there is little or no coordination among state authorities regarding the activities and schemes carried out by these departments, resulting in frequent duplication of functions and service delivery gaps.

SIX

Child poverty, knowledge and policy in Latin America and the Caribbean

6.1 Introduction

This chapter is about children and the knowledge–policy interface in Latin America, and is structured as follows: Section 1 briefly outlines the extent and nature of child poverty and well-being across Latin America using the 3D well-being approach, and Section 2 reflects on the characteristics of the knowledge-generation process in this region. Section 3 discusses opportunities and challenges involved in the knowledge–policy interface surrounding child well-being in Latin America, paying particular attention to the role of the media in shaping policy debates in the region and the rise of civil society in demanding greater accountability and transparency over the last two decades. Section 4 presents a case study of evidence-informed policy change in the context of an NGO-led initiative aimed at mainstreaming children's rights into macro-policy debates about trade liberalisation, good governance and service delivery in Peru. Finally, Section 5 concludes.

6.2 Children and well-being in Latin America and the Caribbean

In this section, we provide an overview of the extent and nature of child poverty and well-being in Latin America and the Caribbean (LAC) across material, relational and subjective dimensions.

Material child well-being

To recap Chapter 1, the material dimension of child well-being concerns practical welfare, standards of living and the objectively observable outcomes that children and adults are able to achieve. In terms of aspects of material well-being, a quick review of child nutrition, child education and child health using the MDGs as a barometer reveals a mixed picture in LAC.

Figure 6.1: MDG 1 – underweight children in LAC

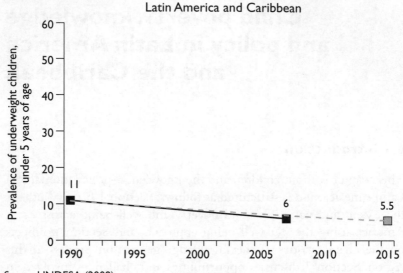

Source: UNDESA (2009).

Figure 6.2: MDG 2 – net primary enrolment in LAC

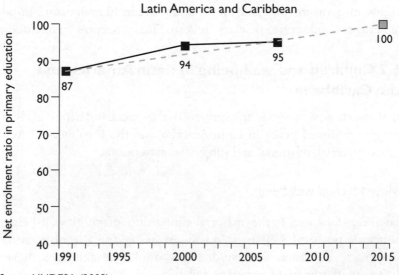

Source: UNDESA (2009).

Figure 6.3: MDG 4 – under-five mortality in LAC

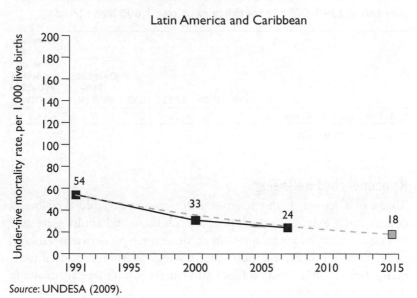

Source: UNDESA (2009).

The story these graphs tell is generally a positive one (also see Table 6.1). The MDGs for underweight children, net primary enrolment and under-five mortality are on track and very positive based on international comparisons – only 6% of children are born underweight, 95% of the relevant cohort of children are enrolled in primary school and under-five mortality is just 24/1,000.

Table 6.1: Children in LAC: selected material well-being indicators

MDG	1990	2005–08	2015 estimate on current trend	MDG target
Underweight children (%)	11.0	6.0	3.1	5.5
Net primary enrolment (%)	86.7	94.9	95.6	100
Under-five mortality (per 1,000 live births)	55.0	24.0	13.7	18.0

Source: UNDESA (2009).

The above picture has, as with Africa and Asia, been complicated by the *Lancet* review of MDG 4 under-five mortality data (You et al, 2009). Indeed, You et al conclude that under-five mortality has declined by half in LAC since 1990 at an annual rate of 4.5%.

Table 6.2: LAC: levels and trends in MDG 4 – under-five mortality, 1990–2008 (mortality rate per 1,000 live births)

	1990	2000	2005	2008	Decrease 1990–2008 (%)	Average annual rate of reduction 1990–2008 (%)
Latin America and the Caribbean	52	33	26	23	56	4.5

Source: You et al (2009: 1–2).

Relational child well-being

To recap Chapter 1, the relational dimension of child well-being concerns the extent to which people – children and adults – are able to engage with others in order to achieve their particular needs and goals. As with other developing-country regions, such relational well-being data are difficult to find for Latin America, but there are growing data-collection efforts.

First, relational well-being indicators are evident in a crude sense in the MDG indicators that relate to children and inequality such as gender (in)equality in education, inequality in under-five mortality and maternal mortality. A brief review of these suggests a mixed picture in LAC.

Figure 6.4: MDG 3 – gender equality in education in LAC

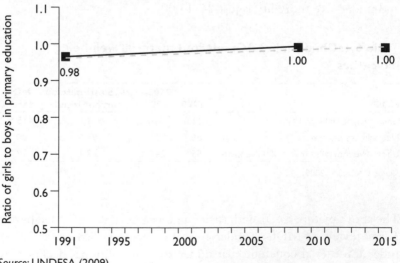

Source: UNDESA (2009).

Figure 6.5: MDG 5 – maternal mortality ratio in LAC

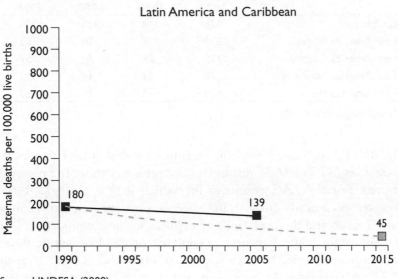

Source: UNDESA (2009).

The story these graphs tell is generally good (also see Table 6.3). MDG 3 (gender equality in education) has already been achieved and MDG 5 (maternal mortality) is on track in LAC. The 2015 Maternal Mortality Ratio (MMR) estimate for LAC is 45.

Table 6.3: Children in LAC: selected relational well-being indicators

MDG	1990	2005–08	2015 estimate on current trend	MDG target
Gender equality in education (%)	98	100	100	100
Maternal mortality (per 100,000 live births)	180	139	45	112

Source: UNDESA (2009).

As noted previously, Hogan et al (2010) recently re-estimated maternal mortality data in *The Lancet*. What is immediately evident when the data are disaggregated by region is considerable variation between Southern Latin America's MMR of 41 and the Caribbean's 254. Other disparities are also evident in recent work by the Economic Commission for Latin America and the Caribbean (ECLAC) (2010) on eight Latin America countries, which found infant mortality of indigenous peoples/territories and non-indigenous people at much higher levels than recorded in national-level censuses.

Table 6.4: MMR per 100,000 live births by LAC region

	1980	1990	2000	2008
Caribbean	426	348	323	254
Latin America, Andean	326	229	156	103
Latin America, Central	125	85	70	57
Latin America, Southern	76	54	44	41
Latin America, tropical	150	113	71	57

Source: Hogan et al (2010).

UNICEF MICS data is available for only a handful of Latin American countries (see Table 6.5), making it impossible to extrapolate regional trends. For the LAC countries for which data is available, birth registration is nearly universal in Belize, Guyana, Jamaica, and Trinidad and Tobago and the prevalence of orphans in these countries is low. Interestingly, while Guyana's percentage of children left without adequate care is nearly twice the rate of orphanhood (11.3% versus 5.7%), in Trinidad and Tobago even orphans (5.9%) do not lack for care (1%). More than one tenth of Jamaican children, on the other hand, are considered vulnerable.

Women's knowledge of HIV prevention hovers around 50% – ranging from 39% in Belize to nearly 60% in Jamaica. Their understanding of mother-to-child HIV transmission averages slightly higher, with Trinidad and Tobago having the lowest rate at 50.3% and Belize the highest at nearly 60%. Marriage of young adolescents is uncommon, although one in five women in Guyana was married before her 18th birthday.

Table 6.5: Selected LAC countries and relational well-being data in UNICEF MICS

	Marriage before age 15 among women (%)	Marriage before age 18 among women (%)	Prevalence of orphans (%)	Children left with inadequate care (%)	Prevalence of FGM/C (%)	Prevalence of vulnerable children (%)
Belize (2006)	n/a	n/a	5.1	4.0	n/a	n/a
Guyana (2006–07)	4.6	21.4	5.9	11.3	n/a	5.3
Jamaica (2005)	1.2	10.4	4.5	3.5	n/a	11.2
Trinidad & Tobago (2006)	1.6	10.7	5.7	1.0	n/a	n/a

Source: UNICEF MICS3, downloaded from www.micscompiler.org/MICS.html

Children and subjective well-being

To recap Chapter 1, the subjective dimension of child well-being concerns meanings that children and adults give to the goals they achieve and the processes in which they engage. Subjective well-being data on impoverished LAC children are almost non-existent. Peru is covered in Crivello et al (2009), and Johnston (2008: 34) reports that children believed that a peer who is 'doing well' is likely to: be conscientious and successful in his/her studies; be good, affectionate, punctual, respectful, polite and obedient; be sociable, have a lot of friends and avoid anti-social behaviour, including gangs and fighting; have his/her family around him/her and be loved and understood by them; be well-off economically (rural site boys only); and be healthy.

Table 6.6: Children in LAC: selected subjective well-being studies of children's perceptions of poverty and well-being

Country and reference	Key findings
India, Vietnam, Peru, Ethiopia Crivello et al (2009)	This article reviews Young Lives' work on developing child-focused, participatory, qualitative methods that capture how children understand their own well-being and how that understanding changes over time. These methods, which included timelines and body mapping, allow research to move beyond simple quantitative measures of child poverty. They also showed that, despite the fact that family well-being was crucial to child well-being, children had unique perspectives that needed to stand on their own. Children, for example, wanted playtime, which adults rarely saw as important. They also wanted to focus on their education, which adults saw as often being secondary to work. Furthermore, children simply saw the world through a different lens. For example, in India adults saw sickness and dirty appearance as two key indicators of child ill-being. Children, on the other hand, chose 'plays in drainage ditch' and 'kills birds' as their top indicators.
Johnston (2008)	Based on a PPA with children, this article's main findings on children's perceptions of well-being were: a child who is 'doing well' is likely to: be conscientious and successful in his/her studies; be good, affectionate, punctual, respectful, polite, and obedient; be sociable, have a lot of friends, and avoid anti-social behaviour, including gangs and fighting; have his/her family around him/her and be loved and understood by them; be well-off economically (rural site boys only); and be healthy.

6.3 Knowledge generation and child well-being in Latin America and the Caribbean

Although still relatively fledgling and less developed than knowledge on Northern childhoods, the generation of research-based knowledge on child poverty and well-being in Latin America is more extensive than that for Africa or Asia. As Karen Wells (2009: 8–9) notes:

> The North American history of childhood forms part of a narrative of general progress and improvement, tempered by increased differentiation by 'race' and class of children's experiences. This is not the case for Latin American history where the themes that preoccupy historians of childhood continue to be the focus of the contemporary sociology of Latin American childhood.... [These include] abandoned children and the structure of the family, criminal children, children and urban disorder, the child-saving movement, the impact of war on children, the practice of informal fostering or 'child-circulation' amongst poor families and street children.

This growing knowledge base is reflected in the number of institutions dedicated to researching childhood well-being (see Table 6.7).[1] As Table 6.7 highlights, there are a number of research institutes with a regional perspective on child well-being, including the International Centre for Research and Policy on Childhood (CIESPI) in Brazil, the Latin American and Caribbean Network of Social Institutions (RISALC) in Chile, the International Centre for Education and Human Development (CINDE) in Colombia and the Inter-American Children's Institute in Uruguay, as well as a sizeable number of organisations that focus on research on children at a national level. Their thematic foci are diverse, and include the documentation of best practices for social programmes focused on women and children, children's media representation, children's education and psychosocial development, and child protection as broadly defined. Given the declining presence of international donors in Latin America over the last decade, the emergence of this epistemic community on child rights and well-being is an important development that should be closely monitored to draw out potential lessons for fostering similar research capacities in other developing-country regions.

UNICEF, ECLAC, the Inter-American Development Bank (IADB) and the World Bank are also increasingly carrying out important research into childhood poverty and well-being in Latin America. UNICEF country and subregional offices on the continent have partnered with a range of institutions (e.g. the New School University, Columbia University and ECLAC's social division) to undertake research on, for instance, children and social inclusion, children- and

Table 6.7: Selected institutions with a research focus on child poverty and well-being in Latin America

Name	Home location	Affiliations and partnerships	Thematic focus
International Centre for Research and Policy on Childhood (CIESPI)	Rio de Janeiro, Brazil	Childwatch partner working in Latin America	CIESPI is a research and reference centre dedicated to research and on-the-ground projects about children and youth and their families and communities. Its goal is to inform policy and practice for this population, thereby contributing to the implementation of children's rights and promoting their full development. http://www.ciespi.org.br/english/index.htm
Centre for the Study and Care of Children and Women (CEANIM)	Chile	Childwatch partner	CEANIM designs and implements evaluations of programmes targeted at women and children. It provides technical expertise to those on the ground and serves to promote best practices in the field. www.accionag.cl/archives/2191
Latin American and Caribbean Network of Social Institutions (RISALC)	Chile	Affiliated to ECLAC, UN working in Latin America	The Network of Social Institutions in Latin America and the Caribbean is comprised of 1,372 governmental, academic, and civil society institutions in the region that are focused on research and indicator development related to a wide range of social issues, including those pertaining to children and youth. http://www.risalc.org:9090/portal/index.php The network has a new thematic web portal on youth, the Ibero-American System for Knowledge on Youth (Sistema Iberoamericano de Conocimiento en Juventud). http://sicj.cepal.org/
International Centre for Education and Human Development (CINDE)	Colombia	Childwatch partner working in Latin America	CINDE is an educational research and development centre, based in Colombia, with local, national, and international presence. Its focus is the creation of appropriate environments to promote the healthy physical and psychosocial development of young children. http://www.cinde.org.co/English.htm
Fundación Paniamor	Costa Rica	Childwatch partner	Fundacion Paniamor is a Costa Rican non-profit, non-partisan, private organisation focused on child rights from a preventive and technical perspective. http://www.paniamor.or.cr/

(continued)

Table 6.7 (continued)

Name	Home location	Affiliations and partnerships	Thematic focus
Institute for Interdisciplinary Studies of Childhood and Adolescence (INEINA-UNA)	Costa Rica		INEINA-UNA aims to conduct research on child and adolescent issues, and provides training and education for students, community members, and faculty. http://www.una.ac.cr/
Caribbean Child Development Centre (CCDC)	Jamaica	Childwatch partner	The CCDC's mission is to support holistic development for Caribbean children through collaborative research to inform policy and programme development, information management and dissemination, training and public service, and advocacy. http://www.open.uwi.edu/academics/ResearchUnit/director-Consortium.php
Documentation Centre on Infancy and Childhood	Mexico	Childwatch partner	The centre works to promote legal, educational, social, and policy changes on infancy, childhood, and youth towards a more inclusive framework coherent with the UNCRC through participatory research, networking, educational training programmes and information sharing. http://www.uam.mx/cdi/
Inter-American Children's Institute	Uruguay	Childwatch partner working in Latin America	The institute's principal purpose is to cooperate with member state governments to promote the development of technical activities and instruments that contribute to the integral protection of children and the improvement of their and their families' quality of life. www.iin.oas.org/IIN/english/index.shtml
Centre for Childhood and Family Research (CENDIF)	Venezuela	Childwatch partner	CENDIF's main objective is the study of children, youth, and their families, as well as various aspects of human development. An important feature of its work is the development and dissemination of alternative practices to expand and improve programmes and services in the areas of education, health, and development of the poorest sectors of society

family-oriented policies, children and the MDGs, children and social protection, indigenous children's rights, children and HIV/AIDS, birth registration policies, children and social protection, as well as violence against children and adolescents (ECLAC and UNICEF, 2005). In addition, as discussed in Chapter 4, the UNICEF MICS and Global Childhood Poverty Study are generating important data and analysis on childhood poverty and well-being in the region. Recently, the IADB has also undertaken research on children and adolescents, including issues related to intergenerational educational mobility, child labour, use of childcare services, child abuse and child health and nutrition services, while the World Bank is supporting a range of impact evaluations on cash transfers and children's human capital development and investments in programmes for at-risk youth.

Finally, there is an embryonic body of research involving children's participation (see Table 6.8). This work has largely focused on methodological challenges to tapping children's perceptions (including limitations of interactive tools such as drawing and photography), but also highlights the importance of play in children's understanding of well-being and the complex trade-offs involved in school attendance versus work activities.

6.4 Knowledge–policy interactions in Latin America and the Caribbean

Latin America is a diverse continent with considerable variation in types and quality of governance, the nature of state–civil society interactions, levels of economic development, human capital and inequality, social policy regimes and so on. Opportunities and challenges for engaging in evidence-informed policy influencing in the region are also quite varied, but some broad trends distinguish the region from the African and Asian contexts discussed in Chapters 4 and 5, respectively. Therefore, this section provides a brief overview of some of the key contours that shape Latin America's knowledge–policy interface, paying particular attention to the media's role in shaping policy debates, as well as the rise of civil society in demanding greater accountability and transparency over the last two decades.

The role of the media

In Latin America, the media has emerged as a key player in policy processes. Liberal political theory has long advocated that an independent press is essential to promote freedom of expression and

Table 6.8: Selected research in peer-reviewed journals about children involving children's participation in Latin America

Reference	Subject	Country	Key findings
Camfield et al (2009)	Value of qualitative methods	Draws on Young Lives and WeD research, including in Peru	This article discusses the challenges and benefits of qualitative methods of understanding well-being in both children and adults. While being time intensive and requiring carefully trained researchers, these methods allow for a more holistic understanding of respondents' perceptions and can be fruitfully combined with quantitative approaches to maximise explanatory power.
Camfield et al (2009)	Researching children's well-being	Draws on Young Lives research, including in Peru	This article begins with the notion that the concept of well-being could draw together the three competing strands of research with children: longitudinal, participatory, and indicator-based. Using Young Lives as an example, the author demonstrates that well-being indicators need to be sensitive to age, gender, and culture, and dynamic enough to allow for change.
Crivello et al (2009).	Qualitative methods used in Young Lives	Young Lives research, including Peru	This article reviews Young Lives' work on developing child-focused, participatory, qualitative methods that capture what children understand about their own well-being and how that understanding changes over time. These methods, which include timelines and body mapping, allow research to move beyond simple quantitative measures of child poverty. They also showed that although family well-being was crucial to child well-being, children had unique perspectives that needed to stand on their own. Children, for example, wanted playtime, which adults rarely saw as important. They also wanted to focus on their education, which adults often saw as secondary to work.

(continued)

Reference	Subject	Country	Key findings
Punch (2002)	Conceptualising children in research and children's participation	Bolivia	This article begins with the notion that how one perceives children's status determines how one hears what they have to say. While children are not used to being taken seriously and adults have a difficult time seeing the world from a child's perspective, various methods offer researchers the opportunity to capture the child as a competent actor. This small study with school children in Bolivia used a combination of drawings, photographs, diaries, and worksheets to maintain child interest and increase reliability. Rural children had little access to visual images and little experience with art supplies, making drawing a sometimes problematic method, particularly for older children who judged the quality of their drawings harshly. Photography, on the other hand, is liable to capturing what is 'now' rather than what is generally important.
Woodhead (1999)	Children's participation in research	Includes case studies from El Salvador, Guatemala and Nicaragua	This study of 300 children used the Children's Perspective Protocol to ascertain which occupations children viewed as desirable and undesirable. Listening to children's perspectives allows stakeholders to ascertain how they weigh risks and benefits and adjust targets accordingly. Children are very clear on the advantages and disadvantages of both work and school – the ability to combine both was viewed as the most desirable outcome in all locations. For example, children reported that they got hot and itchy working in fields, and were often beaten as porters and domestic workers. However, school had its own drawbacks, with children reporting humiliation, beatings and high costs as disadvantages. On the positive side, children enjoyed the money, autonomy and skills they got from work and the literacy and numeracy they learned at school. Children do not see their exclusion from the workforce as a desirable outcome, as the money that they earn is often what keeps them from hunger.

foster informed political debate among citizens. As Norris (2008: 67) argues:

> in the first stage [of democratisation], the initial transition from autocracy opens up the state control of the media to private ownership, diffuses access, and reduces official censorship and government control of information.... [I]n the second stage, democratic consolidation and human development are strengthened where journalists in independent newspapers, radio and television stations facilitate greater transparency and accountability in governance, by serving in their watch-dog roles, as well as providing a civic forum for multiple voices in public debate, and highlighting social problems to inform the policy agenda.

Since the 1980s, authoritarian regimes in Latin America have been largely overthrown by democratising forces, and with this the media has taken on an increasingly important role in shaping policy agendas and providing a civic forum for a plurality of voices in public debate. Indeed, by 2005, Latin America (with the notable exceptions of Cuba, Venezuela and Colombia) enjoyed the highest freedom of the press ranking in the developing world, with a Freedom House average regional score of 62 (Norris, 2008). Moreover, a 2004 UNDP report found that 65.2% of opinion leaders in the region identified the media as the second most powerful institution on the political stage, following private economic power at 79.9%, but ahead of public institutions, which were placed a distant third at less than 50%.

Opinion is, however, divided as to whether the media's power in Latin American policy processes is positive or negative. On the one hand, there are encouraging signs that the media's visibility has been linked with the strengthening of civil society and the democratisation of information flows. This can be seen in the rise of a vigorous alternative community media movement (including over 4,000 community radio stations[2]), the emergence of media monitoring observatories and critique networks (such as Calandria in Peru and the Observatoria da Imprensa in Brazil), a growing interest in media ethics, the right to information, and citizens' participation in media, as well as training in socially responsible journalism (Banfi, 2006).

On the other hand, mainstream media in the region is highly concentrated in the hands of a few media moguls. On average, more than 70% of the national market and audience share is dominated by just four top companies. This structural concentration has resulted in lack of diversity in content and points of view, excluding voices and topics of interest to regional and ethnic minorities from the news agenda (Inter-American Dialogue, 2009). As Briscoe (2009: 1) argues, 'the entire architecture of the region's media ... is criss-crossed by lines linking it to major economic and political actors, whether through corporate tie-ups on one side or unofficial patronage on the other'. Indeed, in some cases, this loss of independent information culminates in intimidation, de facto censorship and even violence against journalists (Banfi, 2006).[3]

The role of civil society

A second critical trend in Latin America over the last several decades has been the emergence of an increasingly vibrant civil society, with many organisations focused on strengthening political transparency and accountability. Following the violation of liberal guarantees during decades of authoritarian rule, special emphasis has been placed since the 1980s on the restoration of basic civil liberties and the language of rights and citizenship. As Craske and Molyneux (2002: 1) argue, 'Rights talk was used to raise awareness among the poor and the socially marginalised of their formal legal rights, but also to call into question their lack of substantive rights ... and to make claims for social justice.' The range of rights that civil society organisations champion has been broad – ranging from health, education and child welfare to indigenous rights and environmental protection – and many have gained representation in deliberative bodies at the municipal level as power was decentralised as part of the democratisation process (Keck and Abers, 2006). Civil society organisations have also increasingly become important players in the provision and communication of new knowledge on policy-related issues, as evidenced in particular by the growth of the think-tank sector in the region since the 1990s.[4] As policy processes, especially those pertaining to economic development, have become more and more complex, information politics has played a critical role in the relationship between state and civil society actors. Uña et al (2010), for instance, highlight the importance of think tanks in securing popular support across class divides for anti-poverty measures in the region through the provision of rigorous expert-led evidence.

However, as Table 6.9 illustrates, the field remains limited in terms of knowledge intermediaries focusing on child well-being. Only a small number of communities of practice are concerned with child well-being at the regional level, and this holds true at the national and sub-national

Table 6.9: Selected communities of practice on child well-being in Latin America

Name	Time frame	Objectives	Type of policy impact
News Agency for Children's Rights (ANDI) www.andi.org.br/	1992	ANDI was created in 2000 and encompasses 11 organisations working closely to spotlight childhood on the media agenda. ANDI aims to strengthen the system of protection of rights; improve means of access, production, and delivery of communication; encourage child and adolescent participation in media and society at large; improve access to and quality of primary education; and direct public policy around childhood and adolescence.	ANDI has achieved important changes in the way journalists and newspaper editors in Brazil and other parts of Latin America report on children. Since 2000, a total of 346 journalists have been trained and honoured.
Argentinean Committee for the Follow-up of the UNCRC (CASACIDN) www.casacidn.org.ar/	1991	This Argentinean coalition of nearly two dozen civil society organisations works to promote the rights of children and adolescents. The main objectives of the committee are to disseminate information on the UNCRC and mobilise the community to effectively protect the rights of children.	CASACIDN's work focuses on: investigating claims concerning threats to and violations of the rights of children and youth; drafting Alternative Reports to the Committee on the Rights of the Child on the Optional Protocol on the sale of children; capacity building and institutional strengthening; and monitoring provincial and national laws on the protection of the rights of children.
Child Rights Network in Mexico http://www. derechosinfancia.org.mx/ Red/red_ing1.htm	2001	The network is a union of 63 Mexican civil organisations, operating in 14 states, which develop programmes to support Mexican children in vulnerable situations.	The network works to strengthen children's institutions, encourage children's participation, ensure that children's rights are on policy agendas, promote knowledge sharing, and, through workshops and training, to move public opinion towards recognising children's rights.

(continued)

Name	Time frame	Objectives	Type of policy impact
Equity for Children in Latin America http://www.equidadparalainfancia.org/	2006	This online forum provides students, professors, academics, and practitioners with an interactive space to learn, research, and communicate on thematic issues related to child poverty, rights, and social issues.	This forum facilitates learning and communication between key children's rights actors. Important foci are social policy and impact monitoring and evaluation.
Ibero-American Network for the Defence of Children's and Adolescents' Rights http://www.redlamyc.info/	2000	This group pulls together 30 national NGO networks from 24 LAC countries – all involved in defending children's rights.	The group works to prioritise children's rights issues on national and regional agendas, facilitate communication between actors in the region, and provide a forum for learning.
Jamaica Coalition on the Rights of the Child http://ccwrn.org/Brochures/Chhave_right2/index.htm	1989	This umbrella body promotes and monitors the UNCRC in Jamaica.	The coalition lobbies the government to ensure that the UNCRC is included in national plans, policies, and programmes. It also assists NGOs in understanding the UNCRC and provides public education.

levels. Partial exceptions include communities focused on child rights monitoring, investigating rights violations, capacity strengthening around children's rights (including for media professionals) and social policy impact assessments. Overall, the communities identified have generally had greater success establishing monitoring processes than impacting substantive policy change and influencing behavioural shifts. The one partial exception is the News Agency for Children's Rights (ANDI) in Brazil, which has contributed to an important shift in the extent and way that journalists in the region report on children's issues, as the following quote highlights:

> ANDI has contributed to the rise in the coverage of topics related to childhood and adolescence in Brazil: from 10,700 articles published in newspapers in 1996 to 161,807 articles in 2004. The quality of coverage also increased in a significant way, with an increase of 45% in the number of articles focused on the search for solutions. In this way, ANDI contributes to forming Brazilian public opinion on the topic, and supporting social actors in order to be able to act and acquire the proper influence on public policy formulation. (Banfi, 2006: 126)

6.5 Case study: children, NGO-led policy advocacy and Peruvian policy processes

Background

We now turn to a case study on policy-influencing efforts to mainstream children's rights into Peru's policy process. Peru shares many of the broader knowledge–policy–practice characteristics outlined in the previous section, and thus provides a useful lens through which to explore linkages between knowledge on childhood poverty and policy change in Latin America. We begin by outlining the policy change objective of this NGO-led policy advocacy endeavour, then discuss how evidence was generated and utilised in an attempt to shape policy debates, as well as eventual policy change outcomes.

Policy change objective and children's 3D well-being

This case study entails efforts by an NGO project, the DFID-funded *Niños del Milenio* project on childhood poverty, to shape policy debates and public attitudes regarding the impact of macro-level policies on children's well-being and the importance of investing in childcare and nurture in post-authoritarian Peru. The Peruvian political context in the first half of the first decade of the 2000s was exceedingly complex and dynamic, characterised by the end of the increasingly autocratic and divisive leadership of Alberto Fujimori and the emergence of a new constellation of political actors, including the election of the nation's first indigenous president, Alejandro Toledo. The country faced a number of simultaneous challenges, including coming to terms with the recent bloody civil conflict, promoting good governance and the end of highly centralised government tendencies, and pursuing an economic growth agenda with equity. Accordingly, raising the visibility of largely neglected child well-being-related issues on the policy agenda would require creative efforts to highlight the linkages between macro-policy debates and children's micro-level experiences if they were to secure any significant traction.

3D evidence generation on 3D child well-being

In order to build a compelling case for macro–micro policy linkages, the project sought to generate evidence on a number of key policy debates from a child-sensitive perspective, ranging from trade liberalisation to human rights and human capital development to political decentralisation. A diverse range of mixed-methods research approaches was employed, including: econometric simulations on the likely effects of the forthcoming free trade agreement (FTA) with the US on children's time use; a child-focused content analysis of the country's Truth and Reconciliation findings on human rights abuses during the 1980–2000 civil war; an impact evaluation of the country's early child development programme, *wawawasis*; and regional reports drawing on secondary data and children's testimonies on their multidimensional well-being to inform public debates leading up to the country's first sub-national elections in 2006. In each case, respected experts carried out the analysis to lend the evidence much-needed legitimacy following a decade of research data being manipulated and overly politicised under Fujimori.

3D approaches to knowledge–policy interaction

The project's approach to knowledge–policy interaction was embedded within the project design, including careful attention to the dynamics of policy narratives/messages, actors/networks and context/institutions.

In terms of political context, like much of the rest of Latin America, Peru presents a paradox. While it has enjoyed uninterrupted democratic governance since the ousting of ex-President Fujimori in 2000, the country faces a growing social crisis marked by persistent poverty, high levels of inequality and relatively widespread dissatisfaction with democracy.[5] Against this backdrop, knowledge interaction efforts, especially those focused on social issues with limited visibility on the political agenda such as children's rights and child well-being, need to go beyond conventional advocacy approaches and be as innovative as possible. Accordingly, the *Niños del Milenio* project undertook a range of creative multimedia evidence-informed approaches to raise awareness among key policy and community-level audiences about the importance of integrating a child-sensitive lens into broader macro-policy debates. These included the development of videos with case study children, participatory digital storytelling initiatives to communicate children's perspectives on poverty and vulnerability,[6] national photo-journalist competitions and travelling photo exhibitions on children's rights, training for journalists on child-related social policy issues, and community radio broadcasts (see Box 6.1 for further details).

Box 6.1: Communication for empowerment

Among the multimedia approaches employed by *Niños del Milenio* were photographic exhibitions drawing from the work of award-winners in national photo-journalist competitions on the multiple facets of children's experiences of poverty. Juxtaposing children's testimonies with political leaders' policy promises, these exhibitions not only served as mirrors for communities and children to reflect on their lives, but also to sensitise authorities to children's experiences of poverty and development. The exhibitions were staged in diverse public spaces, including the Peruvian National Congress building, the Ministry of Women and Social Development, embassies in the US and the UK, regional administrative offices, public universities, the streets of Lima and those of a number of regional cities, policy stakeholder meetings, local schools (in Young Lives countries and the UK), and on the BBC website.

In terms of actors and networks, given the generally weak evidence-based culture within Peru's political circles and the limited presence of international donor agencies that could have played a monitoring and evaluation role vis-à-vis progress on rights-based issues, the media facilitated the communication of research-informed messages in a direct and visible way. The excesses of the Fujimori era, including high-level corruption, human rights abuses and an overly dominant executive branch, exemplified by Fujimori's closure of Congress, had resulted in strong civil society distrust of political institutions. As a result, in the first decade of the 2000s, civil society assumed a strong watchdog role and sought to enhance governmental accountability and transparency by strengthening citizen awareness of their rights. Within this context, and with increasing emphasis on the importance of having credible evidence to underpin policy decisions, the media evolved as a powerful policy actor (Mably, 2006).

A linchpin in this policy-influencing approach was the development of a culturally palatable and politically feasible policy narrative. As Tarrow (1994: 119) argues, collective action does not result from a simple conversion of objective socio-economic conditions into protest, but needs to be framed 'around cultural symbols that are selectively chosen from a cultural tool chest', and which resonate with broader discourses of 'injustice' employed by both domestic and international advocates of social change. The principal policy narrative the *Niños del Milenio* project focused on was the necessity of mainstreaming children's rights to well-being, inclusion and care into macro-level policy debates so as to ensure that the traditionally voiceless were rendered visible on the policy stage. Discussion of childhood poverty is typically limited to sectoral policy debates around health, nutrition and education, but the *Niños del Milenio* project sought to reframe common assumptions about the underlying causes of children's poverty and draw attention to the way that children are often as, or more profoundly, affected by macroeconomic and poverty-reduction policies. As Pais (2002) argues, the child mainstreaming agenda is an ambitious 'one, seeking to involve government and non-governmental actors at international, national, and sub-national levels around the agendas of development, humanitarian aid, peace and security'.

In the Peruvian context, a key example of this mainstreaming approach involved efforts to highlight the potential impacts of trade liberalisation on child well-being and the importance of addressing the specific vulnerabilities of marginalised children in the context of any complementary social protection strategy. While economic simulations suggested that the much-contested FTA with the US[7] would have an overall positive impact on Peruvian growth rates, welfare gains and losses were likely to be unequally distributed across the population and among different types of families (with or without children, male- or female-headed households, urban versus rural, and so on) (Escobar and Ponce, 2005). Changes in household poverty would in turn have uneven impacts on childhood well-being and, in particular, children in jungle, highland and rural households were likely to experience exacerbated poverty due to increasing demand for their or their mother's labour and/or falling household incomes (Escobal and Ponce, 2005). Whereas public debate in Peru has mainly focused on the likely negative impacts on particular sectors (e.g. producers of specific crops such as grain), *Niños del Milenio*'s policy briefs sought to set a new agenda that went beyond the polarised 'pro- and contra-FTA' agenda. Instead, the project argued for more careful social impact analyses of trade that disaggregated intra-household and intergenerational consequences (Vilar et al, 2006).

Another important strand of the *Niños del Milenio* mainstreaming policy narrative focused on the Truth and Reconciliation Committee process and efforts to raise awareness of the little-known experiences of children during the 1980–2000 political violence between the national army and the Maoist guerilla resistance group, the *Sendero Luminoso* (Shining Path), in order to advocate for better child protection mechanisms. Child victims constituted 13% of the total 65,000 fatalities, and poor children from rural areas in particular suffered from forced recruitment, sexual abuse, kidnappings, disappearances, extra-judicial executions, imprisonment and torture. The project synthesised key child-specific findings from the unabridged background report and disseminated these results widely, including through press releases and seminars with high-level officials, in order to highlight systemic problems such as child abuse and discrimination. In addition to drawing attention to the penetration strategies used by the *Sendero Luminoso* guerrillas to recruit new members in schools, the publication highlighted the ways racism and discrimination are expressed in the Peruvian educational system, creating resentment and reinforcing patterns of social exclusion.

Outcomes of a 3D approach

As discussed in Chapter 3, policy change can take a number of forms, from agenda-setting and procedural changes to substantive policy gains and behavioural shifts. In the case of the *Niños del Milenio* project, policy-influencing efforts contributed to a range of child well-being-related changes. Here we focus on three examples. First, as part of the project's efforts to reframe the policy agenda to include children in mainstream political debates, staff cooperated with an umbrella research organisation, the Consortium for Social and Economic Research (CIES),[8] to ensure that children's issues were included as a key debate topic in regional and provincial elections and discussed on the basis of transparent evidence. In order to improve the quality of political debate and strengthen the capacities of regional journalists to engage with political candidates on a range of policy topics, including those related to child-sensitive policies, the project team adopted an approach inspired by the Brazilian-based ANDI media for social change network. This involved collating region-specific data on children's development indicators, developing policy briefings with policy recommendations to address child well-being deprivations and preparing companion question guides that journalists could use to shape their interviews with candidates. A number of public presentations with candidates from three regions (Arequipa, Piura and Cusco) were held in order to encourage candidates to think specifically about their positions on child-related policy issues. Moreover, because this initiative was part of a broader CIES undertaking, including nine other key policy areas, child-specific policy concerns were situated within broader discourses about the impacts of macroeconomic and political issues on families at the micro-level, problems of resource concentration in Lima and regional capitals, and inequalities among and within regions.

A second area of policy impact the project accomplished was contributing to a shift in community-level attitudes regarding childcare approaches through a community radio initiative. Drawing on insights from the project's analytical work on child well-being, this advocacy programme facilitated access to research-based information aimed at improving the quality of the care environment for children living in impoverished communities. It sought to tackle social exclusion barriers by addressing the dearth of easily understood and applied information for low-income and often second-language speakers of Spanish by broadcasting short programmes about early child development and education and the availability of public services and social programmes in a context of poverty. The testimonies in Box 6.2 provide examples of the reactions of participants in focus group discussions organised to evaluate the first phase of the programme. Together they suggest that audio communication approaches that are integrated into people's everyday lives can have an important impact on attitudinal and behavioural change.

The project's contribution to substantive policy and budget changes was more limited, arguably because changes to policy agendas and discourse are likely to take time to contribute to concrete policy shifts. There was, however, one important exception, which highlights the importance of two key ingredients of policy influencing discussed in Chapter 3: the development of culturally resonant and politically feasible messages, and the importance of knowledge intermediaries in facilitating the uptake of new knowledge. In this case, the project's video documentary on Peru's *wawawasi* programme – a government-

Box 6.2: Community radio for parents

"What's important is to pick up the messages about care for children and then pass them on from person to person." (Maria, women's focus group, 25–39 years)

"This radio programme is addressed to everyone ... these messages stay with you once you become a parent." (Héctor, men's focus group, 25–39 years)

"These messages should be provided by the State ... but still what's important is not who communicates these ideas but rather that it actually gets done.... The State should provide us with these types of messages because it is responsible for all of us, responsible for educating the people." (Carlos, men's focus group, 25–39 years)

"I would like a copy of all the messages ... to read every day and to hand out to all my people." (Alejandra, women's focus group, 25–39 years)

subsidised community-run childcare programme in poor indigenous regions – highlighted the positive impact that a relatively inexpensive public policy initiative could have in terms of: (a) access and quality of childcare services; (b) facilitating mothers' opportunities to enter the paid workforce without having to rely on older children (especially daughters) at the cost of the latter's education; and (c) generating employment for some community women as the care providers at the *wawawasi* centres. By linking the need to improve children's micro-level experience of care with broader macro-policy challenges surrounding poverty reduction and employment generation, the documentary proved instrumental in securing a 70% budget increase for the project from the Ministry of Economics. Whereas the project's core funding at the time came from the Inter-American Development Bank, Programme Director Carmen Vasquez has pointed out that 'the video provided an external view of the programme which strengthened arguments about its value internally and the importance of scaling up coverage. For us the video was decisive in our lobbying efforts with the Ministry of Economy and persuading the minister's advisors' (interview, 2004). Accordingly, as of 2005 the ministry began providing 100% of the project's budget. This policy achievement was particularly significant, not only when contrasted with the fate of similar concurrent social programmes within the comparatively weak Ministry of Social Development and Women's Affairs (a number of which were discontinued or faced funding cuts), but also because it underscored the value of a less standardised and more regionally targeted policy design model.

6.6 Conclusions

Three general insights emerge from the discussion on child well-being, the regional overview of knowledge and policy processes and actors working on policy change to improve child well-being, and the empirical study of knowledge–policy interactions in one context in Latin America.

Policy ideas and narratives

In attempting to raise the visibility of 'children's rights' and 'childhood' on the development agenda in diverse political contexts, it is critical to systematically unpack culturally specific understandings of the core cultural concepts with which a research project is engaging – for example, 'childhood', 'family', 'work' – and how these are subject to competing interpretations and reinterpretations in societies undergoing rapid social, political, economic and demographic transitions. It may also be the case that, rather than aiming to persuade others of the value of a specific interpretive lens, advocates could play more useful roles as facilitators, empowering local policy, civil society and media actors to develop their own frameworks to enable them to best make sense of their particular historico-cultural context. A key challenge would, of course, be how to best monitor the efficacy of such advocacy work, especially as the impacts are likely to be diffuse and non-immediate. A related concern may be that if we are to take seriously the challenge of embedding the concept of catalytic validity (i.e. valuing new knowledge on the basis of its potential for social transformation) in development research, then such guidelines may constitute a helpful starting point to encourage policy advocacy projects to think more systematically through dilemmas related to the line between direct policy influencing and supporting knowledge brokers and policy entrepreneurs to undertake a more evidence-informed knowledge intermediary role.

Policy actors and networks

Child-sensitive knowledge–policy initiatives need not be child-focused. An equally valuable approach may entail supporting actors already involved in influencing key development debates such as trade liberalisation debates or the work of the human rights truth and reconciliation committee to embed a child-sensitive component in their broader work. This does not entail influencing actors so that they undertake analysis themselves on child well-being or engage with child-focused policy change efforts, but rather involves persuading them to provide a space where child well-being-related implications can be considered alongside their wider agenda. In the same vein, in attempting to raise the visibility of 'children's rights' and 'childhood', it may also be the case that, rather than aiming to persuade others of the value of a specific interpretive lens, advocates could play more useful roles as facilitators. The focus would thus be on empowering local policy, civil society and media actors to develop their own culturally and context-appropriate frameworks. A key challenge would, of course, be how to best monitor the efficacy of such advocacy work, especially as the impacts are likely to be diffuse and non-immediate.

Context and institutions

Multimedia policy-influencing efforts can play an important role in contexts where there is deep distrust of political institutions, especially following an authoritarian government or conflict environment, as was the case in Peru. The case study therefore highlighted the way in which such efforts can shape substantive policy change and contribute to an array of other policy impacts ranging from agenda-setting to behavioural and attitudinal change. This more nuanced approach to policy impacts also serves to emphasise the cumulative, interactive relationship between different types of policy impact, suggesting that evidence-based advocacy approaches – particularly in complex transitional political contexts – necessitate a longer time horizon. This is especially important in developing countries, where civil society organisations, communities of practice and an independent media are often in their infancy and policy advocacy is still a new enterprise. The challenge is to build on agenda-setting and discursive and procedural change impacts in order to ensure that child-focused development policies are formulated and effectively implemented at the international, national and sub-national levels.

Notes

[1] Note there is no central database of such institutions and the table is the authors' own compilation.

[2] Community radio provides channels to promote cultural recognition and democratic participation for traditionally marginalised communities such as rural workers, indigenous groups and other ethnic minorities. For example, Colombia has around 460 community radio stations focusing on the effects of the internal armed conflict, public services provision and other topics of community interest.

[3] According to Reporters without Borders, seven journalists were killed in Central and South America in 2005. Five more lost their lives to their profession in 2006.

[4] McGann (2007) identifies 408 think tanks in Latin America, many of which emerged in the 1990s. In Argentina, for instance, 19 of the 28 think tanks surveyed by Uña et al (2010) were founded in the 1990s.

[5] Reflecting on the Latin American region as a whole, the UNDP has argued that the roots of democracy remain shallow, with low levels of trust in political institutions, including political parties. This is reflected in the fact that a majority of the population would sacrifice a democratic government in exchange for substantive social and economic progress (UNDP, 2005).

[6] Facilitated by the BBC World Service Trust as part of their global 'Where will we be by 2015' MDG project, the digital storytelling initiative involved supporting a group of children to share their daily life experiences by developing a photo-journal of their surroundings and daily routine. The photographic testimonies highlighted the importance children attach to safety (e.g. the need for safe road crossings, protection from muggers), a clean environment, siblings and time with their parents, and the significant role many of them play in meeting the basic livelihood needs of their families through paid and unpaid work. See: http://www.bbc.co.uk/worldservice/trust/2015/story/2004/06/040609_storiesfromperu.shtml

[7] The FTA was signed by both governments on 12 April 2006, and approved by the Peruvian Congress on 28 June 2006.

[8] CIES is an umbrella organisation with over 30 institutional members among Peruvian academic, research and governmental institutions, and NGOs.

SEVEN

Conclusions

7.1 Introduction

Our book has focused on the relationships between child poverty/ well-being, evidence/knowledge and policy change. We have employed a multilayered model as outlined in the Introduction (see Figure 7.1). These layers seek to understand child poverty and well-being in its material, relational and subjective domains; and the role of ideas, actors and political contexts in shaping related knowledge–policy interactions. Our approach is informed by a multidimensional understanding of power as material, discursive and institutional, and the ways in which power relations shape opportunities for children's own voice (in decision-making), visibility (in knowledge-generation and policy processes) and vision (of well-being).

By focusing on questions about knowledge, policy and power through the lens of children's well-being, the book has unpacked the relationship between different types of knowledge and policy change in a range of contexts and policy sectors in the developing world. It has sought

Figure 7.1: Our approach

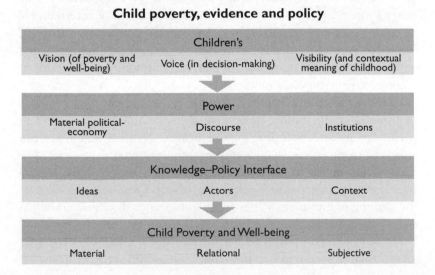

Child poverty, evidence and policy

Children's		
Vision (of poverty and well-being)	Voice (in decision-making)	Visibility (and contextual meaning of childhood)

Power		
Material political-economy	Discourse	Institutions

Knowledge–Policy Interface		
Ideas	Actors	Context

Child Poverty and Well-being		
Material	Relational	Subjective

to draw attention to the importance of combining quantitative and qualitative methodologies, including those that capture children's voices, so as to develop compelling narratives for multiple audiences; framing evidence in accessible and culturally resonant ways to maximise impact in diverse political contexts; as well as the critical role that strategic policy actor alliances can play in knowledge uptake. Here we draw together the main conclusions emerging from the book.

7.2 3D child well-being, methods and policy change

As we discussed in Chapter 1, childhood poverty and well-being are distinct from adult experiences of poverty and well-being, and it is therefore critical that policy design, implementation and evaluation processes are informed accordingly. A 'three-dimensional' human well-being (3D WB) lens is useful to capture this distinctiveness in a holistic way as the approach builds on but goes beyond minimum or 'basic' needs and their legal codification in rights conventions such as the UNCRC. Importantly it focuses on the enabling conditions for a 'flourishing childhood', including material, relational and subjective well-being dimensions.

As we discussed in Chapter 2, in order to capture children's 3D WB, evidence or knowledge-generation processes need to draw on a mixed-methods or 3D approach, combining quantitative and qualitative (both Participatory Rural Appraisal [PRA] and ethnographic) approaches. While there has been growing recognition of the importance of including children's voices in knowledge-generation initiatives, we have argued that such knowledge also has to be complemented by other sources in order to speak to the complexities of international development policy dialogues. In particular, methodological improvements are needed to adequately reflect linkages between child well-being and intra-household dynamics, community–child relations and macro–micro policy linkages.

As we discussed in Chapter 3, a 3D WB lens implies different ways of thinking about policy, policy engagement and advocacy, and in particular an understanding of the power relations that underpin efforts to shape policy change. Importantly, it implies that we need to think about power as multidimensional, including not only control over resources (i.e. material political-economy), but also control over the shaping of prevailing values and identities (i.e. discourse and what counts as knowledge), and control over norms, and conventions and behaviour (i.e. institutions). We have argued that if knowledge is to play a constructive role in policy processes about child well-being then it is important to adopt an iterative 'knowledge interaction' approach to policy change whereby there is an explicit recognition of the power dynamics that shape which types of knowledge are privileged or overlooked by different policy actors. We emphasise that such awareness is especially important in the case of efforts to shape policies related to child well-being given the particular voicelessness of children in many contexts and their exclusion from conventional policy spaces. As such, we also need to think more broadly about types of policy change objectives, to include not just substantive policy and legislative change, but also discursive, procedural and behavioural shifts.

Given the complexities of power relations in the production of knowledge and its use (or otherwise) within the policy process, our case studies from developing-country contexts suggest that there is no single recipe for child-sensitive knowledge interaction and policy-influencing processes, but there are certain prerequisite 'ingredients' upon which we can agree. The three clusters of factors that support such policy change are as follows.

Policy ideas and narratives

Questions about the role of knowledge in policy circles, and the power that shapes the acceptability of some forms of knowledge but silences others, are becoming increasingly salient. In this regard, as important as the development of rigorous evidence to measure progress in enhancing children's well-being and rights is, the ways in which new and existing knowledge is synthesised and presented to diverse policy, practitioner and lay audiences requires particular attention if investments in child-focused research are to have maximum value. Given limited awareness of children's rights issues by civil society and government actors alike, borrowing from framing techniques in other areas of development (or 'frame extension') may be effective in promoting quick buy-in in that the language and its policy implications are already relatively familiar (for instance, drawing on 'mainstreaming' or 'pro-poor budget-monitoring' discourses). However, there is also the risk that such an approach may be perceived as 'yet another special interest lobby', so a careful assessment of existing relations between civil society and the state in a specific context would need to guide such choices.

Investing in innovative strategies to dismantle dominant paradigms that assume that children will automatically benefit from broader and household-level poverty-reduction interventions is also critical. Without an appreciation of the specific and multidimensional nature of childhood poverty, vulnerability and resilience, the fulfilment of children's rights will remain only partial. As such, there is a pressing need to better understand the power dynamics operating to privilege particular narratives about human well-being and the ways in which they serve to subtly obscure new knowledge. In the same vein, it is also important to promote the triangulation of knowledge about children from a wide range of sources, ranging from children's testimonies and participatory photo projects to survey data and budget-monitoring efforts, from guidelines for journalists and key informant discussions to content analysis of African Union policy statements and international rights conventions.

Policy actors and networks

The relative marginalisation of child well-being issues on the development policy stage means that forging alliances among a broad array of governmental and non-governmental actors is critical to ensure that new ideas have a chance of gaining adequate policy purchase. This involves attention to the following issues.

Given the importance of macro–micro policy linkages in shaping children's experiences of poverty and vulnerability, establishing relationships with actors in government agencies charged with mainstream poverty-reduction and economic development issues can be critical to promote child-sensitive policy change. Investing in awareness-raising efforts about childhood poverty and rights among an array of government and mainstream civil society actors as well as the media may also be necessary before new knowledge about child well-being can be effectively integrated into the conceptual frameworks that inform different policy actors' daily practice. Similarly, in view of the relative weakness of actors mandated to work with children (e.g. ministries of social welfare, women and children), an effective policy engagement strategy may necessarily entail attention to capacity-strengthening work with key governmental and/or civil society actors so that these agencies can participate more effectively in policy agenda-setting and budget-allocation decision-making processes.

Different audiences are likely to subscribe explicitly or implicitly to different knowledge hierarchies. Accordingly, drawing on multiple sources of knowledge can be an effective strategy to reach a particular policy audience. As we have argued, evidence that is expert-led (i.e. based on the work of technically trained persons) and evidence derived from citizens' experiences can both be child-sensitive under certain conditions. The choice of advocacy or knowledge interaction approach in part depends on the policy/sector/issue and available entry points for policy influence – some sectors require a high level of technical expertise (e.g. macroeconomic and trade policies, budget processes) and are less amenable to participatory forms of knowledge. However, while it is important to frame research findings with this in mind, it is equally important to work with actors to begin to break down conventional knowledge hierarchies given the complexity and diversity of childhood poverty and vulnerability.

Children's participation in poverty policy processes is still in a fledgling state and the evidence to date suggests that its contribution to tangible policy changes has been limited. However, perhaps just as importantly, our analysis has highlighted ways in which children's participation can contribute to other change objectives. This includes introducing new ideas on to the policy agenda, bringing about procedural shifts (so that children are gradually more routinely involved in citizen consultation processes for example), and gradually transforming the attitudes of those in power towards recognising the potential contribution that children and young people can make to policy debates.

Policy contexts

In light of our growing knowledge base about the impact pathways between macro-level political and economic development shifts, meso-level policy and community responses, and micro-level impacts on children and their caregivers, there is a need for proponents of child-sensitive policy change to embed their policy engagement efforts within a strong understanding of broader policy process dynamics. This can include trade liberalisation processes to shifting aid modalities and PRSP development and monitoring, budget processes and public finance management to post-conflict reconciliation processes. Approaches to knowledge interaction may need to be tailored accordingly. For instance, as our case studies highlighted, in transitional or post-conflict political contexts where trust in political institutions has been eroded or is fragile, employing a multimedia rather than a conventional research communication approach may be important in order to communicate to policymakers and citizens alike.

Our analysis has also highlighted that it is critical to invest more in understanding multiple policy levels – international, regional, national and sub-national levels. Indeed the latter appears to be especially important not only because of the challenges involved in overcoming extant data constraints, but also because this is increasingly where implementation of social policies – which help to mediate the effects

of macro-development policy changes on children and their families
– take place.

Lastly, our case studies underscored that, as important as context-mapping is, policy engagement strategies need to have inbuilt flexibility given that windows of opportunity within a specific context can open and close rapidly with little prior warning. Issues that are seemingly distant from children's lives such as national elections may have a profound impact on the contours of the policy process landscape.

7.3 What next?

All of the above suggests a research and action agenda around (i) conceptual development to understand the specificities of child poverty and well-being in a particular context, to reflexively inform both (ii) empirical knowledge-generation processes about and with children on child poverty and well-being, and (iii) knowledge–policy interactions and how they play out in different developing-country settings.

In terms of future practical steps for both researchers and those involved in policy processes (from inside or outside political institutions) there are four key things that can be done differently – although these constitute more of a change of emphasis and direction than a seismic shift.

First, there is a pressing need to promote greater investment in terms of time, resources and intellectual energy in more collaborative mixed-methods knowledge-generation efforts around child well-being. This type of work is still in a fledgling stage, especially with regard to aspects of well-being that fall outside the Millennium Development Goal agenda (including protection from violence, abuse, neglect and exploitation, and the role that socio-cultural norms and practices play in perpetuating and reinforcing these), but is critical to tap the 3D nature of children's experiences of poverty and well-being.

Second, given the importance of context in shaping the ways in which knowledge about child well-being informs (or not) policy processes, promoting the institutionalisation of systematic context-mapping at the national and sub-national levels within organisations championing children's rights is an essential step if research investments are to both resonate with and remould policy discourses and priorities.

Third, given the limited density of organisations and networks working on the knowledge–policy interface around child well-being in Africa in particular, but also in Asia, it will be important to support intermediary organisations that can help foster communities of practice which can develop feasible and regionally strategic approaches to evidence-informed policy influencing.

Finally, urgent action is required to address the dearth of monitoring, evaluation and learning initiatives relating to knowledge–policy interactions on child well-being. This will require vision and leadership among knowledge and policy actors alike, as well as strategic support from donors and international agencies.

We hope this book stimulates both researchers and those in policy processes to take forward such ideas and discussions and that this raises children's visibility, voice and vision in both knowledge-generation and policy processes.

References

Introduction

Ames, P. and V. Rojas (2009) *Childhood, Transitions and Wellbeing in Peru: A Literature Review*, Young Lives Technical Note No 16, Oxford, UK: Young Lives.

Ansell, N. (2005) *Children, Youth and Development*, London: Routledge.

Ben-Arieh, A. (2005) 'Where are the Children? Children's Role in Measuring and Monitoring their Well-being', *Social Indicators Research* 74: 573–96.

Bielak, A., A. Campbell, S. Pope, K. Schaefer and L. Shaxson (2008) 'From Science Communication to Knowledge Brokering: The Shift from "Science Push" to "Policy Pull"', in D. Cheng, M. Claessens, T. Gascoigne, J. Metcalfe, B. Schiele and S. Shunke (eds) *Communicating Science in Social Contexts*, Springer.

Biggeri, M., R. Libanora, S. Mariani and L. Menchini (2006) 'Children Conceptualizing their Capabilities: Results of a Survey Conducted during the First World Congress on Child Labour', *Journal of Human Development* 7(1): 59–83.

Bird, K. (2007) *The Intergenerational Transmission of Poverty: An Overview*, ODI Working Paper 286, London: Overseas Development Institute; and CPRC Working Paper 99(1), London, UK: CPRC.

Boyden, J. and J. Ennew (eds) (1997) *Children in Focus – A Manual for Participatory Research with Children*. Stockholm, Sweden: Save the Children.

Bradshaw, J., P. Hoelscher and D. Richardson (2006) 'Comparing Child Well-Being in OECD Countries: Concepts and Methods', Innocenti Working Paper, Florence: Innocenti Research Centre, UNICEF.

Camfield, L. and Y. Tafere (2008) 'Children with a Good Life Have to Have School Bags: Understandings of Well-Being among Children in Ethiopia', Paper presented at IYC Resnet Conference, Cyprus.

Camfield, L., N. Streuli and M. Woodhead (2008) 'Children's Well-being in Contexts of Poverty: Approaches to Research, Monitoring and Participation', *Young Lives Technical Note No. 12*. Oxford, UK: Young Lives.

Camfield, L., G. Crivello and M. Woodhead (2009a) 'How Can Children Tell Us about Their Wellbeing? Exploring the Potential of Participatory Research Approaches within Young Lives', *Social Indicators Research* 90(1): 65–109.

Camfield, L., N. Streuli and M. Woodhead (2009b) 'What's the Use of "Well-Being" in Contexts of Child Poverty? Approaches to Research, Monitoring and Children's Participation', *The International Journal of Human Rights* 17(1): 65–109.

Carden, F. (2009) *Knowledge to Policy: Making the most of Development Research*, New Delhi: Sage and IDRC/CRDI.

Cash, D.W., W.C. Clark, F. Alcock, N.M. Dickson, N. Eckley, D.H. Guston, J. Jager and R.B. Mitchell (2003) 'Knowledge Systems for Sustainable Development', *The Proceedings of the National Academy of Sciences* 100(14): 8086–91.

Choi B.C.K., T. Pang, V. Lin, P. Puska, G. Sherman, M. Goddard, M.J. Ackland, P. Sainsbury, S. Stachenko, H. Morrison and C. Clottey (2005) 'Can Scientists and Policy-makers Work Together?', *Journal of Epidemiology and Community Health* 59(8): 632-7.

Clark, W. and C. Juma (2002) 'Mobilizing Science and Technology for Sustainable Development', *Report on the Forum on Science and Technology for Sustainability.* Cambridge, MA.

Corak, M. (2005) 'Principles and Practicalities in Measuring Child Poverty for the Rich Countries', Innocenti Working Paper. Florence: UNICEF and Innocenti Research Centre.

Corak, M. (2006) *Do Poor Children Become Poor Adults? Lessons from a Cross-Country Comparison of Generational Earnings Mobility*, Lewes, UK: Emerald Publishing.

Corsaro, W. (1997) *The Sociology of Childhood.* London, UK: Pine Forge Press.

Court, J., I. Hovland and J. Young (2005) *Bridging Research and Policy: Evidence and the Change Process*, Rugby: ITDG Publishing.

Crivello, G. (2009) *'Becoming Somebody': Youth Transitions Through Education and Migration – Evidence from Young Lives, Peru*, Young Lives Working Paper 43, Oxford: Young Lives.

Culyer, A.J. and J. Lomas (2006) 'Deliberative Processes and Evidence-informed Decision-making in Healthcare: Do They Work and How Might We Know?', *Evidence and Policy* 2(3): 357-71.

Doek, J.E., A.K. Shiva Kumar, D. Mugawe and S. Tsegaye (2009) *Child Poverty: African and International Perspectives*, Antwerp: Intersentia.

Fairhead, J., M. Leach and M. Small (2006) 'Where Techno-science Meets Poverty: Medical Research and the Economy of Blood in the Gambia', *Social Science and Medecine* 63(4): 1109-20..

Fattore, T., J. Mason and E. Watson (2007) 'Children's Conceptualisation(s) of Their Well-Being', *Social Indicators Research* 80(1): 5–29.

Harper, C. and R. Marcus (2000) 'Mortgaging Africa's Future: The Long Term Costs of Child Poverty', *Development, the Journal of the Society for International Development* 43(1): 65–72.

Harper, C., R. Marcus and K. Moore (2003) 'Enduring Poverty and the Conditions of Childhood: Lifecourse and Intergenerational Poverty Transmissions', *World Development* 31(3): 535–54.

Herring, R.J. (2007) 'Whose Numbers Count? Resolving Conflicting Evidence on Bt Cotton in India', *Qsquared Working Paper 44*. Toronto: University of Toronto.

Huebner, E. (2004) 'Research on Assessment of Life Satisfaction of Children and Adolescents', *Social Indicators Research* 66(1/2): 3–33.

Innvaer, S., G. Vist, M. Trommald and A. Oxman (2002) 'Health Policy-makers' Perceptions of Their Use of Evidence: A Systematic Review', *Journal of Health Services Research and Policy* 7(4): 239–44.

James, A. and A. Prout (1990) *Constructing and Reconstructing Childhood: Contemporary Issues in the Sociological Study of Childhood*, London: Routledge.

Johnston, J. (2008) 'Children's Perspectives on their Young Lives: Report on Methods for Sub-Studies', Young Lives Technical Note No 10, Oxford, UK: Young Lives.

Jones, N., H. Jones and C. Walsh (2008) *Political Science? Strengthening Science–Policy Dialogue in Developing Countries*, ODI Working Papers 294, London: ODI.

Joubert, M. (2001) 'Priorities and Challenges for Science Communication in South Africa', *Science Communication* 22(3): 316–33.

Lackey, R. (2006) 'Science, Scientists and Policy Advocacy', *Conservation Biology* 21(1): 12–17.

Land, K.C., V.L. Lamb, S.O. Meadows and A. Taylor (2007) 'Measuring Trends in Child Well-Being: An Evidence-Based Approach', *Social Indicators Research* 80(1): 105–32.

Leach, M. and I. Scoones (2006) *The Slow Race: Making Technology Work for the Poor*, London: Demos.

Liberatore, A. and S. Funtowicz (2003) '"Democratising" Expertise, "Expertising" Democracy: What Does This Mean, and Why Bother?' *Science and Public Policy* 30(3): 146–50.

Lomas, J., T. Culyer, C. McCutcheon, L. McAuley and S. Law (2005) *Conceptualising and Combining Evidence for Health System Guidance*, Ottawa: Canadian Health Services Research Foundation.

Manzini, S. (2003) 'Effective Communication of Science in a Culturally Diverse Society', *Science Communication* 25(2): 191–7.

Marshall, J. (2003) 'Children and Poverty – Some Questions Answered', CHIP Briefing Paper 1. London: Save the Children UK.

Maxwell, S. and D. Stone (2005) 'Global knowledge networks and international development: bridges across boundaries', in D. Stone and S. Maxwell (eds) *Global Knowledge Networks and International Development: Bridges across Boundaries*, New York: Routledge, ch 1.

Mayall, B. (2002) *Towards a Sociology for Childhood: Thinking from Children's Lives.* Milton Keynes, UK: Open University Press.

Moore, K. (2001) 'Frameworks for Understanding the Intergenerational Transmission of Poverty and Well-being in Developing Countries', CPRC Working Paper 8, Chronic Poverty Research Centre (www.chronicpoverty.org/pdfs/08Moore.pdf).

Moore, K. and Lippman, L. (eds) (2005) *What Do Children Need to Flourish?: Conceptualising and Measuring Indicators of Positive Development.* New York: Springer Science and Business Publishers.

O' Neil, M. (2005) 'What Determines the Influence that Research has on Policy-making?', *Journal of International Development* 17(6): 761–4.

Pollard, E.L. and P.D. Lee (2003) 'Child Well-Being: A Systematic Review of the Literature', *Social Indicators Research* 61(1): 59–78.

Redmond, G. (2008) 'Children's Perspectives on Economic Adversity: A Review of the Literature', *Discussion Paper No. 2008-01.* Florence: UNICEF Innocenti Research Centre.

Redmond, G. (2009) 'Children as Actors: How Does the Child Perspectives Literature Treat Agency in the Context of Poverty?' *Social Policy and Society* 8(4): 541–50.

Ridge, T. (2002) *Childhood Poverty and Social Exclusion: From a Child's Perspective.* Bristol: The Policy Press.

Rosenstock, L. (2002) 'Attacks on Science: The Risks to Evidence-based Policy', *American Journal of Public Health* 92(1): 14–18.

Rowe, G. and L. Frewer (2005) 'A Typology of Public Engagement Mechanisms', *Science, Technology and Human Values* 30(2): 251–90.

Smith, B. and K. Moore (2006) 'Intergenerational Transmission of Poverty in Sub-Saharan Africa', *CPRC Annotated Bibliography 3/ CPRC Working Paper 59.* See: http://www.chronicpoverty.org/research-themes-igt.php

Subrahamanian, R. (2005a) 'Childhood Poverty: A Review of Key Issues to Inform the YL Project', Unpublished. Sussex: Institute of Development Studies.

Subrahamanian, R. (2005b) 'Gender Equality in Education: Definitions and Measurement', *International Journal of Behavioural Development* 25: 395–407.

Tafere, Y., W. Abebe and A. Assazinew (2009) 'Well-being of Children in Ethiopia: Country Context Literature Review', Young Lives Technical Note No 17, Oxford, UK: Young Lives.

Weingart, P. (1999) 'Scientific Expertise and Political Accountability: Paradoxes of Science in Politics', *Science and Public Policy* 26(3): 151–61.

White, S. (2002) 'Being, Becoming and Relationship: Conceptual Challenges of a Child Rights Approach in Development', *Journal of International Development* 14(8): 1095–104.

White, S. and S. Choudhury (2007) 'The Politics of Child Participation in International Development: The Dilemma of Agency', *The European Journal of Development Research* 19(4): 529–50.

Woodhead, M. (2001) 'The Value of Work and School: A Study of Working Children's Perspectives', in K. Lieten and B. White (eds) *Child Labour: Policy Options.* Amsterdam, Netherlands: Aksant Academic Publishers.

Woodhead, M. and D.M. Faulkner (2008) 'Subjects, Objects or Participants: Dilemmas of Psychological Research with Children', in A. James and P. Christenson (eds) *Research with Children,* London, UK: Routledge.

Yaqub, S. (2002) 'Poor Children Grow into Poor Adults: Harmful Mechanisms or Over-Deterministic Theory?', *Journal of International Development* 14(8): 1081–93.

Chapter 1

Alkire, S. (2008) *Valuing Freedoms,* Oxford: OUP.

Ames, P. and V. Rojas (2009) 'Childhood, Transitions and Wellbeing in Peru: A Literature Review', Young Lives Technical Note No 16, Oxford, UK: Young Lives.

Barrientos, A. and DeJong, J. (2006) 'Reducing Child Poverty with Cash Transfers: A Sure Thing?', *Development Policy Review* 24(5): 537–52.

Ben-Arieh, A. (2005) 'Where are the Children? Children's Role in Measuring and Monitoring their Well-being', *Social Indicators Research* 74: 573–96.

Bird, K. (2007) 'The Intergenerational Transmission of Poverty: An Overview', ODI Working Paper 286, London: Overseas Development Institute; and CPRC Working Paper 99(1). London, UK: CPRC.

Bourdieu, P. (1990) 'Structures, Habitus, Practices', in *The logic of Practice.* Stanford, CA: Stanford University Press, pp 52–79.

Boyden, J. and J. Ennew (eds) (1997) *Children in Focus – A Manual for Participatory Research with Children.* Stockholm, Sweden: Save the Children.

Camfield, L. (2009) '"Even if She Learns, She Doesn't Understand Properly": Children's Understandings of Ill-being and Poverty in Five Ethiopian Communities', *Social Indicators Research* 96(1): 85-112.

Camfield, L. and Y. Tafere (2009) 'No, Living Well Does Not Mean Being Rich: Diverse Understandings of Well-being Among 11 to 13 year-old Children in Three Ethiopian Communities', *Journal of Children and Poverty* 15(2) 117–36.

Camfield, L., G. Crivello and M. Woodhead (2009a) 'How Can Children Tell Us About Their Wellbeing? Exploring the Potential of Participatory Research Approaches within Young Lives', *Social Indicators Research* 90(1): 65–109.

Camfield, L., N. Streuli and M. Woodhead (2009b) 'What's the Use of "Well-Being" in Contexts of Child Poverty? Approaches to Research, Monitoring and Children's Participation', *The International Journal of Human Rights* 17(1): 65–109.

Chambers, R. (2003) 'The Best of Both Worlds?' in R. Kanbur (ed) *Q-Squared: Qualitative and Quantitative Methods of Poverty Appraisal.* Washington, DC: Permanent Black.

Copestake, J. (2008) 'Wellbeing in International Development: What's New?' *Journal of International Development* 20(5): 577–97.

Corak, M. (2006) *Do Poor Children Become Poor Adults? Lessons from a Cross-Country Comparison of Generational Earnings Mobility*, Lewes, UK: Emerald Publishing.

Crivello G. (2009) *'Becoming Somebody': Youth Transitions Through Education and Migration – Evidence from Young Lives, Peru*, Young Lives Working Paper 43, Oxford: Young Lives.

Crivello, G., L. Camfield and M. Woodhead (2009) 'How Can Children Tell Us About Their Well-Being? Exploring the Potential of Participatory Research Approaches within "Young Lives"', *Social Indicators Research* 90(1): 51–72.

Deneulin, S. and McGregor, J.A. (2009) 'The Capability Approach and the Politics of Social Wellbeing', WeD Working Paper 09/43, University of Bath (www.welldev.org.uk/).

Fattore, T., J. Mason and E. Watson (2007) 'Children's Conceptualisation(s) of their Well-being', *Social Indicators Research* 80: 5–29.

Fitoussi, J., J. Stiglitz and A. Sen (2009) *Report of the Commission on the Measurement of Economic Performance and Social Progress, Paris*, www.stiglitz-sen-fitoussi.fr/documents/rapport_anglais.pdf (accessed 12 November 2009).

Fraser, N. (2000) 'Rethinking Recognition', *New Left Review* 3: 107–20.

Gerhardt, S. (2004) *Why Love Matters: How Affection Shapes a Baby's Brain*, Hove: Bruner-Routledge.

Giovannini, E. (2009) 'Why Measuring Progress Matters', *OECD Observer*, www.oecdobserver.org/news/fullstory.php/aid/2283/Why_measuring_progress_matters.html (accessed 6 October 2009).

Gordon, D., S. Nandy, C. Pantazis, S. Pemberton and P. Townsend (2004) 'The Distribution of Child Poverty in the Developing World', *Report to UNICEF*, Bristol, UK: Centre for International Poverty Research, Bristol University.

Gough I. and J. McGregor (eds) (2007) *Well-being in Developing Countries: From Theory to Research*, Cambridge: Cambridge University Press.

Harper, C., R. Marcus and K. Moore (2003) 'Enduring Poverty and the Conditions of Childhood: Lifecourse and Intergenerational Poverty Transmissions', *World Development* 31(3): 535–54.

Hausermann, J. (1999) *A Human Rights Approach to Development*, London: Rights and Humanity.

Johnston, J. (2008) 'Children's Perspectives on their Young Lives: Report on Methods for Sub-Studies', Young Lives Technical Note No 10, Oxford, UK: Young Lives.

Kahneman, D., Krueger, A.B., Schkade, D., Schwarz, N. and Stone, A. (2004) 'Toward National Well-Being Accounts', *The American Economic Review* 94(2): 429–34.

Layard R. (2006) *Happiness: Lessons from a New Science*, London: Penguin.

Lewis, O. (1996) 'The Culture of Poverty', reprinted in G. Gmelch and W. Zenner (eds), *Urban Life: Readings in Urban Anthropology*, Prospect Heights, IL: Waveland Press.

Lister, R. (2004) *Poverty.* Cambridge: Polity Press.

McGillivray M. and M. Clarke (2006) *Understanding Human Well-being*, New York: United Nations University Press.

McGregor, J.A. (2007) 'Researching Well-being: From Concepts to Methodology', in I. Gough and J.A. McGregor (eds) *Well-being in Developing Countries: New Approaches and Research Strategies.* Cambridge: Cambridge University Press.

McGregor J.A. and A. Sumner (2010) 'Beyond Business as Usual. What might 3-D Well-being Contribute to MDG Momentum?', *IDS Bulletin* 41(1): 104–12.

Maxwell, S. (1999) *What Can We Do With a Rights-Based Approach to Development?*, ODI Briefing Paper, London: ODI.

Moore, K. and L. Lippman (eds) (2005) *What Do Children Need to Flourish?: Conceptualising and Measuring Indicators of Positive Development.* New York: Springer Science and Business Publishers.

Morrow, V. and Vennam, U. (2009) *Children Combining Work and Education in Cottonseed Production in Andhra Pradesh: Implications for Discourses of Children's Rights in India*, Young Lives Working Paper 50, Oxford: Young Lives.

North, D. (1990) *Institutions, Institutional Change and Economic Performance*, Cambridge: Cambridge University Press.

Nussbaum, M. (2000) *Women and Human Development*. New York: Cambridge University Press.

Redmond, G. (2008) 'Children's Perspectives on Economic Adversity: A Review of the Literature', Discussion Paper No 2008-01, Florence: UNICEF Innocenti Research Centre.

Redmond, G. (2009) 'Children as Actors: How Does the Child Perspectives Literature Treat Agency in the Context of Poverty?', *Social Policy and Society* 8(4): 541–50.

Samman, E. (2007) *Psychological and Subjective Well-being: A Proposal for Internationally Comparable Indicators*, OPHI Working Paper. Oxford: OPHI.

Sen, A. (1992) *Inequality Reexamined*, Oxford, Oxford University Press

Sen, A. (1999) *Development as Freedom*. Oxford and New York: Oxford University Press.

Sen, A. (2009) *The Idea of Justice*, Allen Lane: New York.

Shek, D.T.L. (2004) 'Beliefs about the causes of poverty in parents and adolescents experiencing economic disadvantage in Hong Kong' *Journal of Genetic Psychology* 165(3): 272–91.

Shek, D.T.L., Tang, V., Lam, C.M., Lam, M.C., Tsoi, K.W. and Tsang, K.M. (2003) 'The relationship between Chinese cultural beliefs about adversity and psychological adjustment in Chinese families with economic disadvantage', *The American Journal of Family Therapy* 31(5): 427–43.

Smith, B. and K. Moore (2006) *Intergenerational Transmission of Poverty in Sub-Saharan Africa CPRC Annotated Bibliography 3/CPRC Working Paper 59* (www.chronicpoverty.org/research-themes-igt.php).

Subrahamanian, R. (2005a) 'Childhood Poverty: A Review of Key Issues to Inform the YL Project', unpublished, Sussex: Institute of Development Studies.

Subrahamanian, R. (2005b) 'Gender Equality in Education: Definitions and Measurement', *International Journal of Behavioural Development* 25: 395–407.

Sumner, A., L. Haddad and C. Gomez (2009) 'Rethinking Intergenerational Transmission(s): Does a Wellbeing Lens Help? The Case of Nutrition', *IDS Bulletin* 40(1): 22–30.

UNICEF (1999) *The Voices of Children and Adolescents in Latin America and the Caribbean*, New York: UNICEF.

UNICEF (2005) *State of the World's Children*, New York: UNICEF.

White, S. (2008) 'But What is Well-Being? A Framework for Analysis in Social and Development Policy and Practice', WeD Working Paper 43, Wellbeing In Developing Countries, Bath: University of Bath.

White, S. and S. Choudhury (2007) 'The Politics of Child Participation in International Development: The Dilemma of Agency', *The European Journal of Development Research* 19(4): 529–50.

Woodhead, M. (2001) 'The Value of Work and School: A Study of Working Children's Perspectives', in K. Lieten and B. White (eds) *Child Labour: Policy Options*, Amsterdam, Netherlands: Aksant Academic Publishers.

Chapter 2

Aitken, S.C. and T. Herman (2009) 'Literature Review on Qualitative Methods and Standards for Engaging and Studying Independent Children in the Developing World', Innocenti Working Paper, Florence: UNICEF.

Alfini, N. (2006) 'Children's Participation in Policy and Academic Institutions', *Building Participation among Children*, Brighton: IDS.

Ammons, D.N. and Rivenbark, W.C. (2008) 'Factors influencing the use of performance data to improve municipal services: Evidence from the North Carolina benchmarking project', *Public Administration Review* 68(2): 304–18.

Appleton, S. and D. Booth (2001) 'Combining Participatory and Survey-based Approaches to Poverty Monitoring and Analysis', *Q-Squared Working Paper: Centre for International Studies* 14.

Batbaatar, M., T.S. Bold, J. Marshall, D. Oyuntsetseg, C.H. Tamir, and G. Tumennast (2005) 'Children on the Move: Rural–Urban Migration and Access to Education in Mongolia', Ulaanbaatar and London: Save the Children UK, National University of Mongolia and the Childhood Poverty Research Centre.

Becker, S., Aldridge, J. and Dearden, C. (1998) *Young Carers and their Families*, Oxford, UK: Blackwell.

Becker, S., A. Bryman and J. Sempik (2006) *Defining 'Quality' in Social Policy Research: Views, Perceptions and a Framework for Discussion*. Suffolk, UK: Social Policy Association.

Ben-Arieh, A. (2005) 'Where are the Children? Children's Role in Measuring and Monitoring their Well-being', *Social Indicators Research* 74: 573–96.

Ben-Arieh, A. (2006) 'Measuring and Monitoring the Well-being of Young Children around the World', Background paper prepared for the Education for All Global Monitoring Report 2007, *Strong Foundations: Early Childhood Care and Education*, Paris: United Nations Educational, Scientific and Cultural Organisation.

Biggeri, M., R. Libanora, S. Mariani and L. Menchini (2006) 'Children Conceptualizing their Capabilities: Results of a Survey Conducted during the First World Congress on Child Labour', *Journal of Human Development* 7(1): 59–83.

Boaz, A. and D. Ashby (2003) 'Fit For Purpose: Assessing Research Quality For Evidence Based Policy and Practice', ESRC UK Centre for Evidence Based Policy and Practice Working Paper No 11, London: Queen Mary, University of London.

Boyden, J. and Ennew, J. (1997) *Children in Focus – a Manual for Participatory Research with Children*, Stockholm, Sweden: Radda Barnen (Save the Children Sweden).

Brannen, J. (2005) 'Mixed Methods Research: A Discussion Paper', ESRC National Centre for Research Methods Review Paper (www.ncrm.ac.uk).

Brehaut, J. and Juzwishin, D. (2005) *Bridging the Gap: The Use of Research Evidence in Policy Development*, Health Technology Assessment Unit (HTA) Series Initiative #18, Alberta, Canada: Alberta Heritage Foundation for Medical Research (AHFMR).

Cahill, C. (2007) 'Doing Research *with* Young People: Participatory Research and the Rituals of Collective Work', *Children's Geographies* 5(3): 297–312.

Carvalho, S. and H. White (1997) 'Combining the Quantitative and Qualitative Approaches to Poverty Measurement and Analysis', *World Bank Technical Paper No. 366,* Washington, DC: World Bank.

Chambers, R. (2003) 'The Best of Both Worlds?' in R. Kanbur (ed) *Q-Squared: Qualitative and Quantitative Methods of Poverty Appraisal.* Washington, D.C.: Permanent Black.

Clampet-Lundquist, S., K. Edin, J.R. Kling and G.J. Duncan (2005) 'Moving At-Risk Kids to Better Neighborhoods: Why Girls Fare Better Than Boys?' Paper presented at the National Poverty Centre conference *Mixed Methods Research on Economic Conditions, Public Policy, and Family and Child Well-Being,* 26–28 June, Ann Arbor, Michigan.

Cockburn, J. (2002) 'Income Contributions of Child Work in Rural Ethiopia', Working Paper Series No 171, Oxford, UK: Centre for the Study of African Economies (Oxford University).

Cracknell, B.E. (2001) 'Knowing is all: Or is it? Some reflections on why the acquisition of knowledge focusing particularly on evaluation activities, does not always lead to action', *Public Administration and Development* 21(5): 371–9.

Crivello, G., L. Camfield and M. Woodhead (2009) 'How Can Children Tell Us About Their Well-Being? Exploring the Potential of Participatory Research Approaches within "Young Lives"', *Social Indicators Research* 90(1): 51–72.

David, D. and J. Dodd (2002) 'Qualitative Research and the Question of Rigour', *Qualitative Health Research* 12(2): 279–89.

Duncan, S. (2005) 'Towards evidence-inspired policymaking', *Social Sciences* 61: 10-11.

Fattore, T., J. Mason and E. Watson (2007) 'Children's Conceptualisation(s) of their Well-being', *Social Indicators Research* 80: 5–29.

Folbre, N. (2006) 'Measuring Care: Gender, Empowerment and the Care Economy', *Journal of Human Development* 7(2): 183–99.

Folbre, N. and M. Bittman (2004) *Family Time: The Social Organization of Care*. New York: Routledge.

Gaventa, J. (2006), 'Finding the spaces for change: a power analysis', *IDS Bulletin* 37: 23–33.

Gordon, D., S. Nandy, C. Pantazis, S. Pemberton and P. Townsend (2004) 'The Distribution of Child Poverty in the Developing World', *Report to UNICEF*, Bristol, UK: Centre for International Poverty Research, Bristol University.

Graue, M. and D. Walsh (1998) *Studying Children in Context, Theories, Methods and Ethics*. London: Sage Publications.

Hill, M., J. Davis, A. Prout and K. Tisdall (2004) 'Moving the Participation Agenda Forward', *Children and Society* 18: 77–96.

Holland, J. and S. Abeyasekera (eds) (forthcoming) *Who Counts? Participation, Numbers and Power*. London, UK: ITDG Publications.

Holland, J., R. Thomson and S. Henderson (2006) 'Qualitative Longitudinal Research: A Discussion Paper', *Families & Social Capital*, ESRC Research Group Working Paper No 21, London: South Bank University.

Huebner, E. (2004) 'Research on Assessment of Life Satisfaction of Children and Adolescents', *Social Indicators Research* 66: 3–33.

James, A. and A. Prout (1990) *Constructing and Reconstructing Childhood: Contemporary Issues in the Sociological Study of Childhood*, London: Routledge.

James, A., C. Jenks and A. Prout (1997) *Theorizing Childhood*. Cambridge, UK: Polity Press.

Jones, N. with E. Villar (2008) 'Situating Children in International Development Policy', *Journal of Evidence and Policy* 4(1): 53–73.

Jones, N., A. Datta and H. Jones with EBPDN Partners (2009) *Knowledge, Policy and Power: Six Dimensions of the Knowledge–Development Policy Interface*. London, UK: ODI.

Kabeer, N. (2003) *Gender Mainstreaming in Poverty Eradication and the Millennium Development Goals: A Handbook for Policy-makers and Other Stakeholders*, Toronto and London: IDRC and the Commonwealth Secretariat.

Landry, L., Lamari, M. and Amara, N. (2003) 'The extent and determinants of the utilization of university research in government agencies', *Public Administration Review* 63(2): 192–205.

Lansdown, G. (2005) *Understanding the Implications of Human Rights Treaty: Evolving Capacities of the Child*, Florence: UNICEF Innocenti Research Centre.

Lasswell, H.D. and Lerner, D. (1951) *The Policy Sciences: Recent Developments in Scope and Method*, Stanford: Stanford University Press.

Lather, P. (1986) 'Research as Praxis', *Harvard Educational Review* 56: 257–77.

Lewis, J. (2002) 'Gender and Welfare State Change', *European Societies* 4(4): 331–57.

Lloyd-Smith, M. and J. Tarr (2000) 'Researching Children's Perspectives: A Sociological Dimension', in A. Lewis and G. Lindsay (eds) *Researching Children's Perspectives.* Buckingham, UK: Open University Press, pp 59–70.

Lukes, S. (1974) *Power: A Radical View.* London: Macmillan.

Magnuson, K. and T. Smeeding (2005) 'Earnings, Transfers and Living Arrangements in Low-income Families: Who Pays the Bills?', presented at National Poverty Centre Conference *Mixed Methods Research on Economic Conditions, Public Policy, and Family and Child Well-Being*, 26–28 June, Ann Arbor, Michigan.

Mannion, G. (2007) 'Going Spatial, Going Relational: Why "Listening to Children" and Children's Participation Needs Reframing', *Discourse* 28(3): 405–20.

Marshall, J. (2003) 'Children and Poverty – Some Questions Answered', CHIP Briefing Paper No 1, London: Save the Children UK.

Marston, G. and Watts, R. (2003) 'Tampering with the evidence: a critical appraisal of evidence-based policy-making', *The Drawing Board: An Australian Review of Public Affairs* 3: 143–63.

Mayall, B. (2002) *Towards a Sociology for Childhood: Thinking from Children's Lives.* Milton Keynes UK: Open University Press.

Mayoux, L. and R. Chambers (2005) 'Reversing the Paradigm: Quantification, Participatory Methods, and Pro-poor Impact Assessment', *Journal of International Development* 17(2): 271–98.

Monaghan, M. (2008) 'The Evidence Base in UK Drug Policy: The New Rules of Engagement', *Policy & Politics* 36(1): 145–50.

Morrow,V. (1999) '"We are people too": Children's and young people's perspectives on children's rights and decision-making in England', *The International Journal of Children's Rights* 7(2): 149–70.

Moser, C. (2003) 'Apt illustration or Anecdotal Information: Can Qualitative Data be Robust or Representative?' in R. Kanbur (ed) *Q-Squared: Qualitative and Quantitative Methods of Poverty Appraisal.* Washington, DC: Permanent Black.

Moser, C. (2004) *Encounters with Violence in Latin America: Urban poor perceptions from Columbia and Guatemala,* London: Routledge.

Moynihan, R., Oxman, A.D., Lavis, J.N. and Paulsen, E. (2008) *Evidence-informed Health Policy: Using Research to Make Health Systems Healthier,* Report prepared for the WHO Advisory Committee on Health Research, Oslo, Norway: Norwegian Knowledge Centre for the Health Services, http://hera.helsebiblioteket.no/hera/bitstream/10143/33952/1/NOKCrapport1_2008.pdf

Naker, D. (2007) 'From Rhetoric to Practice: Bridging the Gap between What We Believe and What We Do', *Children, Youth and Environments* 17(3): 146–58.

Nutley, S., Davies, H. and Walter, I. (2002) 'Evidence Based Policy and Practice: Cross Sector Lessons from the UK', Paper presented at a seminar on 'Evidence-based Policy and Practice', organised by the Royal Society, Wellington, New Zealand.

Patton, M. (2002) *Qualitative Research and Evaluation Methods.* London: Sage.

Pham, T.L. and N. Jones (2005) 'The Ethics of Research Reciprocity: Making Children's Voices Heard in Poverty Reduction Policy-making in Vietnam', Young Lives Working Paper No 25, London: Save the Children UK.

Platt, L. (2003) 'Putting Childhood Poverty on the Agenda: The Relationship Between Research and Policy in Britain 1800–1950', Young Lives Working Paper No 7, London: Save the Children UK.

Powell, M.A. and A.B. Smith (2009) 'Children's Participation Rights in Research', *Childhood* 16(1): 124–42.

Redmond, G. (2008) 'Children's Perspectives on Economic Adversity: A Review of the Literature', Innocenti Discussion Paper No. 2008-01, Florence: UNICEF.

Ridge, T. (2002) *Childhood Poverty and Social Exclusion: From a Child's Perspective.* Bristol: The Policy Press.

Ruel, M.T., C.E. Levin, M. Armar-Klemesu, D. Maxwell and S.S. Morris (1999) 'Good Care Practices Can Mitigate the Negative Effects of Poverty and Low Maternal Schooling on Children's Nutritional Status: Evidence from Accra', *World Development* 27(11): 1993–2009.

Rycroft-Malone, J., Seers, K., Titchen, A., Harvey, G., Kitson, A. and McCormack, B. (2004) 'What counts as evidence in evidence-based practice?', *Journal of Advanced Nursing* 47(1): 81-90.

Sanderson, I. (2004) 'Getting Evidence into Practice: Perspectives on Rationality', *Evaluation* 10(3): 366–79.

Selener, D. (1997) *Participatory Action Research and Social Change.* Ithaca, NY: The Cornell Participatory Action Research Network, Cornell University.

Shaffer, P. (2003) 'Difficulties in Combining Income/Consumption and Participatory approaches to Poverty: Issues and Examples', in R. Kanbur (ed) *Q-Squared: Qualitative and Quantitative Methods of Poverty Appraisal,* Washington, DC: Permanent Black.

Simons, H. (2004) 'Utilizing evaluation evidence to enhance professional practice', *Evaluation: The International Journal of Theory, Research and Practice* 10(4): 410–29.

Sumner, A. and Tribe, M. (2008) *International Development Studies in the 21st Century: Theory and Methods in Research and Practice,* London: Sage.

Thomas, A. and H. Johnson (2002) 'Not Only Reinforcing But Also Different Stories: Combining Case Studies and Surveys to Investigate How Postgraduate Programmes Can Build Capacity for Development Policy and Management', Paper for 'Combined Methods' Conference, 1–2 July, Swansea: Centre for Development Studies.

Thompson, P. (2004) 'Researching Family and Social Mobility with Two Eyes: Some Experiences of the Interaction between Qualitative and Quantitative Data', *International Journal of Social Research Methodology* 7(3): 237–57.

Thorbecke, E. (2003) 'Tensions, Complementarities and Possible Convergence Between the Qualitative and Quantitative Approaches to Poverty Assessment', in R. Kanbur (ed) *Q-Squared: Qualitative and Quantitative Methods of Poverty Appraisal.* Washington, D.C.: Permanent Black.

Tilley, N. and Laycock, G. (2000) 'Joining up Research, Policy and Practice about Crime', *Policy Studies* 21 (3): 213–27.

Van Blerk, L. and N. Ansell (2007) 'Participatory Feedback and Dissemination with and for Children: Reflections from Research with Young Migrants in Southern Africa', *Children's Geographies* 5(3): 313–24.

White, S. (2002) 'Being, Becoming and Relationship: Conceptual Challenges of a Child Rights Approach in Development', *Journal of International Development* 14(8): 1095–104.

White, S. and S. Choudhury (2007) 'The Politics of Child Participation in International Development:The Dilemma of Agency', *The European Journal of Development Research* 19(4): 529–50.

Woldehanna,T., B.Tefera, N.Jones and A. Bayrau (2005a) 'Child Labour, Gender Inequality and Rural–Urban Disparities: How can Ethiopia's National Development Strategies Be Revised to Address Negative Spill-over Impacts on Child Education and Well-being?' *Young Lives Working Paper No. 20*. London: Save the Children UK.

Woldehanna,T., N.Jones and B.Tefera (2005b) 'Children's Educational Completion Rates and Achievement: Implications for Ethiopia's Second Poverty Reduction Strategy' *Young Lives Working Paper No. 18 (2006-10)*. London: Save the Children UK.

Wood, G. (ed) (1985) *Labelling in Development Policy*, London: Sage.

Woodhead, M. (1999) 'Combating Child Labour: Listen to What the Children Say', *Childhood* 6(1): 27–49.

Woodhead, M. and D. Faulkner (2000) 'Subjects, Objects or Participants? Dilemmas of Psychological Research with Children', in A. James and P. Christensen (eds) *Research with Children*, London: Falmer.

Yaqub, S. (2002) 'Poor Children Grow into Poor Adults: Harmful Mechanisms or Over-Deterministic Theory?' *Journal of International Development* 14(8): 1081–93.

Young, J. (2005) 'Research, Policy and Practice: Why Developing Countries are Different', *Journal of International Development* 17(6): 727–34.

Chapter 3

African Child Policy Forum (2006) *Youth Participation: Concepts, Models and Experiences,* Addis Ababa: ACPF.

Alfini, N. (2006) 'Children's Participation in Policy and Academic Institutions', *Building Participation among Children,* Brighton: IDS.

Bessell, S. (2009) 'Children's Participation in Decision-Making in the Philippines: Understanding the Attitudes of Policy-makers and Service Providers', *Childhood* 16(3): 299–316.

Black, M. (2004) *Opening Minds, Opening Up Opportunities: Children's Participation in Action for Working Children,* London: Save the Children UK.

Boyden, J. and J. Ennew (eds) (1997) *Children in Focus – A Manual for Participatory Research with Children,* Stockholm: Save the Children Sweden.

Brady, B. (2007) 'Developing Children's Participation: Lessons from a Participatory IT Project', *Children and Society* 21:31–41.

Brock, K. and McGee, R. (2004) *Mapping Trade Policy: Understanding the Challenges of Civil Society Participation,* IDS Working Paper, Brighton, Institute of Development Studies.

Brock, K., Cornwall, C. and Gaventa, J. (2001) *Power, Knowledge and Political Spaces in the Framing of Poverty Policy,* IDS Working Paper, Brighton, Institute of Development Studies.

Buse, K., N. Mays and G. Walt (2005) *Making Health Policy,* Berkshire, UK: Open University Press.

Canadian Health Services Research Foundation (2003) *The Theory and Practice of Knowledge Brokering in Canada's Health System,* Ottawa, Canada: CHSRF/FCRSS (www.chsrf.ca/brokering/pdf/Theory_and_Practice_e.pdf).

Cash, D.W., W.C. Clark, F. Alcock, N.M. Dickson, N. Eckley, D.H. Guston, J. Jager and R.B. Mitchell (2003) 'Knowledge Systems for Sustainable Development', *The Proceedings of the National Academy of Sciences* 100(14): 8086–91.

Cornia A., Jolly, R. and Stewart, F. (1987) *Adjustment with a human face protects vulnerable growth,* Oxford: Oxford University Press.

Court, J. and J. Young (2003) 'Bridging Research and Policy: Insights from 50 Case Studies', ODI Working Paper No 213, London, UK: ODI.

Crewe, E. and J. Young (2002) 'Bridging Research and Policy: Context, Evidence and Links', ODI Working Paper No 173. London: ODI.

De Janvry, A. and S. Subramanian (1993) 'Political Economy of Food and Nutrition Policies', in P. Pinstrup-Andersen (ed) *The Politics and Economics of Food and Nutrition Policies Program: An Interpretation.* Baltimore: John Hopkins University Press.

Dopson, S. and L. Fitzgerald (eds) (2005) *Knowledge to Action. Evidence-Based Healthcare in Context.* Oxford, UK: Oxford University Press.

Edwards, M. and D. Hulme (eds) (1996) *Nongovernmental Organisations – Performance and Accountability: Beyond the Magic Bullet,* Hartford, CT: West Kumarian Press.

Escobar, A. and Alvarez, S. (eds) (1992) *The Making of Social Movements in Latin America: Identity, Strategy and Democracy,* Boulder, CO: Westview Press.

Estabrooks, C., D. Thompson, J. Lovely and A. Hofmeyer (2006) 'A Guide to Knowledge Translation Theory', *The Journal of Continuing Education in the Health Professions* 26(1): 25–36.

Etzioni, A. (1967) 'Mixed Scanning: A Third Approach to Decision Making', *Public Administration Review* 27(5): 385–92.

Fanelli, C.W., R. Musarandega and L. Chawanda (2007) 'Child Participation in Zimbabwe's National Action Plan for Orphans and Other Vulnerable Children: Progress, Challenges and Possibilities', *Children, Youth and Environments* 17(3): 122–45.

Fischer, F. (2003) *Reframing Public Policy: Discursive Politics and Deliberative Practices*, Oxford, Oxford University Press.

Fischer, F. and J. Forester (1993) *The Argumentative Turn in Policy Analysis and Planning*, Durham, NC: Duke University Press.

Gerwe, C.F. (2000) 'Chronic addiction relapse treatment: a study of effectiveness of the high-risk identification and prediction treatment model: Part I', *Journal of Substance Abuse Treatment* 19: 415–27.

Grindle, M. and J. Thomas (1980) *Politics and Policy Implementation in the Third World,* Princeton: Princeton University Press.

Haas, A.L. (2000) 'Legislating Equality: Institutional Politics and the Expansion of Women's Rights in Chile', PhD dissertation, Department of Political Science, Chapel Hill, US: University of North Carolina at Chapel Hill.

Hanney, S. (2005) 'Personal Interaction with Researchers or Detached Synthesis of the Evidence: Modelling the Health Policy Paradox', *Evaluation and Research in Education* 18(1–2): 72–82.

Harper, C. and Jones, N. (2009) 'Child rights and aid: mutually exclusive?', ODI Background Note, London: ODI.

Hart, J. (2008) 'Children's Participation and International Development: Attending to the Political', *International Journal of Children's Rights* 16(3): 407–18.

Heidel, K. (2005) *Poverty Reduction Strategy Papers – Blind to the Rights of the (Working) Child? The (I-)PRSPs' Perception of Child Labour: A Problem Outline and Annotated Collection of Source Material*, Heidelberg: Kindernothilfe and Werkstatt Ökonomie.

Hickey, S. and Mohan, G. (2003) *Relocating Participation within a Radical Politics of Development: Citizenship and Critical Modernism*, Draft working paper prepared for conference on 'Participation: From Tyranny to Transformation? Exploring new approaches to participation in development', 27–28 February, University of Manchester.

Hill, M., J. Davis, A. Prout and K. Tisdall (2004) 'Moving the Participation Agenda Forward', *Children and Society* 18: 77–96.

Hinton, R. (2008) 'Children's Participation and Good Governance: Limitations of the Theoretical Literature', *International Journal of Children's Rights* 16: 285–300.

Hogwood, B. and Gunn, L. (1984) *Policy Analysis for the Real World*, New York: Oxford University Press.

Holmes, T. and I. Scoones (2000) 'Participatory Environmental Policy Processes: Experiences from North and South', IDS Working Paper No 113, Brighton: Institute of Development Studies.

Invernizzi, A. and B. Milne (2002) 'Are Children Entitled to Contribute to international policy making? A Critical View of Children's Participation in the International Campaign for the Elimination of Child Labour', *International Journal of Children's Rights* 10: 403–31.

Jenkins, W.I. (1978) *Policy Analysis*, Oxford: Martin Robertson.

Jones, N. and Sumner, A. (2009) 'Does Mixed Methods Research Matter to Understanding Childhood Well-being?', *Social Indicators Research* 90(1): 33–50.

Jones, N., B. Tefera and T. Woldehanna (2008) 'Childhood Poverty and Evidence-based Policy Influencing in Ethiopia', *Development and Practice* 18(3): 371–84.

Jones, N., A. Datta and H. Jones, with EBPDN Partners (2009) *Knowledge, Policy and Power: Six Dimensions of the Knowledge–Development Policy Interface*, London: ODI.

Keck, M.E. and K. Sikkink (1998) *Activists Beyond Borders: Advocacy Networks in International Politics*. Ithaca and London: Cornell University Press.

Keeley, J. and I. Scoones (2003a) 'Seeds in a Globalised World: Agricultural Biotechnology in Zimbabwe', IDS Working Paper No 189, Brighton: Institute of Development Studies.

Keeley, J. and I. Scoones (2003b) 'Contexts for Regulation: GMOs in Zimbabwe', IDS Working Paper No 190, Brighton: Institute of Development Studies.

Keeley, J. and I. Scoones (2003c) *Understanding Environmental Policy Processes: Cases from Africa,* London: Earthscan.

Keeley, J. and Scoones, I. (2006) 'Understanding Environmental Policy Processes', IDS Working Paper No 89, Brighton: IDS.

Kingdon, J. (1984) *Agendas, Alternatives and Public Policies*, Boston: Little Brown and Co.

KNOTS (Knowledge, Technology and Society Group, IDS) (2006) *Understanding Policy Processes: A Review of IDS Research on the Environment*, Brighton: IDS.

Knott, J. and A. Wildavsky (1980) 'If Dissemination is the Solution, What is the Problem?' *Science Communication* 1(4) 537–78.

Lansdown, G. (2001) *Promoting Children's Participation in Democratic Decision-Making*, Florence: UNICEF.

Lansdown, G. (2006) 'International Developments in Children's Participation: Lessons and Challenges', in E.K.M. Tisdall, J.M. Davis, M. Hill and A. Prout (eds) *Children, Young People and Social Inclusion: Participation for What?* Bristol: The Policy Press.

Lasswell, H.D. (1951a) *The Political Writings of Harold D. Lasswell.* Glencoe: The Free Press.

Lasswell, H.D. (1951b) 'The Immediate Future of Research Policy and Method in Political Science', *The American Political Science Review* 45(1): 133–42.

Lasswell, H.D. (1951c) 'Politics: Who Gets What, When, How', in Lasswell (ed) *The Political Writings of Harold D. Lasswell.* Glencoe: The Free Press, 290–461.

Lasswell, H.D. (1951d) *The World Revolution of our Time: A Framework for Basic Policy Research*, Hoover Institute Studies; Series A: General Studies 1. Stanford, CA: Stanford University Press.

Lasswell, H.D. and Lerner, D. (1951) *The Policy Sciences: Recent Developments in Scope and Method*, Stanford, Stanford University Press.

Lavis, J., Lomas, J., Hamid, M. and Sewankambo, N. (2006) 'Assessing country-level efforts to link research to action', *Bulletin of the World Health Organisation*, August, 84(8).

Leach, M., I. Scoones and B. Wynne (eds) (2005) *Science and Citizens: Globalization and the Challenge of Engagement,* London: ZED Press.

Lemieux-Charles, L. and F. Champagne (eds) (2004) *Using Knowledge and Evidence in Health Care: Multidisciplinary Perspectives.* Toronto: University of Toronto Press.

Lindblom, C. (1959) 'The Science of Muddling Through', *Public Administration Review* 19(2):79–88.

Lindblom, C. (1979) 'Still Muddling, Not Yet Through', *Public Administration Review* 39: 97–106.

Lomas, J. (2007) 'The In-between World of Knowledge Brokering', *British Medical Journal* 334:129–32.

Loomis, B.A. and Cigler, A.J. (2002) 'Introduction: The Changing Nature of Interest Group Politics' in A.J. Cigler and B.A. Loomis (eds) *Interest group politics*, 6th edn, Washington, DC: Congressional Quarterly Press.

Lukes, S. (1974) *Power: A Radical View*, London: Macmillan.

Lund, R. (2007) 'At the Interface of Development Studies and Child Research: Rethinking the Participating Child', *Children's Geographies* 5(1/2): 131–48.

Majone, G. (1989) *Evidence, Argument and Persuasion in the Policy Process*, New Haven, CT: Yale University Press.

Mannion, G. (2007) 'Going Spatial, Going Relational: Why "listening to children" and Children's Participation Needs Reframing', *Discourse* 28(3): 405–20.

March, G. and P. Olsen (1976) *Ambiguity and Choice in Organizations*. Bergen: Universitetsforlaget.

Marston, G. and R. Watts (2003) 'Tampering With the Evidence: A Critical Appraisal of Evidence-Based Policy-Making', *The Drawing Board: An Australian Review of Public Affairs* 3(3): 143–63.

Mayo, M. (2001) 'Children's and Young People's Participation in Development in the South and in Urban Regeneration in the North', *Progress in Development Studies* 1(4): 279–93.

Mitton. C., C. Adair, E. McKenzie, S. Patten and B. Waye-Perry (2007) 'Knowledge Transfer and Exchange: Review and Synthesis of the Literature', *The Milbank Quarterly* 85(4): 729–68.

Mniki, N. and S. Rosa (2007) 'Heroes in Action: Child Advocates in South Africa', *Children, Youth and Environments* 17(3): 179–97.

Moses, S. (2008) 'Children and Participation in South Africa: An Overview', *International Journal of Children's Rights* 16: 327–42.

Mosse, D. (2004) *Cultivating Development: An Ethnography of Aid Policy and Practice*, London, Pluto.

Naker, D. (2007) 'From Rhetoric to Practice: Bridging the Gap between What We Believe and What We Do', *Children, Youth and Environments* 17(3): 146–58.

Naker, D., G. Mann and R. Rajani (2007) 'The Gap between Rhetoric and Practice: Critical Perspectives on Children's Participation', *Children, Youth and Environments* 17(3): 99–103.

Newell, P. and Tussie, D. (2006) *Civil Society Participation in Trade Policy-making in Latin America: Reflections and Lessons*, IDS Working Paper 267, Brighton: Institute of Development Studies (IDS), University of Sussex.

Nguyen, T.T.T., M.H. Nguyen and N. Jones (2006) 'Fostering the Right to Participation: Children's Involvement in Vietnam's Poverty Reduction Policy Processes', presented at XVI ISA World Congress of Sociology, Durban, RSA, 23–29 July.

North, D. (1990) *Institutions, Institutional Change and Economic Performance*, Cambridge: CUP.

Nutley, S., Davies, H. and Walter, I. (2002) 'Evidence-based policy and practice: cross-sector lessons from the UK', Paper presented at the Royal Society's Seminar on Evidence-Based Policy and Practice, Wellington, New Zealand.

O'Kane, C. (2002) 'Marginalised Children as Social Actors for Social Justice in South Asia', *British Journal of Social Work* 32: 697–710.

O'Kane, C. (2003) *Children and Young People as Citizens: Partners for Social Change: Learning from Experience*, Kathmandu, Nepal: Save the Children Alliance South and Central Asia Region.

O'Malley, K. (2004) *Children and Young People Participating in PRSPs: Lessons from Save the Children's Experiences.* London: Save the Children UK.

Oxfam GB (2004) *'Donorship' to 'Ownership': Moving to PRSP Round 2*, Oxfam Briefing Paper 51, Oxford: Oxfam GB.

Pais, M.S. (2002) 'Centre of Attention', *CRIN Newsletter* 15: 9-12 (www.crin.org/docs/resources/publications/crinvol15e.pdf).

Pham, T.L. and N. Jones (2005) 'The Ethics of Research Reciprocity: Making children's voices heard in poverty reduction policy-making in Vietnam', *Young Lives Working Paper No 25*, Young Lives.

Pinkerton, J. (2004) 'Children's Participation in the Policy Process: Some Thoughts on Policy Evaluation Based on the Irish National Children's Strategy', *Children and Society* 18: 119–30.

Pomares, J. and Jones, N. (2009) 'Evidence-based Policy Processes: A Systematic Review of the Knowledge-Policy Interface across Policy Sectors', mimeo (unpublished).

Pressman, P. and Wildavsky, A. (1973) *Implementation*, Berkeley, CA: University of California Press.

Pridmore, P. (2003) 'Revisiting Children's Participation: A Critical Review of Child-to-Child Experiences in Kenya and Vietnam', *Anthropology in Action* 10(1): 15–24.

Prout, A. (2003) 'Participation, Policy and the Changing Conditions of Childhood', in C. Hallett and A. Prout (eds) *Hearing the Voices of Children: Social Policy for a New Century.* Abingdon: RoutledgeFalmer.

Ray, P. and S. Carter (2007) *Each and Every Child: Understanding and Working with Children in the Poorest and Most Difficult Situations*, Plan.

Rich, A. (2005) 'War of Ideas: Why mainstream and liberal foundations and the think tanks they support are losing in the war of ideas in American politics', *Stanford Social Innovation Review* (Spring): 18-25.

Sabatier, P. and H. Jenkins-Smith (1993) *Policy Change and Learning: An Advocacy Coalition Approach.* Boulder, CO: Westview Press.

Sanderson, I. (2004). 'Getting Evidence into Practice: Perspectives on Rationality', *Evaluation* 10(3): 366–79.

Save the Children (2005) *Practice Standards in Children's Participation.* London, UK: Save the Children.

Shier, H. (2001) 'Pathways to Participation: Openings, Opportunities and Obligations: A New Model for Enhancing Children's Participation in Decision-making in line with Article 12.1 of the United Nation's Convention on the Rights of the Child', *Children and Society* 15: 107–17.

Simon, H. (1957) *Administrative Behaviour* (2nd edn), New York: Macmillan.

Sinclair, R. (2004) 'Participation in Practice: Making it Meaningful, Effective and Sustainable', *Children and Society* 18: 106–18.

Skelton, T. (2007) 'Children, Young People, UNICEF and Participation', *Children's Geographies* 5(1/2): 165–81.

Stone-Sweet, A., N. Fligstein and W. Sandholtz (2001) 'The Institutionalization of European Space', in A. Stone-Sweet, W. Sandholtz and N. Fligstein (eds) *The Institutionalization of Europe.* Oxford: Oxford University Press.

Sumner, A. and Harpham T. (2008) 'The market for "evidence" in policy processes: The case of child health in AP, India and Viet Nam'. *European Journal of Development Research* 20(4):712–32.

Sumner, A. and Jones, N. (2010) 'Are pro-poor policy processes expert–led or citizen-led?', *International Development and Planning Review* 30(4): 359–76.

Sumner, A. and Tiwari, M. (2009) *After 2015: International Development Policy at a Crossroads*, Palgrave MacMillan: Basingstoke.

Sumner, A., L. Haddad and C. Gomez (2009) 'Rethinking Intergenerational Transmission(s): Does a Wellbeing Lens Help? The Case of Nutrition', *IDS Bulletin* 40(1): 22–30.

Thomas, J. and S. Grindle (1990) 'After the Decision: Implementing Policy Reforms in Developing Countries', *World Development* 18(8): 1163–81.

Tisdall, E.K.M. (2008) 'Is the Honeymoon Over? Children and Young People's Participation in Public Decision-Making', *International Journal of Children's Rights* 16(3): 419–29.

UNICEF (2009) *The Participation of Children and Young People in UNICEF Country Programme and National Committee Activities.* New York: UNICEF.

Upshur, R., E. Van Den Kerkhof and V. Goef (2001) 'Meaning and Measurement: An Inclusive Model of Evidence in Health Care', *Journal of Evaluation in Clinical Practice* 7(2): 91–6.

Van Blerk, L. and N. Ansell (2007) 'Participatory Feedback and Dissemination with and for Children: Reflections from Research with Young Migrants in Southern Africa', *Children's Geographies* 5(3): 313–24.

Walt, G. (1984) *Health Policy: An Introduction to Process and Power*, London, UK: Zed Books.

Walt, G. and L. Gibson (1994) 'Reforming the Health Sector in Developing Countries: The Central Role of Policy Analysis', *Health Policy and Planning* 9: 353–70.

White, S.C. (2002) 'Being, Becoming and Relationship: Conceptual Challenges of a Child Rights Approach in Development', *Journal of International Development* 14: 1095–104.

White, S. and S. Choudhury (2007) 'The Politics of Child Participation in International Development: The Dilemma of Agency', *The European Journal of Development Research* 19(4): 529–50.

Wildavsky, A. (1980) *The Art and Craft of Policy Analysis*, London: Macmillan.

Williams, E. (2004) 'Children's Participation and Policy Change in South Asia', *CHIP Report No. 6*. London: Save the Children UK.

Williams, E. (2005) 'Small Hands, Big Voices? Children's Participation in Policy Change in India', *IDS Bulletin* 36(1): 82–90.

Young, L. and J. Everitt (2004) *Advocacy Groups*. Vancouver, BC: UBC Press.

Chapter 4

Abebe, T. (2009) 'Multiple Methods, Complex Dilemmas: Negotiating Socio-ethical Spaces in Participatory Research with Disadvantaged Children', *Children's Geographies* 7(4): 451–65.

Ahmed, M. (2005) 'Bridging Research and Policy Development', *Journal of International Development* 17(6): 765–73.

Airede, L.R. and B.A. Ekele (2003) 'Adolescent Maternal Mortality in Sokoto, Nigeria', *Journal of Obstetrics & Gynaecology* 23: 163–5.

Amundsen, I. and C. Abreu (2006) *Civil Society in Angola: Inroads, Space and Accountability*, Bergen: CMI.

Bethlehem, T., C. Griffin and L. Camfield (2009) 'Using Qualitative Methods with Poor Children in Urban Ethiopia: Opportunities & Challenges', *Social Indicators Research* 90(1): 73–87.

Bloom, D., D. Canning and K. Chan (2005) 'Higher Education and Economic Development in Africa', Working Paper, Harvard University. Available at: http://siteresources.worldbank.org/EDUCATION/Resources/278200-1099079877269/547664-1099079956815/HigherEd_Econ_Growth_Africa.pdf

Bonn, M., D. Earle, S. Lea and P. Webley (1999) 'South African Children's Views of Wealth, Poverty, Inequality and Unemployment', *Journal of Economic Psychology* 20: 593–612.

Buhler, U. (2002) 'Participation with Justice and Dignity: Beyond the New Tyranny', *Peace, Conflict and Development: An Interdisciplinary Journal* 1: 1–16.

Camfield, L. (2010) '"Even if she learns, she doesn't understand properly". Children's Understandings of Ill-being and Poverty in Five Ethiopian Communities', *Social Indicators Research* 96(1): 85–112.

Camfield, L. and Y. Tafere (2009) 'No, Living Well Does Not Mean Being Rich: Diverse Understandings of Well-being among 11–13-year-old Children in Three Ethiopian Communities', *Journal of Children and Poverty* 15(2): 119–38.

Chowdhury, N., C. Finlay-Notman and I. Hovland (2006) *CSO Capacity for Policy Engagement: Lessons Learned from the CSPP Consultations in Africa, Asia and Latin America*, ODI Working Paper No 272, London: ODI.

Clacherty, G. and D. Donald (2007) 'Child Participation in Research: Reflections on Ethical Challenges in the Southern African Context', *African Journal of AIDS Research* 6(2): 147–56.

Committee on the Rights of the Child (2003) *United Nations Convention on the Rights of the Child (UNCRC), General Comment No 5: General measures of implementation of the Convention on the Rights of the Child*, 34th session, UN Doc CRC/GC/2003/5, downloaded at http://www.unhchr.ch/tbs/doc.nsf/(symbol)/CRC.GC.2003.5.En

Cooper, E. (2007) 'Praxis in a Refugee Camp? Meanings of Participation and Empowerment for Long-Term Refugee Youth', *Children, Youth and Environments* 17(3): 114–31.

Crewe, E., I. Hovland and J. Young (2005) 'Context, Evidence, Links: A Conceptual Framework for Understanding Research–Policy Processes', in J. Court, I. Hovland and J. Young (eds) *Bridging Research and Policy in Development: Evidence and the Change Process*, London, UK: Overseas Development Institute.

Crivello, G., L. Camfield and M. Woodhead (2009) 'How Can Children Tell Us About Their Wellbeing? Exploring the Potential of Participatory Research Approaches Within Young Lives', *Social Indicators Research* 90(1): 51–72.

Fatton, R. (1995) 'Africa in the Age of Democratization: The Civic Limitations of Civil Society', *African Studies Review* 38(2): 72–7.

Fatton, R. (1999) 'Civil Society Revisited: Africa in the New Millennium', *West Africa Review* 1(1): 1–18.

Filmer, D. and Pritchett, L.H. (2001) 'Estimating Wealth Effects Without Expenditure Data-Or Tears: An Application to Educational Enrolments in States of India', *Demography* 38(1): 115-132.

Guyot, J. (2007) 'Participation: Children and Youth in Protracted Refugee Situations', *Children, Youth and Environments* 17(3): 159–78.

Harper, C. and N. Jones, with A. Bennett, A. Datta, J. Espey, T. Kipping, H. Marsden and F. Samuels (forthcoming) 'The Visibility of Children's Rights in Donor Action: An Assessment of Donor Countries' Strategies and Programming', UNICEF Innocenti Research Centre Working Paper, Florence: UNICEF Innocenti Research Centre.

Harper, C., N. Jones, J. Espey, N. Patrick, P. Pereznieto and D. Walker (2009) *EC Toolkit on Child Rights: Child Rights in Poverty Reduction Strategy Processes: Desk Review.* New York: UNICEF.

Heidel, K. (2005) *Poverty Reduction Strategy Papers: Children First! A Case Study on PRSP Processes in Ethiopia, Kenya and Zambia from a Child Rights Perspective.* Heidelberg and Duisburg: Kindernothilfe and Werkstatt Ökonomie.

Hogan, M.C., Foreman, K.J., Naghavi, M., Ahn, S.Y., Wang, M., Makela, S.M., Lopez, A.D., Lozano, R. and Murray, C.J.L. (2010) 'Maternal mortality for 181 countries, 1980–2008: A systematic analysis of progress towards Millennium Development Goal 5', *The Lancet* 375(9726): 1609–23.

ICRW (International Centre for Research on Women) (2006) *Too Young to Wed,* Washington, DC: ICRW.

Jones, N. and F. Tembo (2008) 'Promoting Good Governance Through Civil Society–Legislator Linkages: Opportunities and Challenges for Policy Engagement in Developing Country Contexts', Paper presented at the International Third Sector Research Conference, Barcelona, 9–12 July.

Jones, N. and J. Young (2007) 'Setting the Scene: Situating DFID's Research Funding Policy and Practice in an International Comparative Perspective', a scoping study commissioned by DFID Central Research Department, London: ODI.

Jones, N., B. Gutema, B. Tefera and T. Woldehanna (2005) *Mainstreaming Children into National Poverty Strategies: A Child-focused Analysis of the Ethiopian Sustainable Development and Poverty Reduction Programme (2002–2005),* Young Lives Working Paper 22, Oxford: Young Lives.

Jones, N., M. Bailey and M. Lyytikäinen (2007) 'Research Capacity Strengthening in Africa: Trends, Gaps and Opportunities', A scoping study commissioned by DFID on behalf of IFORD. London: ODI.

Jones, N., B. Tefera and T. Woldehanna (2008) 'Childhood Poverty and Evidence-based Policy Influencing in Ethiopia', *Development and Practice* 18(3): 371–84.

Jones, N., H. Jones, L. Steer and A. Datta (2009) *Improving Impact Evaluation and Use,* ODI Working Paper No 300, London, UK: ODI.

Keenan, C. (2007) 'Meeting Youth Where They Live: Participatory Approaches to Research with Marginalized Youth Engaged in Urban Agriculture', *Children, Youth and Environments* 17(3): 198–212.

King, K., R. Palmer and R. Hayman (2005) 'Bridging Research and Policy on Education, Training and Their Enabling Environments', *Journal of International Development* 7(6): 803–17.

Maguire, S. (2007) 'A Study of the Child Rights Climate within the UK's Department for International Development', research commissioned by Save the Children UK, World Vision UK, Plan International, VSO, ChildHope, Amnesty International, Antislavery International, UNICEF UK and DFID. Available at http://webarchive.nationalarchives.gov.uk/+/http://www.dfid.gov.uk/Documents/publications/child-rights-climate.pdf

Makumbe, J.M. (1998) 'Is there a Civil Society in Africa?' *International Affairs* 74(2): 305–19.

Mamdani, M. (1996) *Citizen and Subject, Contemporary Africa and the Legacy of Late Colonialism*. Uganda: Fountain Publishers.

Marcus, R. and J. Wilkinson (2002) *Whose Poverty Matters? Vulnerability, Social Protection and PSRPs*. London, UK: Chronic Poverty Research Centre (CHIP).

McGee, R. (2004) 'Unpacking Policy: Actors, Knowledge and Spaces', in K. Brock, R. McGee and J. Gaventa (eds) *Unpacking Policy: Knowledge, Actors and Spaces in Poverty Reduction in Uganda and Nigeria*. Kampala: Fountain Publishers.

Naker, D. (2007) 'From Rhetoric to Practice: Bridging the Gap between What We Believe and What We Do', *Children, Youth and Environments* 17(3): 146–58.

Nasong'o, S.W. (2007) 'Negotiating New Rules of the Game: Social Movements, Civil Society and the Kenyan Transition', in G. Murunga and S.W. Nasong'o (eds) *Kenya: The Struggle for Democracy*, Dakar: CODESRIA.

Pham, T.L. (2003) 'Managing Research and Advocacy in Vietnam', presented at a Young Lives Conference, *Childhood Poverty: Longitudinal Studies for Policy Making*, University of London, 8–9 September.

Piron, L. with A. Evans (2004) *Politics and the PRSP Approach: Synthesis Paper*, ODI Working Paper No. 237, London, UK: ODI.

Porter, G. and A. Albane (2008) 'Increasing Children's Participation in African Transport Planning: Reflections on Methodological Issues in a Child-centered Research Project', *Children's Geographies* 6(2): 151–67.

Robson, E., G. Porter, K. Hampshire and M. Bourdillon (2009) '"Doing it right?": Working With Young Researchers in Malawi to Investigate Children, Transport and Mobility', *Children's Geographies* 7(4): 467–80.

Sawyerr, A. (2004) 'African Universities and the Challenge of Research Capacity Development', *JHEA/RESA* 2(1): 211–40.

Saxena, N. (2005) 'Bridging Research and Policy in India', *Journal of International Development* 17(6): 737–46.

Start, D. and I. Hovland (2004) *Tools for Policy Impact: A Handbook for Researchers.* London, UK: ODI.

Sumner, A. and C. Melamed (2010) 'The MDGs and Beyond', *IDS Bulletin* 41(1), Brighton: IDS.

Tarrow, S. (1994) *Power in Movement: Social Movements, Collective Action and Politics*, New York: Cambridge University Press.

Tefera, B. (2003) 'Advocacy in the Ethiopian Context and Implications for Young Lives', presented at the Young Lives conference *Childhood Poverty: Longitudinal Studies for Policy Making*, University of London, 8–9 September.

Twum-Danso, A. (2009) 'Situating Participatory Methodologies in Context: The Impact of Culture on Adult–Child Interactions in Research and Other Projects', *Children's Geographies* 7(4): 379–89.

UNDESA (2009) *Millennium Development Goals Report 2009*, New York: UNDESA, downloaded at http://unstats.un.org/unsd/mdg/ Resources/Static/Products/Progress2009/MDG_Report_2009_ En.pdf

Vandemoortele, J. and Delamonica, E. (2010) 'Taking the MDGs Beyond 2015: Hasten Slowly', *IDS Bulletin* 41(1): 60–9.

Varghese, N. (2004) 'Private Higher Education in Africa', prepared for International Institute for Education Planning, Association for the Development of Education in Africa, Association of African Universities, Paris: IIEP: UNESCO.

Wells, K. (2009) *Childhood in a Global Perspective.* London: Polity Press.

Whitter, S. and J. Bukokhe (2004) 'Children's Perceptions of Poverty, Participation and Local Governance in Uganda', *Development in Practice* 14(5): 645–59.

WHO (World Health Organization) and UNFPA (2006) *Pregnant Adolescents*, Geneva: WHO.

Woldehanna, T., B. Tefera, N. Jones and A. Bayrau (2005a) 'Child Labour, Gender Inequality and Rural–Urban Disparities: How can Ethiopia's National Development Strategies Be Revised to Address Negative Spill-over Impacts on Child Education and Well-being?', Young Lives Working Paper No 20, London: Save the Children UK.

Woldehanna, T., N. Jones and B. Tefera (2005b) 'Children's Educational Completion Rates and Achievement: Implications for Ethiopia's Second Poverty Reduction Strategy', Young Lives Working Paper No 18 (2006–10). London: Save the Children UK.

World Bank (2007) *Building Knowledge Economies: Advanced Strategies for Development.* Washington D.C.: The World Bank

You, D., Wardlaw, T., Salama, P. and Jones, G. (2009) 'Levels and trends in under-5 mortality, 1990–2008', *The Lancet*, published online 10 September, DOI:10.1016/S0140-6736(09)61601-9.

Young, L. and H. Barrett (2001) 'Adapting Visual Methods: Action Research with Kampala Street Children', *Area* 33(2): 141–52.

Chapter 5

Agrawal, A. and J.C. Ribot (1999) 'Accountability in Decentralization: A Framework with South Asian and West African Cases', *Journal of Developing Areas* 33: 473–502.

Ahmad, J., S. Devarajan, S. Khemani and S. Shah (2005) *Decentralisation and Service Delivery*, World Bank Policy Research Working Paper 3603, May.

Ahsan, M. (2009) 'The Potential and Challenges of Rights-based Research with Children and Young People: Experiences from Bangladesh', *Children's Geographies* 7(4): 391–403.

Akehurst, C. and C. Cardona (1994) *An Overview of NPA Decentralisation in Developing Countries*, Innocenti Occasional Papers, Decentralization and Local Governance Series, Florence: Innocenti Research Centre.

Ansell, N. (2005) *Children, Youth and Development.* New York: Routledge.

Bardhan, P. (2002) 'Decentralisation of Governance and Development', *Journal of Economic Perspectives* 16(4): 185–205.

Baker, R. (1996) 'PRA with Street Children Nepal', *PLA Notes* 25: 56–60.

Brock, K., A. Cornwall and J. Gaventa (2001) 'Power, Knowledge and Political Spaces in Framing of Poverty Policy', *IDS Working Paper No 143*, Sussex: Institute of Development Studies.

Chakraborty, K. (2009) '"The Good Muslim Girl": Conducting Qualitative Participatory Research to Understand the Lives of Young Muslim Women in the Bustees of Kolkata', *Children's Geographies* 7(4): 421–34.

Cornwall, A. (2002) 'Making Spaces, Changing Places: Situating Participation in Development', IDS Working Paper No 170, Sussex: Institute of Development Studies.

Cos-Montiel, F. (2005) 'Developing a Research Agenda on Decentralisation and Women's Rights in Latin America and the Caribbean', Background Paper for the IDRC 2005 Gender Unit Research Competition. Ottawa: IDRC.

Crivello, G., L. Camfield and M. Woodhead (2009) 'How Can Children Tell Us About Their Wellbeing? Exploring the Potential of Participatory Research Approaches within Young Lives', *Social Indicators Research* 90(1): 51–72.

Crook, R. and J. Manor (1998) *Democracy and Decentralisation in South Asia and West Africa*. Cambridge: Cambridge University Press.

Crook, R. and A. Sverrisson (2001) 'Decentralisation and Poverty-alleviation in Developing Countries: A Comparative Analysis or, is West Bengal Unique?', IDS Working Paper No 130, Sussex: Institute of Development Studies.

Datta, A., N. Jones and E. Mendizabal. (2010) 'Think Tanks and the Rise of the Knowledge Economy: Their Linkages with National Politics and External Donors', in A. Garce and G. Una (eds) *Think Tanks and Public Policies in Latin America*. Buenos Aires, Argentina: Fundacion Siena and CIPPEC.

Gaventa, J. (2006) 'Triumph, Deficit or Contestation? Deepening the "Deepening Democracy" Debate', *IDS Working Paper No. 264*. Sussex: International Development Studies.

Goetz, M. (2004) 'Decentralisation and Gender Equality', in UNDP (ed) *Striving for Gender Equality in an Unequal World, UNDP Report for Beijing + 10*. New York: UNDP.

Guerra, E. (2002) 'Citizenship Knows No Age: Children's Participation in the Governance and Municipal Budget of Barra Mansa, Brazil', *Environment and Urbanization* 14(2): 71–84.

Halik, M. and P. Webley (2009) 'Adolescents' Understanding of Poverty and the Poor in Rural Malaysia', *Journal of Economic Psychology* (forthcoming).

Harper, C. (2004) 'Breaking Poverty Cycles – The Importance of Action in Childhood', *CHIP Policy Briefing No 8*. London: Childhood Poverty Research and Policy Centre.

Harpham, T., N. Huong, T. Long and T. Tuan (2005) 'Participatory Child Poverty Assessment in Rural Vietnam', *Children and Society* 19: 27–41.

Hastadewi, Y. (2009) 'Participatory Action Research with Children: Notes from the Field', *Children's Geographies* 7(4): 481–2.

Hogan, M.C., Foreman, K.J., Naghavi, M., Ahn, S.Y., Wang, M., Makela, S.M., Lopez, A.D., Lozano, R. and Murray, C.J.L. (2010) 'Maternal mortality for 181 countries, 1980-2008: a systematic analysis of progress towards Millennium Development Goal 5', *The Lancet* 375(9726): 1609–23.

Jabeen, T. (2009) '"But I've Never Been Asked!" Research with Children in Pakistan', *Children's Geographies* 7(4): 405–19.

Johnson, C. (2003) 'Decentralisation in India: Poverty, Politics and Panchayati Raj', ODI Working Paper Series No 199, London: ODI.

Jones, N. (2006) *Gender and the Political Opportunities of Democratization in South Korea*. New York: Palgrave Macmillan.

Jones, N., M. Lyytikainen and G. Reddy. (2007a) 'Decentralization and Participatory Service Delivery: Implications for Tackling Childhood Poverty in Andhra Pradesh, India', *Journal of Children and Poverty* 13(2): 1–23.

Jones, N., M. Mukherjee and S. Galab. (2007b) 'Ripple Effects or Deliberate Intentions: Assessing Linkages between Women's Empowerment and Childhood Poverty', UNICEF/Young Lives Social Policy Paper 002, May.

Lockheed, M. (2006) *Decentralisation of Education: Eight Lessons for School Effectiveness and Improvement*, Washington, DC: World Bank.

Lolichen, P.J., J. Shenjoy, A. Shetty, C. Nash and M. Venkatesh (2006) 'Children in the Driver's Seat', *Children's Geographies* 4(3): 347–57.

Manor, J. (2004) 'User Committees: A Potentially Damaging Second Wave of Decentralisation?' *The European Journal of Development Research* 16(1): 192–213.

McGann, J.G. with E.C. Johnson (2005) *Comparative Think Tanks, Politics and Public Policy.* Northampton, US, and Cheltenham, UK: Edward Elgar Publishing Limited.

Mehrotra, S. (2006) 'Governance and Basic Social Services: Ensuring Accountability in Service Delivery through Deep Democratic Decentralisation', *Journal of International Development* 18(2): 263–83.

Mukhopadhyay, M. (2005) *Decentralisation and Gender Equity in South Asia An Issues Paper*. Ottawa: IDRC.

Pereznieto, P., G. Reddy and K. Mayuri (2007) 'Improving Child-focused Spending in Local Bodies in Andhra Pradesh: Constraints and Opportunities', UNICEF/Young Lives Social Policy Paper 003, May.

Pham, T.L. and N. Jones (2005) 'The Ethics of Research Reciprocity: Making Children's Voices Heard in Poverty Reduction Policy-making in Vietnam', Young Lives Working Paper No 25, London: Save the Children UK.

Powis, B. (2003) 'Grass Roots Politics and "Second Wave of Decentralisation" in Andhra Pradesh', *Economic and Political Weekly* 38: 2617–22.

Reddy, V.R., M.G. Reddy and M.S. Reddy (2006) 'Decentralised Governance and Human Resource Development. Democratic vis-à-vis Participatory Institutions in Andhra Pradesh', Background paper prepared for the Andhra Pradesh Human Development Report. Hyderabad: Centre for Economic and Social Studies.

Sapkota, P. and J. Sharma (1996) 'Participatory Interactions with Children in Nepal', *PLA Notes* 25: 61–4.

Saroj, K. (2009) 'Moving Towards an Outcomes-oriented Approach to Nutrition Program Monitoring: The India ICSA Program', Working Paper No 49483, Washington, D.C.: World Bank.

Stone, D. and A. Denham (eds) (2004) *Think Tank Traditions: Policy Research and the Politics of Ideas,* Manchester: Manchester University Press.

Theis, J. (1996) 'Children and Participatory Appraisals: Experiences from Vietnam', *PLA Notes* 25: 70–2.

UNDESA (2009) *Millennium Development Goals Report 2009*, New York: UNDESA, downloaded at http://unstats.un.org/unsd/mdg/Resources/Static/Products/Progress2009/MDG_Report_2009_En.pdf

UNICEF (2007) 'Progress for Children: A World Fit for Children', Statistical Review, New York: UNICEF.

Vandemoortele, J. and Delamonica, E. (2010) 'Taking the MDGs Beyond 2015: Hasten Slowly', *IDS Bulletin* 41(1): 60–9.

Varghese, N.V. (2004) *Institutional restructuring in higher education in Asia: trends and patterns*, in New Trends in Higher Education Series, Paris: IIEP-UNESCO.

Wells, K. (2009) *Childhood in a Global Perspective*, London: Polity Press.

Westcott, C. and D. Porter (2005) 'Fiscal Decentralization and Citizen Participation in East Asia', in I. Licha (ed) *Citizens in Charge: Managing Local Budgets in East Asia and Latin America*. Washington, D.C.: Inter-American Development Bank.

Williams, E. (2004) 'Children's Participation and Policy Change in South Asia', CHIP Report No 6, London: Childhood Poverty Research and Policy Centre.

World Bank (2005) *Maintaining Momentum to 2015? An Impact Evaluation of Interventions to Improve Maternal and Child Health and Nutrition in Bangladesh.*, Washington, D.C.: World Bank.

World Bank (2009) *Global Monitoring Report 2009: A Development Emergency*, Washington DC: The International Bank for Reconstruction and Development/ The World Bank, downloaded at http://siteresources.worldbank.org/INTGLOMONREP2009/Resources/5924349-1239742507025/GMR09_book.pdf

You, D., Wardlaw, T., Salama, P. and Jones, G. (2009) 'Levels and trends in under-5 mortality, 1990-2008' *The Lancet*, published online 10 September, DOI:10.1016/S0140-6736(09)61601-9.

Chapter 6

Banfi, J.A. (2006) 'A Rich Complex Landscape: Challenges and Advances in Media Development in Latin America', in M. Harvey (ed) *Media Matters. Perspectives on Governance and Development from the Global Forum for Media Development*, Internews Europe. Available at: http://www.internews.org/pubs/gfmd/mediamatters.pdf

Briscoe, I. (2009) 'The Writing on the Wall: Media Wars in Latin America', *openDemocracy* October 12. Available at: http://www.opendemocracy.net/article/the-writing-on-the-wall-media-wars-in-latin-america

Camfield, L., G. Crivello and M. Woodhead (2009a) 'Wellbeing Research in Developing Countries: Reviewing the Role of Qualitative Methods', *Social Indicators Research* 90(1): 5–31.

Camfield, L., N. Streuli and M. Woodhead (2009b) 'What's the Use of "Well-Being" in Contexts of Child Poverty? Approaches to Research, Monitoring and Children's Participation', *International Journal of Children's Right*s 17: 65–109.

Craske, N. and Molyneux, M. (2002) *Gender and the Politics of Rights and Democracy in Latin America*. Basingstoke: Palgrave.

Crivello, G., L. Camfield and M. Woodhead (2009) 'How Can Children Tell Us about Their Wellbeing? Exploring the Potential of Participatory Research Approaches within Young Lives', *Social Indicators Research* 90(1): 51–72.

ECLAC and UNICEF (2005) 'Child Poverty in Latin America', *Challenges* No. 1, September, Chile/Panama: ECLAC/UNICEF Regional Office for LAC.

Escobal, J. and C. Ponce (2005) *Trade Liberalisation and Child Welfare: Assessing the Impact of an FTA between Peru and the United States*. Unpublished mimeo, Lima, Peru.

Hogan, M.C., Foreman, K.J., Naghavi, M., Ahn, S.Y., Wang, M., Makela, S.M., Lopez, A.D., Lozano, R. and Murray, C.J.L. (2010) 'Maternal mortality for 181 countries, 1980-2008: a systematic analysis of progress towards Millennium Development Goal 5', *The Lancet* 375(9726): 1609–23.

Inter-American Dialogue (2009) 'Media and Governance: A Project of the Inter-American Dialogue', February. Washington DC.

Johnston, J. (2008) 'Children's Perspectives on their Young Lives: Report on Methods for Sub-Studies Peru Pilot', *Young Lives Technical Note 10*, Oxford UK: Young Lives.

Keck, M.E. and R.N. Abers (2006) 'Civil Society and State-Building in Latin America', LasaForum XXXVII(1): 30–2. Available at: http://irtheoryandpractice.wm.edu/seminar/papers/Keck.pdf

Mably, P. (2006) 'Evidence-Based Advocacy: NGO Research Capacities and Policy Influence in the Field of International Trade', *IDRC Working Papers on Globalisation, Growth and Poverty*, No. 4. Available at: http://www.idrc.ca/uploads/user-S/11727031851GGPWP4-NGO.pdf

McGann, J. (2007) *The Global 'Go-To Think Tanks': The Leading Public Policy Research Organizations in the World, 2007.* Available at: http://www.fpri.org/research/thinktanks/mcgann.globalgotothinktanks.pdf

Norris, P. (2008) 'The Role of the Free Press in Promoting Democratization, Good Governance and Human Development', in *Media Matters: Perspectives on Advancing Governance and Development from the Global Forum for Media Development,* Internews Europe. Available at: http://www.internews.org/pubs/gfmd/mediamatters.pdf

Pais, M.S. (2002) 'Centre of Attention', *CRIN Newsletter* (15): 9–11. Available at: http://www.crin.org/docs/resources/publications/crinvol15e.pdf

Punch, S. (2002) 'Research with Children: The Same or Different from Research with Adults?', *Childhood* 9(3): 321–41.

Tarrow, S. (1994) *Power in Movement: Social Movements, Collective Action and Politics*, New York: Cambridge University Press.

Uña, G., C. Lupica and L. Strazza (2010) 'Think Tanks and Poverty in Latin America: The Role of Thinkers in the Marketplace of Social Policies in Argentina, Chile and Mexico', in A. Garce and G. Una (eds) *Think Tanks and Public Policies in Latin America*. Buenos Aires, Argentina: Fundacion Siena and CIPPEC.

UNDESA (2009) *Millennium Development Goals Report 2009*, New York: UNDESA, downloaded at http://unstats.un.org/unsd/mdg/Resources/Static/Products/Progress2009/MDG_Report_2009_En.pdf

UNDP (2005) *Democracy in Latin America 2004*, Mexico City: UNDP.

Villar, E., Pereznieto, P. and Jones, N. (2006) 'Trade Liberalisation and Child Wellbeing: Potential Impacts of the Peru–US Free Trade Agreement', *Young Lives Policy Brief 3*, Oxford UK: Young Lives.

Wells, K. (2009) *Childhood in a Global Perspective*. London: Polity Press.

Woodhead, M. (1999) 'Combating Child Labour: Listen to what the Children Say', *Childhood* 6(1): 27–49.

You, D., Wardlaw, T., Salama, P. and Jones, G. (2009) 'Levels and trends in under-5 mortality, 1990–2008', *The Lancet*, published online 10 September, DOI:10.1016/S0140-6736(09)61601-9.

OECD's Social Institutions and Gender Index (SIGI)

A valuable new measure of gender equality for researchers and policymakers, also offers some indicators that are relevant for children. While the SIGI composite index includes five broad components aimed at assessing women's status in countries around the world – civil liberties, ownership rights, physical integrity, family code and son preference – the latter three of these sub-indices are particularly applicable to children. All were given equal weight in the data presentation in the following tables.[1]

Africa

Rankings, which are available for over 100 non–OECD countries, indicate that gender inequality is pervasive and severe in sub–Saharan Africa. The Sudan was the least equitable country in the region, with a combined score of 0.53. Mali was not far behind, with 0.47. On the other hand, Mauritius, Botswana and South Africa scored comparatively well, under 0.08. The regional average score was not quite 0.20.

Child-focused SIGI scores for African countries

Country	Score	Family code	Physical integrity	Son preference
Mauritius	0.01435	11th 0.04	23rd 0.22	1st 0.00
Botswana	0.05497	53rd 0.32	15th 0.17	1st 0.00
South Africa	0.07869	73rd 0.42	23rd 0.22	1st 0.00
Namibia	0.08171	58th 0.35	34th 0.26	89th 0.25
Kenya	0.09121	63rd 0.37	46th 0.28	1st 0.00
Burundi	0.09304	57th 0.34	60th 0.39	1st 0.00
Madagascar	0.0954	70th 0.41	60th 0.39	1st 0.00
Tanzania	0.10118	81st 0.50	22nd 0.20	1st 0.00
Ghana	0.10155	61st 0.37	80th 0.40	1st 0.00
Malawi	0.12555	60th 0.36	88th 0.47	1st 0.00
Senegal	0.13435	99th 0.60	45th 0.26	1st 0.00
Congo, Democratic Republic	0.13566	66th 0.39	81st 0.41	1st 0.00
Rwanda	0.1376	56th 0.33	91st 0.52	1st 0.00

(continued)

Child-focused SIGI scores for African countries (continued)

Country	Score	Family code	Physical integrity	Son preference
Cote d'Ivoire	0.14128	79th 0.49	85th 0.43	1st 0.00
Zimbabwe	0.14377	80th 0.49	59th 0.37	1st 0.00
Swaziland	0.14514	86th 0.52	60th 0.39	1st 0.00
Lesotho	0.16621	94th 0.57	—	1st 0.00
Benin	0.16761	84th 0.51	87th 0.47	1st 0.00
Mauritania	0.17087	71st 0.42	103rd 0.60	1st 0.00
Angola	0.17182	89th 0.54	—	89th 0.25
Equatorial Guinea	0.1737	82nd 0.50	91st 0.52	1st 0.00
Nigeria	0.17487	71st 0.42	89th 0.48	89th 0.25
Congo, Rep.	0.18523	101st 0.62	—	1st 0.00
Togo	0.1875	96th 0.59	86th 0.44	1st 0.00
Cameroon	0.18813	89th 0.54	90th 0.48	1st 0.00
Uganda	0.19018	102nd 0.64	81st 0.41	1st 0.00
Eritrea	0.20066	76th 0.46	106th 0.69	1st 0.00
Central African Republic	0.207	92nd 0.56	101st 0.58	1st 0.00
Mozambique	0.20837	109th 0.70	60th 0.39	1st 0.00
Burkina Faso	0.20965	88th 0.54	104th 0.63	1st 0.00
Zambia	0.21231	108th 0.69	60th 0.39	1st 0.00
Niger	0.23021	104th 0.65	99th 0.52	89th 0.25
Gambia, The	0.23359	103rd 0.64	102nd 0.60	1st 0.00
Ethiopia	0.23485	55th 0.33	109th 0.77	1st 0.00
Gabon	0.23686	107th 0.68	91st 0.52	1st 0.00
Liberia	0.26893	87th 0.53	107th 0.76	1st 0.00
Guinea	0.27116	105th 0.67	105th 0.65	1st 0.00
Chad	0.28689	111th 0.79	84th 0.43	1st 0.00
Guinea-Bissau	0.30349	—	107th 0.76	1st 0.00
Sierra Leone	0.3359	98th 0.60	110th 0.80	1st 0.00
Somalia	0.36444	—	113th 0.84	1st 0.00
Mali	0.47125	112th 0.80	114th 0.97	1st 0.00
Sudan	0.52619	106th 0.68	111th 0.82	101st 0.50

The family code indicator, which includes variables that measure the percentage of adolescent girls who have ever been married, the acceptance of polygamy, women's rights to their children and female rights of inheritance, indicates that sub-Saharan Africa has a long way to go before women enjoy the same rights as men. Mauritius, with a score of 0.04, is the only country in the region in which family law is relatively equitable. No other country scores below 0.32, most score well above 0.5, and some, Mali, Chad and Mozambique, score in excess of 0.7.

Girls' and women's physical integrity is also vulnerable in most of sub-Saharan Africa. That indicator, which includes variables for FGM and violence against women and girls, ranges from 0.17 in Botswana to 0.97 in Mali, with the majority of countries clustering between 0.4 and 0.6.

Son preference 'reflects the economic valuation of women'[2] based on the number of women that are missing due to sex-selective abortion or higher female infant mortality. Few countries in the region exhibit a preference for boy children when measured in this manner, the exceptions being Namibia, Angola, Nigeria, Niger and the Sudan.

Asia

As can be seen in the following tables, it is useful to evaluate subregions independently. Overall, South Asia is a far less equitable place for women than East Asia. Average composite scores for the former are over 0.25 and for the latter do not quite reach 0.09. Of course, there is significant variation in both subregions. Afghanistan has the highest score in Asia, with nearly 0.60. Sri Lanka, on the other hand, also a Southern Asian country, has a score of not quite 0.04. The score variation in East Asia is not quite as extreme, it ranges from close to zero for the Philippines to 0.32 for China.

Child-focused SIGI scores for East Asia

Country	Score	Family code	Physical integrity	Son preference
Philippines	0.00451	8th 0.04	3rd 0.09	1st 0.00
Thailand	0.0157	41st 0.16	15th 0.17	1st 0.00
Hong Kong, China	0.02155	26th 0.10	1st 0.00	89th 0.25
Singapore	0.02244	25th 0.10	34th 0.26	1st 0.00
Cambodia	0.03238	38th 0.14	48th 0.30	1st 0.00
Vietnam	0.04421	6th 0.03	60th 0.39	1st 0.00
Lao PDR	0.04568	51st 0.32	23rd 0.22	1st 0.00
Mongolia	0.0506	30th 0.12	48th 0.30	89th 0.25
Myanmar	0.06807	35th 0.14	60th 0.39	89th 0.25
Malaysia	0.07298	53rd 0.32	—	1st 0.00
Indonesia	0.10353	59th 0.35	79th 0.39	1st 0.00
Chinese Taipei	0.10736	—	3rd 0.09	101st 0.50
Korea, Democratic Republic	0.11797	—	91st 0.52	1st 0.00
Timor-Leste	0.12494	—	83rd 0.43	89th 0.25
China	0.32038	1st 0.00	48th 0.30	122nd 1.00

Child-focused SIGI scores for South Asia

Country	Score	Family code	Physical integrity	Son preference
Sri Lanka	0.03708	46th 0.23	15th 0.17	1st 0.00
Nepal	0.16084	62nd 0.37	48th 0.30	101st 0.50
Bangladesh	0.21125	95th 0.58	2nd 0.04	101st 0.50
Bhutan	0.21808	43rd 0.21	54th 0.35	118th 0.75
Pakistan	0.268	64th 0.38	47th 0.28	118th 0.75
India	0.31928	100th 0.61	15th 0.17	118th 0.75
Afghanistan	0.58961	110th 0.72	91st 0.52	122nd 1.00

The previously explained family code indicator shows similar ranges, from zero in China to 0.72 in Afghanistan. Overall, South Asia again compares unfavourably to East Asia and the Pacific. Led by Afghanistan and India (0.61), the region's average sub-score is 0.44, markedly different from the 0.15 of the eastern area.

In terms of women's physical integrity, a different pattern emerges. The subregions are nearly identical, with the eastern region actually having a slightly higher score. Afghanistan and the Democratic Republic of Korea tie, intra-regionally, for last place in terms of violence against women. Bangladesh has the lowest score (0.04) indicating the strength of the nation's laws that protect women's safety.

Son preference is a major issue for a variety of Asian countries. China and Afghanistan both score 1.0, indicating a very strong preference for sons. While a variety of countries, including Thailand, Cambodia, Vietnam and Lao PDR, do not have missing girls, others, such as Papua New Guinea, Bhutan, India and Pakistan, score 0.75. Overall, son preference is stronger in Southern Asia.

Latin America

As can be seen in the following table, there is less score variation in this region than in either Asia or Africa. The range is tighter, from a low of 0.004 in Paraguay to a high of 0.08 in Haiti, as is the magnitude of actual difference. While Haiti's score is 20 times that of Paraguay, in Africa there was a 50-fold score difference between the Sudan and Mauritius and in Asia there was an 80-fold difference between China and the Philippines. The regional average is only 0.02, indicating a high level of gender equality in terms of the indicators captured in the index.

Jamaica is the region's shining star when it comes to the family code indicator – it ties for first place, indicating that there are no gender

Child-focused SIGI scores for Latin America

Country	Score	Family code	Physical integrity	Son preference
Paraguay	0.00365	19th 0.07	3rd 0.09	1st 0.00
Panama	0.00521	—	8th 0.11	1st 0.00
El Salvador	0.00522	17th 0.06	3rd 0.09	1st 0.00
Argentina	0.00557	13th 0.05	9th 0.13	1st 0.00
Ecuador	0.00636	24th 0.09	3rd 0.09	1st 0.00
Costa Rica	0.01043	23rd 0.08	15th 0.17	1st 0.00
Colombia	0.01179	21st 0.07	15th 0.17	1st 0.00
Bolivia	0.01446	13th 0.05	23rd 0.22	1st 0.00
Uruguay	0.01458	15th 0.05	23rd 0.22	1st 0.00
Venezuela, RB	0.01533	21st 0.07	23rd 0.22	1st 0.00
Peru	0.01784	15th 0.05	33rd 0.24	1st 0.00
Puerto Rico	0.02128	—	23rd 0.22	1st 0.00
Chile	0.0213	34th 0.14	23rd 0.22	1st 0.00
Cuba	0.02357	28th 0.12	34th 0.26	1st 0.00
Nicaragua	0.02619	33rd 0.13	34th 0.26	1st 0.00
Brazil	0.02765	19th 0.07	48th 0.30	1st 0.00
Dominican Republic	0.03058	28th 0.12	34th 0.26	1st 0.00
Trinidad and Tobago	0.03365	39th 0.15	15th 0.17	89th 0.25
Guatemala	0.04003	27th 0.11	54th 0.35	1st 0.00
Jamaica	0.04227	1st 0.00	54th 0.35	1st 0.00
Honduras	0.04877	44th 0.22	54th 0.35	1st 0.00
Haiti	0.08196	65th 0.38	54th 0.35	1st 0.00
Regional average	0.023	0.104	0.22	

differences in how family law is applied to men and women. Haiti, at 65th place with a score of 0.38, has the lowest score in the region. The regional average is 0.104 and most countries rank in the top quartile. The physical integrity indicator, which captures violence against women, has a much higher regional average (0.22). Paraguay again has the lowest score with 0.09, and Jamaica, Honduras and Haiti tie for the highest with scores of 0.35. Data indicate no regional preference for sons, with the exception of Trinidad and Tobago, which have a score of 0.25.

As in Asia, it may be important to examine subregions, which have distinct cultures and traditions, independently. As is indicated in the following table, the data bear out this proposition. South America ranks as the most equitable and the Caribbean as the least.

Latin America SIGI by subregion

Subregion	Composite score	Family code	Physical integrity
South America	0.014	0.07	0.19
Central America	0.023	0.12	0.22
Caribbean	0.039	0.15	0.27

Notes

[1] Composite scores range from zero to one – with higher scores indicating more gender inequality.

[2] See http://genderindex.org/content/social-institutions-variables

Index

Note: the following abbreviations have been used: t – tables; f – figures

Child and Youth Network 13*t*
Child and Youth Research and
Training Programme (University
of the Western Cape) 100*t*
child-centred approach 7, 29, 32, 53
Childhood 68
Childhood Education, Institute for
100*t*
Childhood Poverty Research and
Policy Centre (CHIP) 30, 68, 100,
141
Children in Need Network (CHIN)
110*t*
Children's Geographies 68
The Children's Institute 100*t*
Children's Rights Project 100*t*
Childwatch 68
Childwatch International Research
Network 163
Choudhury, S. 20, 49*t*, 70, 84*t*
Christian Relief Development
Agency (CRDA) 117, 119
Chronic Poverty Research Centre 30
civil society organisations (CSOs)
Africa 106–7, 108–10*t*, 111, 113,
116–17
Latin America/Caribbean 186–7
Civil Society for Poverty Reduction
106
Clacherty, G. 104*t*
Clampet-Lundquist, S. 39*t*
Coalition to Fight Against Child
Exploitation (FACE) 150*t*
Cochrane Collaboration 51
Collaborative Research and
Dissemination (CORD) 140*t*
Colombia 34, 193
Committee for Liaison between
Social Organisations for the
Defence of Child Rights
(CLOSE) 109*t*
Committee on the Rights of the
Child 112*t*
communities of practice 107, 108–10*t*,
11, 147–50*t*
community radio 189–90, 193
Consortium for Research on
Educational Access, Transitions and
Equity (CREATE) 141
Consortium for Social and Economic
Research (CIES) 188, 193
Convention on the Elimination of all
forms of Discrimination Against
Women (CEDAW) 11*t*, 22

Convention on the Rights of
the Child, see *United Nations
Convention of the Rights of the Child*
Cooper, E. 104*t*
Council for the Development of
Social Science Research in Africa
(CODESRIA) 99*t*
'critical change' criteria 27, 28*t*
Crivello, G. 44*t*, 97*t*, 98, 138*t*, 173*t*

D

Datta, A. 146
decentralisation 144–5, 153
Delamonica, E. 94*t*, 95*t*, 123, 136*t*,
137*t*
Demographic and Health Survey
(DHS) 94*t*, 95*t*
Development Studies, Institute of 54
Directorate-General for Development
and Co-operation (Belgium) 101*t*
Donald, D. 104*t*
donor agencies/investment 101–2*t*,
139–40, 186

E

Economic and Social Research
Council (ESRC) 14
education 9, 51, 107, 118, 133–4*f*, 152,
154, 155, 156, 159
Africa 90*f*, 91*t*, 92*f*, 107
Asia 125, 128–9*f*, 132*t*
Education for All campaign 107
Educational Psychology, Department
for (Kenyatta University) 99*t*
End Child Prostitution, Child
Pornography, Child Trafficking for
Sexual Purposes (ECPAT) 110*t*,
148*t*
Ethiopia 39*t*, 40, 100, 116, 117
expert-led policy advocacy 112–20
maternal mortality ratio (MMR)
(MDG 5) 94*t*
participatory research 104–5*t*
research institutions 99*t*
subjective well-being 97*t*, 138*t*
under-five mortality (MDG 4) 95*t*
Ethiopian Development Research
Institute (EDRI) 116
European Union (EU) 102*t*
evaluation standards/principles 28*t*
Evans, A. 115
evidence-based policy movement
25–9, 56, 64, 111*t*, 114–15

F

Family and Gender Studies, Institute of 140*t*
Fanelli, C.W. 74*t*
Fattore, T. 44*t*
Faulkner, D. 50*t*
female genital mutilation/cutting (FGM/C)
  Africa 95, 96*t*, 122, 239
  Asia 137*t*
Finance and Economy, Ministry of (MOFED) (Ethiopia) 116, 117
Fischer, F. 64–5
Fitoussi, J. 13
Foreign Affairs, Ministry for (Sweden) 102*t*
Foundation for Child Well-being 13*t*
Fragile Families and Child Well-being Study 38
Fraser, N. 15

G

Gambia 96*t*, 109*t*
Gaventa, J. 29, 55
Gender Empowerment Measure (GEM) (UNDP) 12
gender equality (MDG 3)
  Africa 9, 22, 32, 92*f*, 93*t*, 118, 237
  Asia 133–4*f*, 136*t*, 155, 163
  Latin America/Caribbean 240, 241
German Development Cooperation (GTZ) 101*t*, 102
Ghana 94*t*, 95*t*, 99*t*, 102, 103, 105*t*
Ghana Centre for Democratic Development 106
Ghana NGO Coalition on the Rights of the Child (GNCRC) 109*t*
girls 18, 22, 32, 39, 96, 122, 138, 238, 239, 240
Global Childhood Poverty Study (UNICEF) 69, 103, 141
Gordon, D. 13
Gough, I. 15
Guatemala 34
Guinea Bissau 96*t*
Guyot, J. 104*t*

H

Halik, M. 139*t*
Harper, C. 68, 102*t*
Harpham, T. 86, 138, 139*t*, 143*t*
Hart, J. 74*t*
Hastadewi, Y. 142*t*
Hausermann, J. 9
Heidel, K. 74*t*
Help Age International 111*t*
Heritage Foundation 63
Herman, T. 41*t*
Hill, M. 45*t*, 75*t*
Hinton, R. 75*t*
HIV 94, 95, 122, 137, 155
Hogan, M.C. 93, 94*t*, 136*t*
Holland, J. 51, 52
households 11, 30, 32
household surveys 35*t*
household-level poverty 21, 29, 40, 98, 118, 187–8
Hovland, I. 117
Huebner, E. 45*t*
Human Development approach (UNDP) 10, 66
Human Development Index (HDI) 14

I

incrementalism models of policy processes 54
India 18, 97*t*, 138*t*, 140*t*, 142*t*, 143*t*, 146, 148*t*, 149*t*, 151–60
India Alliance for Child Rights (IACR) 148*t*
Indonesia 136*t*, 137*t*, 142*t*, 149*t*, 150*t*
infant mortality *see* under-five mortality (MDG 4)
Inter-African Committee on Traditional Practices (IAC) 108*t*
Inter-agency Group for Child Mortality Estimation (IGME) 122
Inter-American Development Bank 190
interactive model of policy processes 54
interceptor/receptor models of policy processes 54
'interest group influence' theories 58–9
international agencies 111–12*t*
International Development, Department for (DFID) (UK) 30, 102*t*
International Development Research Centre (IDRC) 107
International Labour Organization (ILO) 30
International Monetary Fund (IMF) 60

Y

Z